More Praise for

OUR TURN

WOMEN WHO TRIUMPH
IN THE FACE OF DIVORCE

"Women who were divorced in midlife. . . . turned out to be a whole lot happier after getting through the transition."

—*Los Angeles Times*

"Provocative. . . . Women who divorce in midlife are not the pathetic wrecks desperate for new husbands that folks often imagine."

—*USA Today*

"Women facing divorce will find encouraging words and valuable advice here."

—*Publishers Weekly*

"Has important things to say. . . . There's plenty of sound advice. . . . [that] will be welcome to many."

—*Kirkus Reviews*

**An Alternate Selection
of the Psychotherapy Book Club**

OUR TURN

Women Who Triumph in the Face of Divorce

Christopher L. Hayes, Ph.D.
Deborah Anderson
Melinda Blau

POCKET BOOKS

New York   London   Toronto   Sydney   Tokyo   Singapore

POCKET BOOKS, a division of Simon & Schuster Inc.
1230 Avenue of the Americas, New York, NY 10020

Copyright © 1993 by Dr. Christopher Hayes, Deborah Anderson, and Melinda Blau

Library of Congress Cataloging-in-Publication Data

Hayes, Christopher L.
    Our turn : women who triumph in the face of divorce / by
Christopher L. Hayes, Deborah Anderson, Melinda Blau.
      p. cm.
    Includes bibliographical references and index.
    ISBN 0-671-74006-7
    1. Divorced women—United States—Psychology. 2. Divorced
women—United States. 3. Middle-aged women—United
States—Psychology. 4. Middle-aged women—United
States. I. Anderson, Deborah Y., 1946– . II. Blau, Melinda,
1943– . III. Title.
HQ834.H38 1993
306.89′082—dc20   92-34096
                                      CIP

First Pocket Books trade paperback printing March 1994

10 9 8 7 6 5 4 3 2 1

Cover design by Christine Van Bree

Printed in the U.S.A.

*To the Women
Whose Honesty and Courage
Gave Life to This Book*

Contents

Contents

New Beginnings: Shattering the Myths of Mid-Life Divorce

Today I look back on July 19 as a new beginning.
I am a very lucky person.
I am alive and strong and healthy, emotionally and physically.
I am so glad to be who I am.
My life did not end four years ago.
A new and wonderful and exciting life began.
Not only am I a more interesting person, but I am also stronger,
   freer, and very capable of taking care of myself
   and making my own decisions.
Divorce is not easy, but one does not die.
Thank you, God, for making me me.

> —Lorraine Feldman's divorce diary, final entry

Portrait of a Survivor

"Do you need a hand?" inquired a concerned male voice.

"I have two hands, two feet, and a strong backside," the woman shot back sharply. She wasn't in trouble; she was only pausing at the top of the mountain for a moment to catch her breath and appreciate how far she had come. "If I need help, I'll ask—but I'd rather do this *on my own!*"

Lorraine Feldman chuckles as she relates this telling anecdote—a particular memory that seems to separate the "before" and "after" of her life. "That poor guide could never have known that this was more than a mountain-climbing lesson. It was an exercise in my own survival.

"*Discovery, adventure, survival*—those were new words for me. Going back twenty-five or thirty years, if you were to ask my ex-husband about me, he'd probably tell you that my idea of adventure was a trip to the Eatontown Mall and discovery was a closeout sale on shoes!"

1

Yet there Lorraine was, rafting down the Colorado River and hiking up rugged mountain trails with people she barely knew. She had scaled the treacherous mountainside fearlessly, climbing hand over foot, the jagged stone edges often cutting into her fingers. "At an earlier time in my life, I would have taken the guide's hand, because I always thought that I needed help. First from my father, and then from my husband—my chosen 'guide' for life. But then my husband decided to be someone else's guide."

Perched atop that slippery peak in Colorado, Lorraine was finally guiding herself. It was a long way from the flatlands of New Jersey to the peaks of the Rocky Mountains, but at that moment, Lorraine knew she had survived her husband's infidelity, survived his abandonment, and survived their divorce. "That was my first real adventure. I was really doing something on my own, not connected to Marv, not connected to the kids. It was *mine*. When I was married to Marvin, I would never have done it— alone or with him. In those days, nothing was as important as being part of a family."

Being a good wife and mother was *everything* to Lorraine Feldman, even if it meant sacrificing her own identity. A product of her time and typical of women who married in the fifties and sixties, Lorraine internalized the message: *Home and children are the most important aspect of your life.* Even as a child she knew that marriage was her admission ticket to Adult Life.

Eternally in the shadow of a handsome, athletic older brother who was "going places" with his life, Lorraine Davidson was adored but not necessarily encouraged to *be* anything. Her upper-middle-class Jewish parents valued education—for girls as well as boys. But Lorraine knew that she was sent to an Ivy League college for a different purpose than her brother. Just as tennis and riding lessons enabled Lorraine to feel at ease at the club or at the riding stables—places you could meet rich, eligible young men—a college education would train her to keep up her end of the conversation. Someday, she would be a tremendous asset to a husband moving up the career track; she would help him get into the right social circles.

Understandably, Lorraine's view of life was vastly different from that of her brother, who eventually went to law school: It was not, "What will I be?" but "Whose wife will I be?" Not "What kind of interests will I have?" but "What kind of family will I have?" And not "How will I take care of myself?" but "Who will take care of me in the happily-ever-after?" At twenty-one, Marvin Feldman seemed to be the answer to everything.

Given this mindset, it's not surprising that after twenty-two years of marriage, Lorraine was crushed when her husband, Marvin, walked out on her. Reeling from the shock of his betrayal, she believed her life had ended. Her three children, aged nineteen, seventeen, and fourteen at the time, didn't need her as much as they once did, and now Marvin was throwing her away too.

To her credit, Lorraine instinctively began to help herself heal. A few months before the breakup, she had started working part-time as a realtor. When Marvin left, she upped her hours, knowing that keeping busy would help her through the long and painful days. Sadly, she got scant support from most of her old friends, who were still married and felt threatened by a suddenly-single woman in their social midst. So, she made a new friend—a woman in her office who had gone through the process a year before. "I've just become a statistic," Lorraine declared for her coworkers to hear.

Lorraine's private agony was very much a matter of public record. Her husband was the big-fish mayor in their small-pond town on the Jersey shore, a community substantial enough to handle a bustling summer tourist trade and small enough to be galvanized by year-round gossip. So, when Mayor Feldman splashed, just about everyone in town felt the waves.

Knowing that her neighbors were aware of, if not all talking about, Marvin's affair, Lorraine often felt humiliated, but she managed to hold her head high. "People would ask how my husband was, and I'd just say, 'Fine.'" As for the stress, she says, "I would get in the car and scream, and I'd keep driving around, screaming. Next thing I knew, I'd be whistling—and then laughing out loud. I also started jogging. I was up to a mile. I lost a lot of weight."

Almost four years lapsed between Lorraine's and Marvin's initial separation and the actual divorce. During that time, the ups and downs of the legal process and the wrangling over money and past debts proved as painful and exhausting as the emotional trauma. "I am so tired within. I am physically tied up in knots when I must encounter Marv," wrote Lorraine in her diary. "Just when I think things are sliding along on an even keel, he hits me with a new wallop."

The diary itself—which spans the four years, from the days of her early suspicions about Marvin's lies and infidelity to Lorraine's trek up the mountain—also helped her get through. "I had no one else to talk to. I just wrote down what I had to say."

Lorraine's growth was very much like that of a butterfly emerging from the cocoon—the "cocoon" being her marriage. The butterfly's wings—damp, weak, and a bit shaky at first—are soon hardened by the outside air, and new strength courses through its veins. So it was with Lorraine. Her eyes began to sparkle again. She stopped screaming in the car. She began to date, to make new friends, and to talk to real people, instead of just confiding in her diary. The little girl who had put herself on the back burner for a domineering father, an older brother, and then a husband, was finally playing front and center stage.

The Myths of Mid-Life Divorce

Lorraine Feldman is truly a survivor. After her divorce, she reawakened aspects of herself that had been repressed during her marriage, and at the same time, she rediscovered the girl she had left behind. Seeing her today, it is hard to believe that words such as *discovery* and *adventure* were ever foreign to her vocabulary. She relishes life. Warm, confident, and quick-witted, her glow is infectious. It is abundantly clear that this ebullient and now successful real-estate broker is recovered from the devastation of her divorce and firmly rooted in her own life. Today, in her mid-fifties, she is remarkably youthful-looking and energetic, despite her mocking disclaimer, "You should have seen me in my *forties!*"

Though she is unique—the star of her own individual story— in many ways Lorraine Feldman is also the personification of hundreds of other women who participated in a groundbreaking research project: the "Divorce After 40" study conducted by the National Center for Women and Retirement Research. The first ever to focus specifically on mid-life women and divorce, the study captures the voices of 352 women throughout the country. Their message—as evidenced in the survey data—clearly challenges the cultural status quo and flies in the face of many widely held beliefs about divorced mid-life women.

MYTH #1: *It's too late for women to change if they're divorced and over forty.*

MYTH #2: *Divorce debilitates women and causes them to lose control over their lives.*

MYTH #3: *The dream of every divorced woman is remarriage.*

MYTH #4: *Sex is no longer part of divorced women's lives.*

MYTH #5: *Divorced women are lonely.*

MYTH #6: *Mid-life and older women "live through" their children after divorce.*

MYTH #7: *Divorced women fear old age.*

It's no wonder that such myths abound. Prior to the "Divorce Over 40" study, researchers offered a dreary prognosis for mid-life women after divorce. "[Older] divorced women suffer from loneliness exaggerated by an empty bed at night and a lack of shared activities for the weekend," summarized one psychologist. "The end of marriage becomes a loss of identity," wrote another, implying that without husbands divorced women are washed up and dried out.

However, that picture doesn't describe the throngs of divorced women who enrolled in the PREP (Pre-Retirement Education Planning for Women) seminars offered throughout the country by the National Center for Women and Retirement Research*— workshops originally developed to assist married women with their life-planning needs. Some were newly divorced and struggling to figure out how to navigate through a storm of emotional and financial changes; they viewed the seminars as an opportunity to gain survival skills. Others, divorced two or more years, were beginning to spread their wings, looking for ways to increase their ability to be independent and to shed the last vestiges of dependency.

Many of these women were already living dynamic, vibrant

---

* For a description of the Center and a detailed discussion of the study, see the Appendix, pages 263–65.

lives. They had resumed their schooling, gone back to work, embarked on new relationships. They wanted to learn money-management skills and get advice about protecting themselves in the future. Suddenly single—whether by choice or by default—most felt unburdened for the first time in their lives. And they weren't risking remarriage if it meant being restricted. They were out to discover who they were.

The discrepancy was puzzling: were the divorced women attending the PREP seminars atypical or was mid-life divorce somehow misrepresented or misunderstood by previous researchers? To find out, the Center for Women and Retirement Research launched the first survey of mid-life divorced women—forgotten women who, according to conventional wisdom, had little hope for a fulfilling life after divorce, unless, of course, they found a man.

Aided by an academic advisory panel, the center developed a comprehensive 17-page survey designed to explore mid-life and older women's adjustment patterns after divorce. The questionnaire contained 77 items—a mix of quantifiable multiple-choice questions and fill-ins—and focused on six critical areas of adjustment after divorce: employment, finances, legal matters, emotional health, building a new life, and perspectives on retirement.

Demographically, the study focused on what might be termed "typical" white middle-class American women, front-runners of the Baby Boom generation and their slightly older counterparts. The women were of a variety of religious backgrounds, from all parts of the country, and married an average of twenty-three years. The survey respondents' average age was forty-five at the time of the divorce; they had two children whose average age was twenty. Although the average marital income ranged from the high six figures to an average of $45,000 during marriage, most women dropped to a devastating $15,000 one year after divorce. Sixty-five percent were employed at the time of their divorce, having had six to ten years of work experience prior to the breakup.

The survey was mailed to women who had called the center's hot line for information, to women divorced after the age of forty who were recruited from local chapters of various women's organizations, and to women who responded to ads, bulletins,

6

and other public-relations efforts promoting the study. "No one will fill out a seventeen-page questionnaire!" declared the skeptics on the advisory panel. They couldn't have been more wrong. In fact, the response was overwhelming—of the approximately three thousand surveys mailed, 352 were answered and returned.

The survey respondents were eager to share their experiences. A number of them indicated that filling out the survey was a cathartic experience. Many noted they had experienced a lack of support for their choices and their growth after divorce. After all, family and friends base their ideas of what is "right" for divorced women on the myths. Thus, the women reported, every item on the questionnaire served as a benchmark of their progress; their answers validated how far they had come since their divorce. Most of them wished they could have known then what they knew now.

The Survey Unbound: Debunking the Myths

Once responses to the "Divorce Over 40" survey began pouring in, it quickly became clear that what was happening in the PREP seminars was not an isolated phenomenon. The survey respondents' comments also mirrored what the study's findings proved: these women were not only surviving but *thriving* in their post-divorce lives.

I would like to say that, after two years, I am happier and more at peace than I have been in my life. I have a group of friends who take "mind" trips, play cards, go to plays and out to dinner. I have a better relationship with my children. My family is proud of me. I worked two jobs until I got a promotion at the full-time position I'm in. I feel much better about myself, and I know I can make it on my own.

Clearly, these divorced Cinderellas simply did not fit into the slippers society had made for them. They weren't waiting for Prince Charming—and they weren't putting themselves out to pasture. Many of them were rewriting the myths as they went along, not only having to battle the emotional dragons of divorce but having to stand up to society's stereotypes as well. Consider some of the myths in light of the findings:

MYTH #1 *It's too late for women to change if they're divorced and over forty.* Not only do they change their lives, divorced women over forty actually grow *more* adaptable as they age. Instead of retreating from life after divorce, an overwhelming eighty-two percent experience a renewed sense of independence and strength to survive difficult times. The vast majority (eighty percent) have a more positive self-image and higher self-esteem after divorce as well.

MYTH #2 *Divorce debilitates women and causes them to lose control over their lives.* On the contrary, nearly two-thirds of these women find that the process inspires them to gain control over their lives for the first time. They are able to redefine themselves and, in the process, reawaken their own hopes and dreams. The energy formerly invested in their marriages and the nurturing once lavished only on husbands and children are rechanneled toward developing a strong, self-reliant sense of identity.

MYTH #3 *The dream of every divorced woman is remarriage.* Divorced women *rarely* dream of remarriage. Although fifty percent of the survey respondents say that the hardest part of being suddenly single is the loss of sharing a life with someone on a daily basis and having a regular companion for social events, five years after divorce, three-quarters of these women place a high premium on their own privacy and independence. Instead of wanting to remarry, they want the time to get to know themselves.

Many, in fact, fear losing their newfound independence to a second marriage. Of the women between the ages of forty and forty-four, twenty-nine percent *prefer* to remain single, and that figure increases among the older age groups—forty-one percent between forty-five and forty-nine opted not to remarry, and forty-six percent between fifty and fifty-nine. It would appear that the older the woman, the better she understands what it means to sacrifice her independence. Also, she has fought longer and harder to achieve autonomy.

MYTH #4 *Sex is no longer part of divorced women's lives.* Approximately one-third of the women in the study experience *more* sexual enjoyment after divorce. It's not surprising that sex (and sexual experimentation) becomes a more important and more satisfying aspect of life after divorce: the majority of women did not experience sexual enjoyment in marriage! Many came from

8

repressed sexual backgrounds, and all were products of a culture that exhorted young women to be "good girls." Although it was not a question included in the survey, more than ninety percent of the women later interviewed were virgins on their honeymoons; and even if they dared to have premarital sex, their husbands were their first and only lovers! While a few women—about five percent of the interviewees—reported extramarital affairs while still married, for most, the freedom of divorce allowed them to first sample a bit of this and that from the sexual smorgasbord they had missed out on during the sixties and seventies when sexual mores were changing at a fast and furious pace.

MYTH #5 *Divorced women are lonely.* Most divorced women are anything but lonely. Although almost half of our women cite "growing older alone" as the hardest aspect of being single after so many years of marriage, an equal number begin dating again. More important, many stop defining themselves in terms of their relationships with men. Instead, they seek the company of other women and embark on new relationships that support their new life-styles. Eight out of ten feel that female friends are more helpful than any other source of support.

MYTH #6 *Mid-life and older women "live through" their children after divorce.* While seventy percent express concern about their children, mid-life divorced women certainly do not live through their children. In fact, the subject of children rarely came up in any of the seventy follow-up interviews! It's important to remember that most of the survey respondents had teenage children or grown children, even grandchildren. The average age of their children at the time of the divorce was twenty years old, and only a third had children living at home after the divorce. Clearly, a mid-life mother has a different perspective on children than a younger woman or a woman emerging from shorter-term marriage, who generally has younger children.

In short, the study indicates that women are most concerned with their own survival and personal growth—not with their children. Most feel competent as mothers: only fifteen percent report that they worry about raising their kids alone. The good news is that as they learn to stand on their own, divorced women become more competent mothers. Six out of ten perceive divorce as a better situation for their children. Of them, seventy-seven percent report having a better relationship with their kids as well.

MYTH #7 *Divorced women fear old age.* Certainly, some women worry about getting sick, about living alone, and most of all, about surviving financially—but their concerns are not as dominant as one might expect. One survey question in particular is most telling. Asked, "When you look ahead to your retirement years, what do you see?" nearly half answered "good health and productivity" and "more time with family," and fifty-six percent saw "more time with friends" in their futures. Seventy percent envisioned "involvement in interesting activities."

Those don't sound like the predictions of women worried about aging! In fact, on the down side, only one out of ten imagined that "sickness and dependency" were in store for their later years. We suspect that women's fears about aging—understandable in a sexist, ageist world—are mediated by the exhilaration of finding new lives after divorce. Relishing the present, the future feels far away and somehow not so important.

Seeing Their Own Reflection

Clearly, the survey spoke volumes of new and vital information about mid-life women and divorce. First and foremost, the findings proved that divorced women at mid-life can defy the cultural odds. Although, many of our women experienced hard times financially and many continue to face dismal economic futures, *psychologically and socially, the vast majority of women thrive in the face of divorce.*

During the next phase of the study, when we conducted in-depth interviews with seventy women, a second, equally important discovery, emerged. As it turned out, Lorraine's trek to the top of a mountain in Colorado by herself expressed a developmental leap taken by the vast majority of women in the study. The interviews throughout this book are dotted with similar parables.
• Joann Cress dared to drive her car across a bridge to a neighboring borough for the first time; Helga Gross traveled alone to the Far East. The distance didn't matter—*they traveled on their own.*
• After thirty years of sterile, monochromatic furnishings—her husband's taste—Anne Garner moved into her own apartment. That it was a tiny studio, one room strewn with colorful thrift-shop bargains, didn't matter—*it was her taste.*

• Never having worked a day in her life, Paula Oslow became a waitress. That her salary was meager at first didn't matter—*she was finally able to support herself.*

As researchers, we had gone from the dry task of analyzing flat, cold data to the warm, three-dimensional experience of interviewing. Suddenly, the astounding and eminently hopeful findings literally leapt off the page. In fact, seeing the women's faces behind the facts and figures and listening to their views not only made the findings come alive, it brought us to another important discovery about mid-life divorce: *Divorce can be a critical developmental springboard that inspires women to change in ways they hadn't dreamed possible.*

That is not to say that divorce—the *event*—doesn't often create chaos, hurt, confusion, anger, and loneliness. Nevertheless, divorce—the *process*—can be a surprising milestone in adult development that forces most women to come to terms with their own identities. We don't mean to imply that women must leave their marriages in order to grow. The key here is how they respond and adapt to crisis and change.

Clearly, divorce is *not* the only crisis that engenders women's growth; it just happens to have been the subject of the study and of this book. Children growing up and leaving home, a sudden drop in income, a spouse's illness or death, facing a personal problem, such as alcoholism, and a host of other challenging life events that precipitate *change*—the hallmark of adult development—can also stimulate a woman's growth. Indeed, some of the women in the study began to nurture themselves and develop their identities within the context of marriage, taking part-time jobs or seeking new careers, going back to school, or in other ways venturing beyond the confines of the cocoon.

Of all of life's crises, however, only divorce forces women to stand on their own, usually without the societal support accorded widows. When the judge's gavel finally falls, even the best-prepared face a totally new beginning. Divorced women must finally go through a process of separation—an apt term—in order to become fully functioning human beings. Whereas they may once have needed a father or a husband to see what they looked like, now they can look in the mirror and see their own reflection.

Naturally, not all women relish their new status the minute they are separated. Many are initially traumatized by the upheaval of divorce. The empty space next to them in bed, the missing setting at the dinner table, the once-annoying stubble in the bathroom sink now gone—it all seems to intensify the feelings of loneliness and defeat. Distress and anxiety are par for the course, but the degree and duration of postdivorce stress are clearly related to how a woman sees herself and how strong a sense of separate identity she possesses.

Ultimately, divorce compels most women to discover themselves. "We made it!" they exclaim. "We've finally found ourselves, and . . . *it's our turn!*" These survivors have a right to be proud. In addition to confronting their own self-doubts, they had the courage to confront society's stereotypes as well. They are not merely recovering from divorce, they are *discovering* themselves. In the words of one woman:

> I'm forty-seven years old and happier than I've ever been in my life. I like who I am and therefore don't regret where I've been. I focus on the positive parts of a twenty-three-year marriage and let the rest go. No anger, resentment, or bitterness for baggage. New horizons are easy to see.

A New Look at Divorce and Women's Development

Why is our prognosis for mid-life divorced women so different from that of researchers in the past, who have concluded that these women are unable to cope with the roller coaster of emotions and are ill-equipped to make the kinds of changes that divorce demands? For one thing, few professionals have focused on mid-life women and divorce. Ours was the first national study to examine a large population in which this phenomenon occurred. Moreover, we believe that other researchers have failed to take a key component into consideration: how women develop during the mid-life years.

The idea that adults go through different stages of development is a relatively new area of exploration in the field of psychology. Historically, because children's growth is quite visible, development was thought to occur only between birth and adolescence, the time when teenagers scrutinize their parents' values and beliefs, experiment with various options, and standing on the threshold of adulthood, decide the core issues of identity: *Who am I?* and *What do I believe in?* It is now generally agreed, however, that development is a continuing, lifelong process.

Just as a three-year-old learns to climb a stepladder when she is confronted by the challenge of reaching a toy on a too-high shelf, adults also continue to adapt and change in response to the various challenges they encounter—changes within themselves, changes in their relationships, and changes in the world at large. But when children or adults aren't permitted to go through the inevitable ups and downs of psychic and emotional growth (for example, the three-year-old's mother always gets the toy for her), development can be slowed, if not stalled altogether.

So it was with the vast majority of mid-life women who participated in this study. Rather than riding the waves of adolescent crisis and making life choices that suited their needs and fulfilled their potential as separate human beings, they adopted their parents' values and followed society's edicts. Many of our participants expressed sentiments similar to those of Gail Leperk, fifty-four, who married at age nineteen after a year and a half of college: "I did not have any personal goals for myself that I can remember. Getting married and raising a family would be a big enough job."

The women in the study did not lack interests nor were they short on motivation. Many, in fact, were talented and competent as teenagers. They were beginning to struggle with their identities. But they grew up in a time when being single was viewed as a personal tragedy. Once marriage entered the picture—or even the prospect of it—these women were like pieces of driftwood in an ocean of societal forces. They had little control over the powerful currents that carried them over the threshold. Most women who were career oriented at the end of high school ultimately felt the way forty-seven-year-old Peggy Kennedy did: "The times didn't allow it. Basically, they looked at girls as getting married and settling down. I had some conflicts, I wanted to do one thing, but the world out there was telling me to do another. So what do you do?"

Oddly enough, even during the seventies—a time of resistance, liberation, revolution, and change—the vast majority of the women in the study observed the women's movement from the sidelines. Certainly, a few were drawn to the new ideas; they joined consciousness-raising groups, dabbled in New Age pursuits, or worked for women's organizations, but they were clearly in the minority. Anyway, just because a woman joins a group, trots off to an empowerment weekend, buys a vibrator, or reads *The Joy of Sex* doesn't mean she's a born-again feminist! In fact, to most of these women, the idea of liberation seemed overwhelming, which is not surprising when you look at how carefully schooled they were on the finer points of being a good wife and loving mother.

Who Are Our Women?

The study surveyed an older and a younger group of women. Forty-six percent were women mostly in their fifties and early sixties who married during the 1950s; and fifty-four percent were in their forties and had married in the 1960s. We didn't find as many differences between the two age groups as we anticipated. Granted, each cohort was a product its time; for instance, the older women grew up listening to swing and bop on shiny, black 78 rpm records, while the younger ones played rock and roll on 45s. But as girls and as young wives and mothers, none of these women were encouraged to nurture their own development. Society set it up that way.

Post–World War II America was preoccupied with the pursuit of "the good life." Men were urged to go out into the world and grab a piece of the prospering American pie. Early in life, they were exhorted to be ambitious and competitive, to choose a profession or find a good job. After all, they had to *be* something. And, of course, they had to earn money—even if they were pushed into fathers' businesses or into stultifying jobs that years later would leave them feeling impotent and empty. All that mattered was being a good provider; their women would keep the home fires burning.

The older women in the study, born predominantly between 1931 and 1940, were teenagers and children during the Great Depression; they remembered wartime rationing and the day we dropped the atom bomb. But once the war was over, Rosie the Riveter, a symbol of women "pitching in" during wartime (she was certainly not viewed as *a working woman*), was pushed out of the factory and into the kitchen.

Film titles of the forties summed up the tenor of the times: *It's a Wonderful Life, The Best Years of Our Lives, Made for Each Other,* and *Every Girl Should Be Married.* Many of our older women recall going to Saturday matinees, dreaming that someday a future husband would be as kind and compassionate as Jimmy Stewart, as brave as Kirk Douglas, as suave as Cary Grant.

Television, fast becoming part of every American household by the early fifties, also helped to spread the word, especially to the younger women in the study, born between 1941 and 1950. If the older women nourished their white-picket-fence dreams by going to the movies, their younger counterparts in the study pieced together their visions of the happily ever after by watching the patient, understanding, ever-cheerful wives and mothers on shows such as *Donna Reed, Leave It to Beaver,* and *Ozzie and Harriet.*

It was a time of "nesting." Ozzie had his role and Harriet hers, and they fit together as snugly as pieces of a jigsaw puzzle, each dependent upon the other. Couples who worked hard could save money and, hopefully, afford to move into their dream house, one of the new ranch-style homes that first appeared in 1946. Life was getting easier for "the little woman," or so the advertisements touted. Electrical appliances made cleaning quicker, power detergents were guaranteed to avoid "ring around the collar," and soap promised not to leave a "bathtub ring," a phrase coined by Procter and Gamble in the early fifties.

Whether they were born in 1933 or 1943, most women were bound by the societal edict: *Get married and have children.* They were conditioned to fulfill their husbands' needs, not their own, and to nurture their children's dreams, not their own. Understandably, well into adulthood, many still hadn't explored what *they* wanted out of life, because it violated the code of self-sacrifice and devotion in which they had been so carefully schooled.

Thus, most of the divorced women in our survey, regardless of their age, had to reckon with cataclysmic social, political, and economic upheaval, changes ushered in while they were cloistered inside the cocoon of marriage. In fact, that's what makes a divorced woman who exits a long-term marriage different from one whose marriage lasts less than ten years: she enters marriage in one cultural milieu and emerges into a completely different one.

Divorced and in mid-life, many women suddenly found them-

15

selves alone and at sea—a circumstance even more devastating because the loss often coincided with their children leaving home as well. Their nests were empty and their cupboards were in jeopardy of becoming bare. Having willingly surrendered their own ambitions over the course of their long-term marriages, some had limited work histories as well, which often translated into economic, as well as emotional, calamity.

When Women Change the Rules of Marriage

Not all women in the study were completely constrained by their conditioning. In varying degrees, some began to effect change in their lives while they were still married. Typically, when interests and activities that weren't connected to the family became more important to a woman than maintaining the cultural status quo, it elicited what we began to call the where's-my-dinner? response from her husband. Somehow having dinner on the table was a reassuring symbol in traditional households. It was part of the deal—he was the producer and she the caretaker.

"My first job was to put the two pieces of baloney between the slices of bread—and that's it!" commented Anne Garner, who became increasingly involved in the PTA, her church, and other volunteer work when she was in her forties—more than twenty years into her marriage. Her extended absences didn't sit right with her traditional husband. So as not to "rock the boat," Anne started packing lunch the night before! At times, she would even leave a freshly baked cake on the kitchen counter for her family—a domestic peace offering. Bringing this theme into the 1990s, Geena Davis as "Thelma," in the movie *Thelma and Louise,* is careful to leave her husband's dinner in the microwave before she escapes home for her joyride!

"You're not acting like yourself," groused husbands, wondering what had "gotten into" wives who had decided to take a college course or dabble in part-time work. Some advised their women to get professional help to "fix" whatever was wrong! As Frances Slender remarked, the way her husband saw it, "Everything was my fault. As long as I stayed home and did things his way, everything was fine."

Debby Black, fifty-five, a frizzy-haired redhead in flamboyant thrift-shop clothing whose smile lights up the room, had been

16

married eleven years when a crisis precipitated a major change in her marriage. Her husband's prosperous apparel business was faltering, so Debby took a sales job at a local store to bolster the family income—"temporarily," of course. Because of her flair, the part-time position quickly blossomed into a full-time career. Debby, who admits that in high school she "did things to make people notice me," always longed for the world outside the cocoon. "I hated the socializing with the husbands on a Saturday night, where they sat in one corner and we—the women—were in another corner."

Debby fumed whenever Mike referred to her work as "her toy," implying that her job was something she could play at, when she had finished the duties of her *real career*—taking care of him and the children. At first, Debby modified her work hours to get home in time for dinner. However, she got a taste of being in the "real world," and a year later when Mike's business was back on track, Debby refused to back down when her husband asked her to quit working altogether.

"As I look back, I have to say that was the beginning. It eventually led to the downfall of the marriage." Debby's successes as a working woman not only gratified her ego, they took her into a different social setting. "I began to be in contact with people other than the females with the babies and the children."

Women like Debby know that having their own money or even talking about money will somehow unbalance their relationships. So, they become jugglers and magicians, camouflaging their growth and change, creating the illusion that their husbands have the proverbial upper hand.

"I buried it," admits Debby Black, referring to her growing desire to put more time into her career. "I didn't let him know. It was easier to keep peace." Debby spent several years dancing around this issue of money and her career, so that Mike wouldn't be intimidated. She eventually earned more money than he, and when she finally left the marriage, she felt guilty for having broken the rules.

As described from the wives' perspectives, few husbands were able to understand and support either their wives' emotional needs or their desire to have even a modicum of financial independence. However, we certainly don't mean to imply that it was the man's "fault." They, too, were victims of the culture

17

that shaped them, which is a theme that resonates throughout this book.

Just as women were not expected to take care of themselves, men were not expected to be nurturing fathers, emotionally expressive communicators, or artful and sensitive lovers. They just had to show up—and bring home a paycheck. Now, without warning, their wives seemed to be changing the rules, demanding more of them emotionally and sexually, wanting their own paychecks. Underneath many a husband's anger were feelings of impotence and despair.

"What could be wrong with our marriage?" an utterly dumbfounded Mike Black would ask Debby. "I've given you this beautiful home, two wonderful children. I don't run around with women. I don't drink. I don't gamble."

Debby, who understood Mike's confusion, concluded that he wasn't a bad man. Rather, he was the product of generations of men who had a limited emotional repertoire and rigid role definitions of how husbands and wives were supposed to act.

Indeed, in many of the mid-life marriages seen through the lens of the "Divorce Over 40" study, the women were on one track and the men on another, living parallel lives. In most cases, it was a gradual process, but it's hardly an accident that so many of these marriages broke down when they did. During the mid-life years, many of these women became acutely aware of their husbands' lack of communication skills. Some tried in vain to push for more conversation, but, under pressure, the men— uncomfortable in the realm of emotions because of their own conditioning—withdrew even more. Despairing of getting their husbands' validation, some women started to redefine themselves.

Though half of the women in the survey sought counseling before their marriages ended—their most frequent complaint being "He never talks to me"—three out of five indicate that it was not helpful. Undoubtedly, much larger cultural issues stood in the way. Even if their husbands had been more willing and receptive, therapy probably could not have saved many of these marriages. These women were so different from the "girls" they once were, there was no turning back.

"I found that I was doing things that I always wanted to do but couldn't because my husband didn't want to," said Paula Oslow, who walked out of her twenty-one-year marriage on her fortieth birthday. "One day, I finally said to my husband, 'If I don't leave, I'll die.'

"He thought I meant suicide, but I told him, 'No, I'll just cease to exist.' "

Forging New Identities After Divorce

When she walked down the aisle, the typical woman in the study had bought the fairy tale and, with it, the notion of romantic love. She believed she had found The One, and it was forever. She believed she would get everything she needed from her husband and her children.

Decades later when he left her—or she, finding the marriage empty, left him—she realized how wrong she had been. She wondered if they ever had really loved each other, or if either of them even knew what love was. She also discovered that her marriage, and the roles she had played in it, had deprived her of the one thing she would need to get on with her life: a separate identity.

Divorce may be a drawn out and terrifying prospect; however, being a divorced women is like being a creature who is compelled to deal with an alien environment: she must adapt—deal with life as a single woman—or "die." That means forging a new identity, one that enables her to walk alone in a Noah's Ark world. It is an arduous task at best.

Forty-eight-year old Joann Cress, a teenage bride whose story will unfold throughout this book, is typical of many of our women: "My goal in life was to get married, be a wife and mother. I wanted to make him happy, I wanted to make a nice home and have a nice family. I saw his role as the decision maker. Eventually, it got to be where I didn't do anything for me at all. I was Mrs. Cress, and there was no Joann!"

In a sense, some women in the study, a small minority, cannot adapt to their new status; they "die" in the aftermath of divorce. They cannot recover from the narcissistic blow of their husbands' departure, overcome feelings of inadequacy, or learn to make independent decisions. So, they remain stuck in the past, unable to reconcile their sense of loss, unable to see their own reflections when they look in the mirror.

When we look at where such a woman is developmentally,

invariably we find her "frozen." Her growth was stalled in marriage, and she simply could not jump-start herself after divorce. A woman who does not quite feel like a grown-up is ill-equipped to face life as a single woman, as this survey respondent reflects:

> I was in shock—this was not my desire. I was very lonely and ashamed to admit I was divorcing. I was raised in an environment where divorce was just simply not considered. I felt a great sense of resentment against my ex and fear that I would not be able to care for myself financially. I was angry that I was left on my own and sad at the end of what at times had been a very good thing. I was thrown out into the work force at a time when I was looking forward to my husband's retirement and more opportunities for travel and entertainment.

Rarely is there growth without pain. In the immediate aftermath of her divorce, Joann Cress notes, "I felt terror—sheer terror, for there had always been someone else to fall back on, and now it was just me. I was scared, but I felt as though a large weight had been lifted from my shoulders. I was much happier. I learned to stick to my guns. Even though my family wanted me to come back home, I said I finally *was* home."

Especially in the first year after the breakup, many women in the study have similar feelings. Some doubt whether they will be able to function as single women, meet their own needs, and achieve their goals. They also worry about their children; surprisingly, however, that concern appears at the bottom of most women's lists.

Between the second and fourth year, the vast majority become more confident; feelings of achievement soar; the family unit reorganizes; new relationships are formed and old ones are repaired. It's not hard to understand this continuing spiral of success and self-esteem. As a divorced woman is forced by her circumstances to stand on her own two feet and fend for herself, she begins to grow up. Gradually, feeling more secure about herself, she is able to crystallize her vision of what she wants out of life—and to get it. Joann Cress, already past the five-year benchmark, resonates with hope—as do most women at that point: "I'm strong and have a mind of my own. I don't see myself as a weak person. I'm happier making decisions for myself, and I like being independent. My rewards come from my job and my friends. I threw away Donna Reed, pearls, and everything else I thought I had to be. I'm more like Jane Fonda—a whole new me!"

The Good News/Bad News Paradox

While the vast majority of mid-life divorced women adapt to their new status psychologically and emotionally, many of these same women face financial destitution in later life. On the average, our women plunge to a postdivorce income that averages between $10,000 and $15,000—hardly enough to keep them in the style to which many of them have become accustomed! It's a devastating paradox: they overcome extreme adversities to become self-sufficient, and at the same time, they fail to recognize that without financial planning they can be thrown back into dependency in the future.

It's no surprise that most women deferred to their husbands' financial power and knowledge. They came by this attitude logically. Their mothers had virtually no economic power; and their fathers bolstered the cultural clichés. Fathers rarely passed on to daughters the kinds of business advice they conveyed to their sons. Some of them even denigrated their daughters for *thinking* about college and careers. "My father didn't value women much," forty-four-year-old Lisa Frazier realizes. "He used to say, 'Why should a woman go to college if she's going to get married, make babies, and bake meat loaf?' "

In cases where fathers applauded their daughter's girlhood and teenage accomplishments—more the exception than the rule—it was achievement, not a paycheck, that mattered. "My father's greatest compliment to me was, 'You think like a man,' but it was my brother who had to get a paying job every summer, who was urged to save money," recalls Fran Sargent, who grew up in a materialistic, upper-middle-class home in the Lake Shore area of Chicago. "I did volunteer work. My brother brought home the paycheck. All I had to be was *industrious*—I didn't need to make *money*."

After divorce this dependent mentality has a disastrous effect. *Ninety percent of the women in the study have no long-term financial*

21

goals! Worse, they continue to be stymied when it comes to confronting the financial realities of living on a limited or fixed income.

The economic consequences that many women face are severe. Not only will many enter their twilight years economically impoverished, they will be psychologically and socially at risk as well. They may not be able to afford proper health care, not to mention the basics of food, clothing, and shelter. A woman's self-esteem is also tied to her financial situation. Restricted incomes will limit her social life and the kinds of activities in which she can participate. For some, friendships may be lost in the bargain: thirty-eight percent say empty pocketbooks keep them from making friends after the divorce.

The message of the bad news is clear. At the very least, divorced women must learn from their own experiences, and their lessons should be heeded by *all* women. Many of the women in the study failed to participate in financial decisions within the marriage; and in the divorce process they also tended to stay in the dark about their finances. They relegated responsibility for determining an adequate settlement to others—lawyers, tax experts, real-estate brokers, parents, well-meaning friends—which often has a disastrous impact on their future life-style, as this survey respondent points out:

> The latter years in one's life come very quickly. Without financial protection for those years, we who did not understand the importance of pensions, investments, and so on were doomed to a life on the edge of poverty in our later years. Many of us who are now in our fifties and sixties were ignorant of financial protection, usually because our husbands (and society) deliberately kept us that way. Most of our own attorneys compounded the bad situation by patronizing us and not fighting to protect us in our later years.

Such mistakes are compounded further when many of these same women, out in the world and on their own after divorce, still fail to take their financial futures into their own hands. It's crucial to mention, too, that this lack of financial prowess cuts across all educational levels. Women with Ph.D's are just as likely to ignore these financial realities as women who barely made it through high school!

Introduction

In order not to become a poverty statistic, all women must take heed; you can't look at retirement issues a few months before you retire. As one of our survey respondents advises, younger women (divorced or not) ought to start planning now:

> Times are different now. There is no excuse for ignorance in these matters. Information can be found in all the women's magazines, on TV, and, literally, wherever one looks. Women must take advantage of this information and use it—before, during, and after the divorce.

Where We Go from Here

Most of the women in the study were able to find themselves and to achieve personal and professional fulfillment after divorce. And while the statistics do not bode well when one looks at the economic picture—by the year 2000, there will be nineteen million women over the age of sixty-five, many of whom may be divorced and looking at poverty by then—the study demonstrates that women are capable of beating the odds.

This book, and the women's voices it echoes, are a testament to women's resilience and courage. Their journeys, often harrowing, usually hopeful, are as different as the women themselves, and yet each woman's story has within it a universal quality, a basic truth that we (and they) hope will inspire and comfort other women.

Section One: Growing Pains. When many of the women in the study emerged from their marriages, many were victims of "the cocoon effect." They first had to learn what it meant to find their separate identities and to stand on their own—an agonizing but rewarding process. In the first section of this book, we examine this process of adult development and, in particular, how divorce spurs a woman's psychological growth.

In Chapter One, we explain adult development and examine what we call rediscovery, a process through which the women in the study circled back to the point in time when so many of them had abandoned their developing identities in favor of marching down the aisle. According to some developmental psychologists, a man grows from his accomplishments and his independence, and a woman grows from her relationships, gaining a sense of self from her connections. However, our findings tell another story—and we hold that women need *both* types of growth experiences. Women need to be connected and, at the same time, to be autonomous. (So do men, but it is women who are the focus of this book.)

As we will describe in detail, developmental level, not chronological age, is the determinant of women's growth—and is a primary factor in her marriage and her postdivorce adjustment. We identified four developmental patterns in women:

• *Pausers* put their lives completely "on hold," forsaking their needs for those of their families. During marriage, they have virtually no sense of separate identity. The ideas they have when they first get married—about love, children, friendship, fidelity, themselves—change very little over the years.

• *Slow Motions*, who represent the most pervasive pattern in the study, take small, hesitant steps to become independent and nurture their own identities during marriage. These women are primarily concerned with their families and keeping up their part of the marital exchange, but they also allow themselves to be increasingly separate. As the years pass, Slow Motions, who were seemingly content with the circumscribed boundaries of their roles early in the marriage, begin to gradually transform their lives and shape their own identities.

• *Rewinders* never make peace with the cultural mandate. They always feel a little bit out of sync with their more domesticated peers; most have kids, but more because it was "the thing to do" than because they thought they would relish the role. In the seventies, Rewinders became increasingly disturbed by the gap between the stagnation of their own lives (and the boredom of their bedrooms) and what they perceived was happening to younger, unmarried, or more liberated women. Like Slow Motions, they explore new options and search for ways to nurture themselves during marriage, but they do it "on the edge"—having affairs, taking drugs, acting impulsively.

• *Players* are independent women who have a strong sense of identity: they know who they are and what they believe in. Therefore, they are able both to be in relationships and to give to others without sacrificing their own needs. They look for men with similar qualities, who will support their growth, and whom they will support in return. Hardly any of our women were

Players during their marriages, but eight out of ten became Players after divorce.

In Chapter Two, "Emotional Survival," we look at what happens when divorce strikes. Rather than rehashing the old news about the "emotional divorce"—and the fact that after divorce women experience a variety of core emotions such as anger and loneliness—we look at a new phenomenon unearthed by the study: "emotional clustering," a whirlwind of erratic and volatile feelings. Every woman has a different emotional cluster, a different rhythm of recuperation; the ebb and flow of emotions are uniquely her own, which is why talking about predictable stages or offering any kind of prescriptive model of divorce can't possibly work. We also explain how the emotional pain of divorce, particularly in the first year, is related to the pain of searching for one's identity after so many years of living by other people's definitions. Even a consideration such as who did the leaving is really not as important as where a woman is in developmental terms.

In Chapter Three, "Dollars and Nonsense," we see that the way a woman handles finances in the immediate aftermath of divorce is also a function of her inner growth. Money is the last frontier of independence, but because of their conditioning, most women don't know how to garner "green power." We look at the high cost of being taken care of; how women confuse cash with caring and, consequently, delude themselves about both money and their marriages. Most important, we examine what happens during the legal process to women who have abdicated responsibility for their financial lives and, making matters worse, can't separate their feelings from their finances. It's not a very pretty picture. From bargaining with adversarial ex-spouses to the hiring and handling of lawyers to slogging their way through the legal process, women are disadvantaged. However, some do better than others, and from those women we hear valuable lessons about getting an equitable financial settlement.

In Chapter Four, "Letting Go," we draw heavily on the survey findings to illustrate the many ways women do nurture their own identities after divorce, which, not so incidentally, eases the pain of separation. We stress not only the importance of taking risks and getting out—out of the house, out of old habits and ruts, out of relationships that are no longer nurturing—but also the importance of going inside. Some women use therapy; others turn to spiritual pursuits; many do both. In order to let go of the anguish, they must journey deep within themselves and take responsibility for their part in the breakup of the marriage.

Section Two: Moving On. Our survey indicates that two to three years after divorce, most women begin to resolve the identity crisis that divorce precipitates. This section looks at how the rediscovery process inspires social, emotional, and financial changes in women's lives and how a woman's growth in each of these arenas helps her move toward a stronger sense of self.

In Chapter Five, "Sex and the Suddenly Single Older Woman," we examine the attitudes about sex that most of our women— "good girls" of the forties and fifties—brought to their marriages; how they changed or didn't change over the years; and what they experienced when they stepped out of the cocoon. We look at dating in the nineties and hear from the women themselves about the men they meet, what they fear, and how their age does—or doesn't—matter. Finally, we look at sexual development as a barometer of psychological development. A woman's intentions, the kind of man she chooses to have sex with, even lovemaking itself, are revealing indicators of her developmental growth.

In Chapter Six, "You've Got To Have Friends," we probe women's friendships, which are considered by an overwhelming majority of women to be the most important element in healing after divorce. Again, we look at the developmental aspect: the kind of relationships a woman pursues and nurtures is closely linked to how strong a sense of identity she has. We look at what happens to old friends left over from the married years; how new friends are found; why some friendships are toxic. And we see that good friendships are clearly a buoy in times of trouble and a training ground for other intimate relationships as well.

In Chapter Seven, "The Old Gray Mare," we look at the physical effects of divorce and explore the double whammy of growing older and growing older alone. We look at women's health during marriage: how women often blame themselves for ailments or simply disregard what their minds tell them through their bodies, only to pay the piper after divorce. We explore the myths of menopause, which, to many women's surprise, marks a reawakening of sexuality and new feelings of freedom. Once again, the developmental picture cannot be overlooked; fears of growing older wane as women learn to stand on their own.

26

Chapter Eight, "Broken Ties/Mended Lives," chronicles the changes in women's relationships after divorce: with their children, their ex-husbands, and their families, particularly their parents, as well as their ex-families. We look at the legacy of divorce: what mothers tell their children; the lessons they wish to impart; how they see themselves as role models for a new generation.

We deal with children this late in the book for two important reasons: First, while women express concerns about their children, their major focus (and the focus of this book) is their own survival and how divorce affects them. Second, the real "news" unearthed by this study regarding children is how a mother's developmental growth affects them. Just as the formation of a separate identity impacts on women's emotional adjustment, their sex lives, and their friendships, so does it affect their relationships with their children. One interviewee after another told the same story: "When I got my life together, my relationship with my children improved."

In Chapter Nine, "Do as We Say, Not as We Did," the women share the economic lessons they learned. We offer some concrete information about the importance of long-range financial planning after divorce and more than a few warnings on the subject, as well. We demonstrate that neither an opulent predivorce lifestyle nor a sizable financial settlement guarantees economic stability after divorce. And while it is clearly harder to consider financial planning when you don't have enough money for groceries—let alone for savings accounts or investments—suggestions from other women's experiences can be a guide for taking steps to change your economic future.

In the Epilogue, "Where Are They Now? Parting Words from Women on the Road to Rediscovery," the women whose lives have unfolded on these pages tell where they are now and offer thoughts about divorce.

A Final Note

Although this is a book about the aftermath of divorce, it is also a book about change. It is a book that can be read by any woman who feels "stuck" in her life and who wants to better understand the emotional and cultural forces that assault her.

Think of *divorce* in its broadest sense, as a symbol of change. You don't necessarily have to end a relationship to learn how to "give change a chance," as Joann Cress put it.

Likewise, this is not a book just for mid-life and older women. The "cocoon effect"—in which marriage stifles a woman's growth and prevents her from developing a separate identity—may be alive and well among certain members of the up-and-coming generation too. It's obvious that some younger women have simply traded one fairy tale for another. They use words such as "romantic," "appreciative," "communicative," "understanding," and "family-oriented" to describe the qualities they seek in a mate, which does not sound all that different from what their mothers were looking for two or three decades ago. Similarly, their perspectives on intimacy are shaped by illusions. A nineteen-year-old undergraduate student wrote the following in a term paper for an adult-development course:

> A good example of intimacy in a marriage can be demonstrated in the play *Romeo and Juliet.* It was love at first sight between these two teenagers. And their love became so intense that they performed the act of sex. . . . In addition to this play, there are many books, movies and television programs that display how to be intimate with your husband. Some are the soap operas *General Hospital, All My Children,* and the movie *Parenthood.*

While their mothers believed that staying at home, raising kids, and being a dutiful wife was everything, some younger women believe they can *have everything* through "egalitarian" relationships. Prince Charming is now a man who bares his soul and shares equally in all things, from finances to child rearing. But society has not yet made it possible for true equity to exist between men and women. Men still earn more, institutionalized child care does not exist, and the workplace makes scant provision when both Mom and Dad work, which is the case in about sixty-seven percent of all families. And, as with generations of women before them, it's women who are taking up the slack.

In the face of such pressure, the pendulum is swinging back, and some women seem to be stalking the "good provider" once again. In an interview with Kate Rand Lloyd, the former editor of *Working Woman,* she tells us:

The myth is still alive with many young women who are attending college. Many do not want to do it *all*—like their mothers or older sisters. They see their mothers trying to juggle both a career and a family and being perpetually exhausted and knocking themselves dead. I remember some years ago when Princeton first accepted girls, a friend of mine was an assistant dean. And I was talking so rhapsodically about how women were so independent. But she said that Princeton was full of "nouvelle gold diggers"—very smart young girls who want to find a very rich husband!

The process of finding one's identity can at times feel overwhelming, but it is ultimately liberating for the vast majority of women who embark on the voyage. The experience of divorce is analogous to dealing with an aging parent or seeing a loved one through a terminal illness. You spend months readying yourself emotionally to put that person into a nursing home or admit him or her to a hospice. But when death finally comes, the real mourning process begins. Unlike mourning a death, though, the good news about divorce is that mourning the loss of a marriage gives rise to an entirely new life.

This is a book about women's development and, in particular, about how the pivotal transition of divorce impacts on that process and propels women's growth. It is a book for all women of all ages, married or single. Divorce should be viewed as neither a panacea nor a death knell. However, there is much to be learned from women who have negotiated one of life's more precarious paths.

SECTION 1
Growing Pains

◇

1

Rediscovery:
Circling Back to Find
the Girls They Left Behind

> The best way I can explain it, is that I walked around
> with a brown paper bag on my head and suddenly it
> flew off!
>
> —Phyllis May, interviewee,
> describing her growth after divorce

Everygirl's American Dream

For years, Joann Cress was an obedient little girl to her
overbearing husband. When Tony took her cigarettes away, she
didn't smoke. When Tony told her how to fold diapers, she did
it *his* way. When she asked for money, Tony determined how
much she needed, and he made her beg for every penny. "It was
always his money, not our money. He made all the decisions.

"I had a growing dissatisfaction over the years, but I knew
nothing about myself. I always felt it was my role as wife to
maintain the family." Like many of the women in the study,
Joann confused love with control. If Tony balked and barked at
her, it meant he cared.

"I'll finally be taken care of," she remembers thinking as she
danced with her new husband to the strains of "More"—their
wedding song. It was 1966. She was eighteen years old; Tony
was twenty-two—an "untouchable" (because he was four years
older) whom she had always worshipped from afar. "He was a
good catch—a good provider—the one I had been saving myself
for."

The "baby" in a family of five, Joann had a typical fifties family:
her strict Irish father ruled the roost, and Mom suffered in
silence. The kids went to repressive parochial schools, leaving
Joann with an overdeveloped conscience and an underdeveloped

sense of self-esteem. Ever on the social fringe and ashamed of her hand-me-downs ("I always felt like a poor person"), Joann envied the popular girls in high school who giggled with each other in the hallways and rushed home after school every day to see Dick Clark's *American Bandstand* and to practice the Stroll in each other's living rooms.

Tony was her ticket. When he asked her to marry him, Joann began to feel that she deserved a place in the world too—a piece of the American Dream. "Tony seemed to know a lot more than me. I thought he was wiser, and I would listen to his ideas before my own."

But married life was stark and hollow. "Tony wouldn't let me work, because it 'looked bad' for him. And I didn't get any satisfaction from cleaning or doing the laundry." Typical of other women in the study, Joann didn't blame her husband; she thought it was her fault. And she began to search for something that would make things better. Within six months, she was pregnant.

Children were as much a part of Everygirl's dream as the house in the suburbs. Indeed, though ninety percent of our interviewees were virgins when they got married, a third got pregnant on their honeymoons! Considering how young most of the women were, it's impossible not to think of them as children having children.

"Childbirth wasn't the thrilling experience I thought it would be," admits a wiser Joann today. "I gained weight and felt unattractive." And the baby didn't magically unite Joann and Tony. "Nothing changed. He didn't share my happiness." Nor did he share her burden.

Around the time their second son was born, Joann discovered that Tony had been having an affair. "He did it when I was *pregnant*," she says, still amazed. "Of course, then I took the blame, thinking that I was just not woman enough for him. I had gained weight, so obviously, *I* was the problem."

Tony swore the affair would be his last, and Joann agreed to give her errant husband another chance. She went back to the security and shelter of her marriage—back into the cocoon. "I had two children, kept the house, loved him, made him a sandwich, and filled his Thermos in the morning. It was all I knew."

Identities Lost and Found: Four Developmental Paths

Looking at Joann Cress today, a commanding and confident forty-eight-year-old brunette, it's hard to believe that she was once a timid teenage bride whose credo was "peace at any price." But for many years Joann's individual identity got lost in the Mr.-and-Mrs. shuffle of marriage. She married young, before she had a chance to find out who she was and what she wanted out of life. A "Joann-Without-Tony" barely existed, because Joann never had a chance to fully accomplish the most important task of later adolescence: the formation of a separate *identity*, a consistent and reliable sense of who she was and what she believed in.

When Joann got married, she lacked the basic developmental tools of adulthood, and where was she going to get them? Her marriage was like a cocoon, a barrier between her and the outside world. And though she had reservations about her life, for many years she tried to ignore the inner voices that plagued her.

During their marriages, many women were like Joann, casualties of a marital subculture that crushed their emerging identities. Typically, the older women were wed in the fifties and the younger ones in the sixties, a time when most women married young and gave little thought to goals other than becoming wives. Unlike young men—who, as boys, were urged to separate from their parents, to make independent decisions about their lives, and to become responsible for themselves in the "real" world—for most of these women, the journey from childhood to adulthood was a narrow, nonstop route, and the final destination was marriage.

As wives and mothers, they could easily tick off a list of their husband's or children's needs and desires, but most had no sense of what *they* wanted. Twenty or thirty years later, divorced and stripped of the roles that once defined them, many of them are understandably at a loss. Decades of social change have passed them by, and, suddenly, they find themselves single and living in a totally different world.

Interestingly, some women are better prepared for the impact of single life than others, and many of the better-prepared ones experience a new surge of growth when they get divorced. Some of the others take longer to adjust to the changes. And some never adapt at all.

35

Delving into their stories and analyzing the differences between the various ways they recuperated, the study found an important relationship between a woman's mid-life development and how she handles divorce: *postdivorce adjustment is correlated with predivorce independence.* So, the stronger a woman's identity in marriage, the smoother (and sometimes faster) her "rediscovery" process after divorce. Conversely, a woman who flounders in the aftermath is usually one whose emotional development was arrested or stunted during her marriage, a woman who has a poorly-defined identity and low self-esteem.

In the "Divorce Over 40" study, each woman's course of development was unique. By examining their lives before and after divorce, however, it became clear that three basic elements affected each woman's rediscovery process.

1. How much she bought into the traditional cultural "package" society offered women in the forties and fifties.
2. How much she was able to "hear" the message of the women's movement during the seventies.
3. How capable she was—as an individual—of responding to her own internal voice and allowing herself to change.

Based on the above elements, the study isolated four predominant types of identity searchers. Their developmental paths, which influenced both the climate of their marriages and how they weathered divorce, are analogous to the various functions on a videotape player. A woman's growth and development continues, on "play," unless it is interrupted by pushing "pause," which freezes the picture and stops the developmental process, or "slow motion," which slows the developmental process, or "rewind," which replays an earlier portion of her life, the rebellious teenage years. Thus, we have our four types: *Players, Pausers, Slow Motions,* and *Rewinders* (for a bird's-eye view, see the chart on pages 38 and 39):

• *Pausers*—Women who bought the cultural package lock, stock, and barrel. After they got married, they put their own lives "on hold." The paradox was that while they supported their husbands' growth, raised children, and ran their households, their own emotional growth and psychological development was stifled. Their one-liners about marriage tell it all: "I felt like I was on the same level as the children," one woman admits. "He was the professor; I was the pupil," says another. "The overseer and the slave," tells a third. Pausers were completely resistant to, if not downright threatened by, the message of the women's movement. They didn't search for their identity, nor make developmental strides until divorce forced them to.

• *Slow Motions*—Women who, like Joann Cress, believed in the fairy tale—at first. However, secretly, many harbored gnawing feelings of vague discontent. They represent the most pervasive pattern in the study. Joann "made mental notes" about her relationship. "My girlfriends would talk about their husbands— how much they did, how they were with the kids—and I would think, 'That's not what I have in my marriage.'" Likewise, Gail Leperk says she "stored my insights in an imaginary black box that I knew I'd open some day." And after her sixth child, Anne Garner recalls, "I felt that I should be happy, but I wasn't!"

Some Slow Motions were subtly influenced by the women's movement, but only allowed themselves to cheer quietly from the sidelines so that their husbands wouldn't notice. Other Slow Motions *thought* they weren't affected at all. Years later when they divorced, however, they realized that they had been swayed by the changing times, if only on a subliminal level. In either scenario, Slow Motions usually take small, hesitant steps toward independence during marriage, gradually and over many years. They begin to build a separate identities by going back to school, taking part-time jobs, doing volunteer work, comparing notes with their girlfriends. Consciously in some cases, unconsciously in others, they stockpile these experiences. When they divorce, they can sort through their inventory and survey all that they have accomplished, which enables them to launch a new enterprise: themselves.

• *Rewinders*—Women who never made peace with the cultural mandate but didn't have the inner strength to buck societal pressure. They got married and tried to fit in. But they always feel out of sync with their more domesticated peers. Most have children, but they became mothers because it was "the thing to do," not because they thought they would relish the role.

The message of the women's movement was thrilling to Rewinders, for it broadcast and confirmed everything they suspected about their lives but never dared to express. It gave them

FOUR DEVELOPMENTAL PATHS—

DEVELOPMENTAL CATEGORIES	Did She Believe in the Cultural "Package" of the '40s and '50s?	Could She "Hear" the Message of the Women's Movement in the '70s?
PAUSER	Totally—and thought it would bring her happiness and everything she ever needed.	Not at all! If she did, she was threatened by the idea of "liberation."
SLOW MOTION	Only early in marriage; she wanted it all but also wondered what was missing from her life.	Yes, on a conscious or unconscious level; she began to change herself and "the rules" of her marriage accordingly.
REWINDER	Never quite liked the mold, but tried to fit in it anyway; always felt out of sync with her more domesticated peers.	Loved the ideas and felt validated by them! Read many books, got involved in consciousness-raising groups and other aspects of the movement.
PLAYER	Sifted through the package—kept what suited her identity and discarded the rest.	Took what appealed to her; most of the ideas spoke to principles she already believed in.

A BIRD'S-EYE VIEW

Can She Listen to Her Own Internal Voices? (*See note below)	After Divorce . . . The Advantages	After Divorce . . . The Disadvantages
No, she has too many defenses; trusts other people's opinions and ideas more than her own; low self-esteem.	Cautious about her moves, she takes time to sort out her feelings and is less apt to make rash decisions or sudden changes.	She may be in denial about her marriage, and the fantasy of a husband's return may stop her from finding herself.
She observes and listens to authority but quietly begins to make her own choices; increasing self-esteem.	Building esteem over the years, she can now look in the mirror and tally up her accomplishments to piece together a new identity.	She may need to give herself a push —if she has trouble recognizing or refocusing her own talents and achievements.
Makes impulsive, erratic decisions based on "the moment," not on her inner needs; willingness to experiment masks low self-esteem.	Adventurous and experimental, she has already learned what it means to take risks—an important prerequisite to becoming a Player.	She may bury the past without coming to terms with it or rely on destructive coping strategies to get her through the rough times.
Yes, trusts her inner instincts to guide her; well-defined identity and high self-esteem.	Understanding that adult development is a fluid, continuing process, she can always weather the stressful times.	Believing she has such a firm command of her own life, she may underestimate the toll of divorce.

* Other factors that affect this include: personality; parents' attitudes; ethnic, religious, and socioeconomic background; where she lives; her husband's attitudes and his receptiveness to change; children; work history; and various outside influences that touch her life over the years—from school and work to teachers, counselors, and other women.

"permission" to live life the way they had always wanted: their way and on the edge—very much like recalcitrant adolescents.

• *Players*—Independent women who have a strong sense of identity. They know who they are and what they believe in. In adolescence, they answered the essential questions of identity, so that they were able to sift through the cultural package and take what suited their needs. The same held true for the messages of the women's movement. Because they are able to be in relationships and to give to others without sacrificing their own needs, Players look for men with similar qualities, who will support their growth, and whom they will support in return.

Few of the women in the "Divorce Over 40" study were Players during their marriages. Some were Pausers and Rewinders; most were Slow Motions. No value judgment is intended. One developmental path isn't better than the others—just different. Depending on one's perception, one route might seem slower, another more circuitous or slightly more difficult. Also bear in mind that labels are limiting. These descriptions are meant to be representative composites—not definitive portraits. Within each of the categories are wide variations and many shades of gray.

Furthermore, each woman is a unique individual. A constellation of unforeseeable factors informs her journey: Among other variables are her personality; her family history; her socioeconomic, religious, and ethnic background; where she lives; her husband's attitudes and his receptiveness to change; her children; her work history; and diverse influences that touch her life over the years—from school and work to teachers, counselors, and other women.

No book, indeed, no study, could possibly tease out the particular significance that such factors—each as unique as the women themselves—play on growth and development. One thing is clear: In concert, the sum of those factors clearly affects how a woman responds to the inner voices of discontent during her marriage and how she views herself and conducts her life after divorce.

Ultimately, more than eight out of ten women in the study became Players—regardless of which developmental path they traveled during marriage. The rediscovery process enabled them to circle back to fill in their developmental gaps and thereby nourish their nascent identities.

Portraying women's growth by using a videotape metaphor for

the rediscovery process is not only graphic, it is also fitting: In a number of interviews, women are struck by the absence of their images in family albums, motion pictures, and videotapes compiled over the years. As wives and moms, it was their job to chronicle family lore; they were *behind* the camera, directing, coaxing, making sure that all the memorable moments were immortalized. But when these women later tried to reminisce, it was as if they hadn't existed all those years. They aren't *in* any of the pictures! Luckily, divorce allows them to step into the frame, view and review their lives in a new light, and, finally, to become Players, starring in their own stories.

Pausers: Like Mother, Like Daughter

"It's degrading," Kathryn Mason announced indignantly at her first interview, almost a year after her divorce. "He threw me away for a younger woman, like I was some piece of garbage. And that's what I feel like—I'm humiliated" At forty-eight, Kathryn, a quintessential Pauser, didn't have a clue about who she was. The incongruity between her inner and outer self was striking.

Extremely attractive and youthful in appearance, she was a broken woman inside, plagued by a tangle of guilt and rage. Slim and stylish, she often appeared on the society pages in La Jolla, California, where she was active in a number of charities. A member of one the city's most prominent clubs, an avid golfer and tennis player, she might have stepped out of the pages of *Town and Country*. Nearly a year had passed since her husband of thirty years walked out, but she still wore a large diamond engagement ring and wedding band. The word *I* was missing from Kathryn Mason's vocabulary. Every sentence began with *he*.

"He *is* coming back—this is just a phase. Lots of men go through it," she declared, confessing that she still set a place for him at the dinner table—even though he had moved out most of his belongings. She thought it was better, too, to tell their three children that their father had "gone on a vacation."

"It's not that we had a perfect marriage, but I was a good wife to him," she insisted, clutching a wad of soggy tissues in one hand, smoothing her hair with the other. Kathryn Mason was not letting go easily.

OUR TURN

Kathryn had married Jerry Mason for his ambition and drive. She admired him, and his success meant that she had "made it" too. No matter how abusive and impoverished her marriage seemed to an observer, Kathryn saw it as an anchor. An only child, in many ways she had unwittingly recreated her parents by marrying Jerry. He was jealous like her mother, who always accused Kathryn of being a "Daddy's girl" and of "stealing" her father's attention; and he was controlling and self-centered like her strict disciplinarian father. Her husband proved to be as elusive as her father too: "When I went into labor with Jerry, Jr., my mother had to take me to the hospital because Jerry was so busy."

Predictably, Kathryn plunged into motherhood, wearing her three children's accomplishments as badges of honor. She could recite every detail of her children's lives but knew very little about her workaholic husband. "We were like two ships passing in the night," Kathryn admitted, following with a quick disclaimer, which is typical of many Pausers who haven't yet come to terms with their shattered marriages: "But that's how it was with most of our friends. The man made a living, and the woman took care of the home. Of course his needs came first."

Sex was infrequent, always when Jerry wanted it, and never particularly satisfying to Kathryn. "I suspected that Jerry was meeting his needs outside the marriage." Obviously, being alone was worse than being cheated on. Kathryn came by this credo honestly: her mother had confided in her a few years before that she, too, had "put up" with Kathryn's father's affairs.

Many Pausers simply follow their mother's lead, going from daddy to husband, rarely questioning the transition from one household to the other. They *function* like adults on the outside, as Kathryn did, moving effortlessly in her social circle, taking care of the kids, but inside Pausers are not fully developed. The beliefs they held as teenagers—about love, children, friendship, fidelity, themselves—are carbon copies of their mother's beliefs. "My mother always told me, 'You stick by your man even though you have problems. You try to make it work.' "

Kathryn had erected a wall of denial, an emotional barricade that "protected" her from feeling the pain of Jerry's infidelities. After he walked out, her well-honed defenses prevented her from accepting that the marriage had really ended. "I knew Jerry was having affairs all those years, but those were just affairs. I never thought he'd leave me." Like mother, like daughter.

Kathryn, like most Pausers, changed very little over the years —even during the seventies. "Liberated from *what*?" she asked, shocked that an interviewer would even question her about the women's movement. She had a handsome, successful blue-blazered husband on her arm; what more did she need?

For some Pausers the day of reckoning comes when their husbands abandon them or when the first set of legal papers is delivered by their husband's attorney. Others, like Kathryn, take longer. And some never break through their denial.

Interviewing Kathryn again two years later, it is evident that her carefully mortared facade finally crumbled. It had begun when her mother died. "Jerry refused to go the funeral because he said he couldn't stand my mother. I told him that it was still important for me that he be there, but he just hung up on me."

No longer sheltered by the cocoon of marriage, Kathryn explains, "I was thrust into a hostile world. I realize now I had always lived by other people's definitions." Initially, the idea of life without a man (or parents) terrified Kathryn, but with the help of a therapist, she mustered the courage to face her past.

She went through tremendous emotional pain in confronting her feelings of loss and her anger—anger at Jerry and anger at her mother for perpetuating "the lie" about marriage. But, finally, Kathryn was beginning to try on a new identity and to reclaim the adolescent she had left at the altar, which is not an easy feat for a Pauser. Each faltering step in the "real" world was a struggle, but every inch Kathryn crept forward, she took a major stride toward independence.

"I've taken up my art again, you'll be pleased to hear," she says proudly, recalling how her husband once tore up her paintings in a jealous rage and forced her to quit art school. "There was a time I couldn't do *anything* unless Jerry approved of it. I don't have to worry about *that* anymore."

Slow Motions: Stockpiling During Marriage

When they were married, some of the Slow Motions in the study were almost as conservative as Pausers. They only inched their way out of the cocoon, always feeling the tug of the home front. Many were hesitant and ambivalent about cultivating new interests or making personal commitments. They worried that their children would suffer if they were absent from home for long hours, that their husbands would be threatened by their growth, that their parents, friends, and neighbors would think less of them. They often doubted whether they had a right to make such "selfish" choices.

Still, something unconsciously tugged at these Slow Motions, and a voice deep inside urged them to look closer in the mirror. So while they resisted, many also did a fair amount of exploration and questioning. Whether they finished the schooling they had dropped, worked for pay, or accelerated their volunteer activities, Slow Motions spent more and more time away from home. Such activities, as well as friendships with other women, enabled them to slowly stockpile their emotional and social resources, which served them well after divorce.

However, because their personal metamorphosis was largely unconscious, they didn't necessarily connect any of the changes in their lives with the women's movement. In fact, only after their marriages had ended and we posed the question, "Were you affected by the women's movement?" did some of our Slow Motions realize that the changes happening to women at large must also have touched them. A woman may have *thought* that she wasn't swimming in the new social and cultural currents, but her life told another story.

Alice Hampton, now fifty-two, is a case in point. She married the first time, at sixteen, because she had to. The second time, she was in love. "He was introverted, artistic, interesting, and sensitive." Jack, an older man, seemed to come from the same kind of background as hers. Perhaps he reminded her of the father who abandoned her as a child. At twenty-five, Alice settled into her new husband's life-style. They moved back East to live in *his* apartment, which was furnished in *his* taste, and they worked side-by-side to support *his* at-home consulting business. Alice was "oblivious" to the women's movement.

"I was consumed by my marriage. I was too busy working with my husband to notice," she insists. Describing her husband, Jack, as someone with "no social skills," Alice spent years covering his tracks, trying to make up for what he lacked. She didn't think twice about it. They never argued about how money was spent.

"If I wanted something, I could go buy it. The only struggle we had over money was the way it came in. There were always more bills than money. At times, there was a lot of work, and then the money would flow more evenly.

"All this time, we were in his bubble. I loved his life. It was his goals, his dreams," she says. Without realizing it, she then describes a change in her life-style reminiscent of many Slow Motions' marriages: "When I turned forty, I decided to start doing things for myself. I wanted to get rid of the bubble. I loved my husband, but I knew that this was as good as it was going to get. We had great sex for twenty-some years, but I needed to start taking care of myself."

It was 1977. Instead of working until ten o'clock every night, as she had always done to please her workaholic husband, Alice quit at four. She also staked out a tiny area in the corner of the living room and made it *hers*. "I started sewing again. I loved it."

Typical of many Slow Motions' husbands, Jack bristled when Alice made a place for herself. "He resented that I had an interest other than him. He'd walk into the living room and mutter offhandedly, 'Oh, you're sitting in that little hole of yours.' " Jack's resentment grew over the next several years, and so did the gulf between them. Alice begged him to go to a counselor with her, but he refused. "He didn't talk much, so I never knew what he was thinking."

Perhaps Jack Hampton viewed his Slow Motion wife's new stance as a form of treason. In any case, it is clear that when Alice let him know that she wanted to nurture her own interests and that she didn't believe in his "pipe dreams" anymore, he found a younger woman who would. Today, Alice doesn't believe "the other woman" broke up their marriage. "He didn't cheat on me—we had a very good sex life. He loved me, and I loved him. But when I was changing and he couldn't change, is when he had to move on . . . or out . . . whatever!"

Alice didn't want the marriage to end. "I don't know if I would have left him—I might have just put up with it. I didn't have a bad life." She was forty-seven, she had an eleven-year-old daughter (the two children from her first marriage were already in their late twenties), and she was frightened.

At first, Alice Hampton had no idea how many "chips" of self-esteem she had stored away over the years. She felt the proverbial pull: "I had given him the best years of my life." Then, with the hindsight of a Slow Motion who has gotten in touch with her own identity, she adds, almost parenthetically, "That's actually not so. Now I look a helluva lot better and am much healthier than I was way back then!"

When Slow Motions start ministering to *their* needs, rather than tending exclusively to their brood, people around them take notice. They are usually applauded by teachers and coworkers as they make strides toward independence, but not necessarily by the men in their lives. Some husbands think it's "cute" that the "little woman" ventures into the world . . . unless she rocks the boat too much.

When Caroline Breed went back to school—at age thirty-nine —her husband Tom was initially supportive. But when Caroline made dean's list and won a scholarship in her second year, Tom realized she was actually *serious* about working toward a career. "All of sudden, according to him, my major was 'something anybody could do.' At that point, things started coming apart."

Caroline admits that early in life she was inoculated with the cultural serum of the times. A fourth-generation southern "lady," she remembers coming home from Walt Disney's *Cinderella* when she was twelve or thirteen. "My parents and I were sitting around the kitchen table, eating a watermelon that Mother had cut up, and my mind was filled with these marvelous images of happiness ever after and this wonderful person who would carry me away. Prince Charming was definitely what I was looking for!"

Describing her parents, Caroline observes, "Daddy had lots of personality—he was a great salesman—but it was Mother who held it all together.

"But she only worked *at home,*" Caroline adds, inadvertently conveying the message that her mother's efforts were somehow less meaningful because she did the bookkeeping in the oak-paneled library of the rambling mansion that had been in the family for generations. That *job* became part of the *housework.* As a little girl who sat behind Daddy's massive desk and delighted in "playing office," Caroline thought of women as capable, but their *real* role was to bolster the men in the family and to keep the home fires burning. Naturally, that's how she saw her future "job" too.

Caroline Breed was a model wife. Married at nineteen, she quit college and went to work as a secretary so that her husband could finish his degree. By the early seventies, Tom was moving up the corporate ladder, and Caroline was right beside him, supporting his every step. When Tom bought rental houses, Caroline cleaned them up, managed, and rented them. When Tom started a consulting business on the side, Caroline ran off his blueprints.

Other than her three young children and Tom's work, however, Caroline had nothing of her own to ease the loneliness when Tom traveled, an increasingly frequent event. "I didn't have any expectations that my husband would fulfill my emotional needs, but I don't know where I thought I was supposed to get them met." Conditioned as a good Catholic girl, Caroline believed the suffering was quite natural. "I was trained to sacrifice, trained to be a martyr—you got points for that!"

An affair was also out of the question. "I'm very monogamous —that was instilled in me from early on too. I missed the sexual revolution altogether!"

Caroline did volunteer work for a while, setting up a program to teach English to the Vietnamese refugees who were flooding into St. Louis at the time. "It became a model for others, and I won a Missouri State PTA Life Membership." What she remembers most, however, is that Tom was too busy to show up when she was given the award. "I can still be brought to tears when I talk about it."

Talking to Tom did no good. All he cared about was making more money. They were doing less and less together, and he was lost in his career. "I was so much into his needs that I was pulling away from my own," she remarks. Then she went back to school.

The marriage came apart "slowly and painfully." During the last two years, Caroline now knows, Tom rented post-office boxes out of town, shifted money around, and finally declared bankruptcy. "He spent time plotting this." Meanwhile, Caroline found mentors at college who would support her in ways that Tom would—or could—not. The Breeds had also been going to a family therapist for two years, originally referred because one of their twin daughters was having temper tantrums—a common reaction for a child caught in a morass of unaddressed marital problems. But it was too late to save the marriage. Threatened by Caroline's increasing self-assurance, Tom ultimately filed for divorce.

Like Alice Hampton, Caroline admits that she would rather have kept the marriage together. "I felt railroaded by the therapist into accepting that it was over." Both women tried hard to hold on to their husbands—as did many Slow Motions who felt their marriages crumbling. However, in both cases, after divorce these women were able to view and review their growth, finally acknowledging the independent accomplishments they had unknowingly stockpiled over the years. They could look in the mirror and see at least a faint outline of their identities, the beginning of the *I*, which helped them heal from their husbands' betrayal.

Slow Motions: Moments of Truth

In contrast to the Slow Motions who were largely unaware of their own metamorphosis, except in retrospect, some Slow Motions, like Joann Cress, began to change on a very conscious level. In fact, some Slow Motions can point to a particular moment in time when they had what the early *Ms.* magazine called a "click" experience.

"It happened a few years after Tony's first affair—the day I found a woman's lipstick in Tony's car," recalls Joann Cress. This time, she didn't confront him. "I figured this was the way Tony was going to be. That was when I started working on myself."

It was 1973. A decade earlier, Betty Friedan, writing *The Feminine Mystique,* inspired several generations of so-called traditional women to question whether being "just a wife and mother" was enough. By then, the fledgling women's movement was already tackling questions of equal pay, sex discrimination, and women's health and organizing lobbying groups such as the National Organization for Women (NOW). At the grass-roots level, women had begun to form consciousness-raising groups and to arm themselves with knowledge about finances and the law—once the sole dominions of men. For the Slow Motions among them, such gatherings marked the first time they allowed themselves to trust other women, to admit their discontent, and to talk about how men—fathers, husbands, employers, teachers, doctors—had been treating them. They shared confidences, they got angry, and they started to change.

Joann's friend had convinced her to enroll in a women's rights course offered at the local high school. "She thought it might be 'good' for us." It was Joann's first foray into her own consciousness. The teacher warned her and her classmates, all married women in their thirties, that times were changing. She urged them to establish credit in their own names. A woman couldn't necessarily count on a man to take care of her for the rest of her life. "Look around the room," she admonished. "Many of you will be divorced or widowed one day, and you have to prepare yourselves."

"I really admired the woman who taught that course," says Joann, who adds that the teacher inspired her to assert her equality at home too. "She made her own husband help around the house and take care of the children. After all, they were *his* kids too. That floored me!" remembers Joann. "I always felt that this was the way women should be—but I had never heard anyone talk about actually *doing* it.

"That teacher turned on a light bulb in my head, and I said to myself, 'Hey! You've been living in the Dark Ages.'" Joann is quick to point out that her metamorphosis "did not happen overnight." Over the next fifteen years, she continued to chip away at the walls of the cocoon, making the slow, often agonizing, passage toward a separate identity. She listed her own name in the phone book; she opened her own bank account with the $100 prize she won in a bowling tournament; she even took a part-time job.

"I felt that if I went to work, I could handle the money and make decisions." Joann first worked at home, in the auto supply business Tony ran as a sideline to his regular job. But when he refused to write her a real paycheck with social security taken out, she went job hunting. Thereafter, Joann gained increasing self-respect and power in her marriage. Her ability to earn money and her insistence on having separate banking and charge accounts gave her a separate financial identity as well.

"I saw that I could still be independent and married too. I learned that I was entitled to a life with friends outside the marriage and to activities of my own."

Tony tried to hang on to any shred of control, and Joann kept surprising him. "When I got a job, I was not afraid of him anymore." Once, when Joann's car wouldn't start and she told him about it, Tony announced, "Okay, Miss Independence. You're a working woman. You want to go to work, you get it fixed." To his astonishment, she did.

The "final blow," as Joann calls it, was the day Tony demanded that she relinquish the checkbook for their joint account, "From now on, I'll handle everything for the house, but you'll be responsible for any bills with your name on it. You work—so why should I give you any money? I'm tired of this." Joann was even more floored by Tony's next statement: "You'll see that by my doing this that I love you."

"I just looked at him. My mouth dropped," recalls Joann. "Without even thinking, the next words out of my mouth were, 'I want a divorce.' He was speechless. I had never uttered the word *divorce* before. I told him, 'I don't need you. I'm strong enough to stand on my own.' "

The burgeoning women's movement and the experimentation of the Me Decade may have come too late to define some Slow Motions' marriages—but not too late to affect them. Phyllis May's transformation began when she enrolled in est, one of the many mind-expanding empowerment and awareness courses popular among the self explorers of the seventies. "By that time, I was already going through problems in my marriage. Taking that course made me see a lot about myself and the life I had been leading. It brought out my sense of strength. I realized that I was a terrific person. I had a gift for gab, too." She later took a self-actualization course. "I realized *I* was searching for recognition too."

Today, Phyllis, fifty-five and ten years divorced (and the author of the "brown paper bag" quote at the beginning of this chapter), is a vivacious Player who has no trouble expressing herself and knows what she wants out of life. She admits, however, that she wasn't always so self-assured. "If I just wanted to talk, I couldn't do that with him. He couldn't deal with the fact that his wife—a woman—was the center of attention. That didn't go with the circle of friends we had. The women stayed in the background."

Though they dipped into the changing currents of the times, Slow Motions like Joann and Phyllis were hardly at the forefront of a revolution. Typically, it took years for even the most radical Slow Motions to leave their marriages, if, in fact, they left at all. Joann Cress did. However, just as often, the reverse was true.

Phyllis May's husband left her for a younger (more malleable) woman. And when other Slow Motions' husbands walked out, many undoubtedly thought their increasingly independent wives had gone "too far."

Rewinders: Jumping on the Bandwagon

Nowhere was a revolution more evident than in our Rewinders households. Increasingly disturbed by the gap they perceived between themselves and younger, unmarried, or more liberated women, many of them embraced the women's movement and the counterculture with a passion. Like teenagers walking across a narrow precipice or playing chicken in speeding cars, Rewinders dare what Pausers or Slow Motions would never chance. But their searching always skirts "the edge."

Sometimes their experimentation—be it physical, sexual, or spiritual—leads Rewinders down blind alleys, into bad relationships, overindulgence of alcohol and drugs, promiscuity. The aftershock of such behavior plagues some Rewinders for years, but the mistakes are, at least, *theirs*. "I know I got into serious trouble with drugs and alcohol after my divorce," one interviewee, now a member of Alcoholics Anonymous, admitted, "but, in a strange way, I believe that going wild got me to where I am today—willing to face my life as a sober person."

As was true for many Slow Motions, books often opened the door for Rewinders to a different consciousness, but a Rewinder's response is always more extreme, if not melodramatic. "It changed my life!" exclaims forty-four-year-old Rewinder Lisa Frazier, referring to *The Women's Room* by Marilyn French, a novel often mentioned in interviews.

"When I read *The Women's Room*—about all the things I never had the opportunity to experience—I said, 'Oh, my God!' I started to cry and I started to shake. My hands trembled, and I sobbed, and I sobbed into the morning. I never got to sleep that night. I knew that I was married to the wrong guy. I knew that I hadn't stretched or grown. I hadn't explored anything!"

Typical of Rewinders who are given to hyperbole, Lisa made a sudden and, in her mind, irreversible decision: "Right then and there, I *had* to change my life." A Rewinder, impulsive and brash, often relies on quick-fix solutions. She lacks a long-term perspective because she cares most about what is happening in the moment and has little regard for the consequences of her actions and little understanding of her own inner landscapes. She stays stuck in the turbulence and turmoil of adolescence. And because she is perpetually distracting herself from the real business of growing up, she has trouble understanding the difference between rebellion and true independence.

"It took me a long time after I left Harvey to face myself," admits Helga Gross, a sprite of a woman, full of boundless energy, who, at sixty, defies ageist stereotypes. "What a trip!" she exclaims, reflecting on her Rewinder journey. Helga, whose family came here in 1939 seeking refuge from Hitler, never felt as if she fit in. Ashamed of her hardworking "greenhorn" parents—their accents, the way they dressed, the linoleum on their kitchen floor—she dreamed of becoming rich, which, to her, was "American." Her strict, distant father ridiculed Helga's "big ideas," but she was determined to escape his brutal reign and prove him wrong.

Harvey was her ticket out. Unfortunately, her husband denigrated her just as her father did. Helga felt empty and insecure as a young wife and never quite comfortable in the role of mother. "I remember crying a lot. I tried to defend myself and stick up for what I believed, but I'd always end up with this fear that he would leave me."

In the meantime, Helga and Harvey had begun to acquire the trappings of "the good life." "We were not rich, but we had enough money to buy a house, we had a maid, we had two cars, and we belonged to a club in the summer. I got manicures and had a standing beauty parlor appointment twice a week. I had become one of those women I had always wanted my mother to be!"

But it wasn't enough. So, when her three children were in school, she started gambling, playing bridge four, sometimes five, times a week for up to fifteen dollars a game, which was a fair amount of money in those days. "I was good at it—it made me feel better about myself. I remember being disappointed if Harvey was going to be home, because it meant that I had to cancel my card game. It became my life—I would have rather played cards than *anything!*"

In the late sixties, she decided to finish college. When "a long-haired hippie" at school introduced her to marijuana, Helga's consciousness was both altered and raised. "I read *The Feminine Mystique,* and I said, 'You mean somebody *else* is asking these things. You mean somebody *else* is having these feelings?'

"I stopped playing cards because I was starting to think differently than the other women. They were talking about weddings and bar mitzvahs and clothes, and I was rejecting all those things. Even though I was *living* like them, my head wasn't there. They were worried about where their kids were going to college or the drug problem, and here I was—smoking pot, listening to rock 'n' roll, and worrying about my *own* life!"

In retrospect, Helga believes that, among the other influences, marijuana played a major role in her transformation. "Pot made me lose my fear of Harvey and also changed my perception of me. I liked my uniqueness, instead of feeling ashamed of it. When I didn't smoke, the fear would come back."

Harvey disapproved of everything Helga did. Smoking marijuana had become "cool" in their social circle, and on occasion he smoked with her—at parties or when he wanted to get Helga "in the mood"—but he resented her getting high without him. So Helga began to hide it. "I would act like a sixteen-year-old, crouching in my bedroom to smoke a joint," she laughs, "or I'd smoke in the bathroom before he came home, stuff towels under the door, and spray perfume to disguise the smell!"

Ultimately, Helga walked out on Harvey. "I had given him all the things women gave in those days, but I can't say I gave him love." Helga thought that leaving Harvey meant she was free. But it would be many more years before she admitted to herself how desperately she wanted a "daddy" to take care of her, before she began to look at her own dependency. Only recently, twelve years after her divorce, did Helga finally "grow up."

Rewinders such as Helga prove that adolescence is not the sole province of teenagers. Just as an adolescent must question, even rebel against, parental and societal values, testing, assessing, and trying on new life-styles so that she can "find herself," a Rewinder tries to figure out who she is and what she wants out of life. The problem is, she gets stuck there, often clinging to the worst aspects of adolescence.

Sometimes, women on this developmental path act and dress

like teenagers. At sixty, for instance, Helga still dresses in faded jeans and funky T-shirts; her conversations are punctuated by phrases like "Hey, man!" and "Far out!"

Like teenagers who want to try on new identities, Rewinders may even change their names. In marriage, Helga went by the name of Helen Winer, the Americanized version of her first name combined with her husband's last name. After her divorce twelve years ago, Helen, the manicured lady from an affluent suburb of Philadelphia, stopped shaving her legs, moved to New Mexico, and began calling herself Helga Gross, the maiden name she had once found so embarrassing as the child of German-Jewish immigrant parents.

"I moved out West because I wanted the anonymity. I didn't want to be stuck with Helen Winer anymore, so I went where no one knew me. I felt, for the first time, that I could really be *me* —understand who I was, what my interests were, how *I* wanted to live my life. In a lot of ways, I felt like a teenager again—no, maybe for the first time."

Becoming a Player: What's Age Got to Do with It?

When the study was first launched, we expected that a woman's ability to get back on track developmentally—to redefine herself and to come to terms with being alone—would be related to chronological age. We hypothesized that the older group of women in the study, now between fifty and sixty years old, would be more resistant to change than women ten years younger and that it might be difficult for them to develop into Players.

After all, the younger women in the study were old enough to be schooled by the traditional fifties but young enough to be corrupted by the more liberated seventies. Older women, on the other hand, had been more strongly indoctrinated to believe that intellectual curiosity, self-interest, independence, and even sexuality were the provinces of men.

We were wrong, and time and again, our interviewees proved it. Not only Rewinders like Helga Gross, but also less daring Slow Motions, like fifty-seven-year-old Ellen Garland, who remembers when she first "picked up on" the women's movement: "In 1964, when I read Betty Friedan's book, *The Feminine Mystique,* I said, 'Holy cow!' I realized that I had this vague discontentment a lot of the time. I knew that I wasn't using everything that I had to use. I remember thinking, 'This is not a life!' I remember thinking, 'I'm not even thirty.' "

Similarly, Evelyn Dorrin, fifty-six, recalls herself, over twenty years ago, buying and savoring her first copy of *Ms.*, whose cover featured an octopuslike woman juggling her many responsibilities. "I saved it, and every time we moved, it came with me. It's still in the house somewhere!"

Granted, some of the women in the older group were Pausers who shunned the message of the women's movement, but so were some younger women. But the reverse is obviously true, as well. Many of our older women were drawn to the women's movement. In fact, one of the few Players among our interviewees, Melanie Spade, is sixty-two! The bottom line is that *developmental age, not chronological age, is the key determinant of postdivorce adjustment.*

On the Road to Rediscovery: Becoming a Player

Thus, the process of forging an identity can happen at *any* point in a woman's life, so even women whose development is frozen (Pausers), delayed (Slow Motions), or wildly erratic (Rewinders) during marriage have a chance to grow up after divorce—and become Players. It bears repeating that, while the developmental paths are different, none is necessarily better than the others.

In fact, as the chart on pages 38–39 shows, each pattern has its own strengths in the aftermath of divorce. A Pauser, who, like the tortoise in the fabled race, takes her time and evaluates every plan with precision and care, is not likely to make impetuous moves that she might later regret. A Slow Motion, who takes gradual steps toward independence, has a reservoir of strengths to draw on after divorce. And a Rewinder, impatient in her marriage, always stretching and searching (albeit sometimes down a blind alley!), has already become adept at risk taking, an important aspect of postdivorce adjustment.

Likewise, after divorce each type has different needs. The Pauser has to give herself a push, the Slow Motion must recognize and channel the power she has unwittingly amassed, the Rewinder has to temper her wild instincts and be more selective about the kinds of risks she will take.

The "Divorce Over 40" study demonstrates that no matter which developmental path women take during marriage, after divorce, all must undergo the rediscovery process. Pausers, Slow Motions, and Rewinders have to reclaim parts of their lost identities. Even Players, who seem to know themselves and know what they want out of life, often have to reassess their identities in light of their new status. In all cases, this "circling back" is a subtle, internalized, and individualized process, usually spanning two or more years. On the road to rediscovery, however, a woman will begin to notice a distinct difference in her own behavior:

• *She attempts to answer that key question, Who am I?* After years of being *with* someone, she finally decides what she wants to *be*. We can't express this phenomenon better than spunky fifty-six-year-old Betty Duprey, who left her husband of thirty years: "Leaving the marriage was my leaving home for the first time. I was going out to look for my identity. I wanted to come out as *Betty* Duprey, and I wanted to be accepted without Mr. Duprey next to me."

Interestingly, many parents from the "old school" of staying married no matter what questioned their daughter's motives for leaving long-term marriages. Betty's parents secretly worried that Betty had been unfaithful to her husband, but Betty guessed their suspicions and told them: "It's not another man—it's *me!*"

• *She takes risks.* Joann Cress, who started on the road to rediscovery in the final years of her marriage, first took small risks, such as cutting her hair even though she knew Tony preferred it long. Years later, in fact, Tony blamed their failed marriage on that haircut. "If I really cared about him, I would have let my hair grow long!" Joann also took big risks, such as going back to college, even though it was extremely difficult for her. "For the first time I was being judged as Joann Cress. I had always had someone else to fall back on. If I didn't do well, I had no one to blame but myself. I was not used to that."

Of course, what feels like a risk to one woman may not feel like a challenge to another. For Joann, a fifty-minute drive to a town several parkways and a suspension bridge away was a monumental step toward self-sufficiency. She wanted to visit her ailing mother; Tony didn't want her to go. But he could no longer forbid Joann to use the car as he had done in the early years of their marriage; she now had a job and a car of her own. So, he tried to scare her. "You can't do it," he warned. "You can't

handle the highways, and you've never driven across a bridge."
Joann defied him. "I was petrified—but I did it . . . without any
help from anyone!"

• *She begins to listen to and trust an authority within her.* Players listen
to themselves, rather than depending on what their parents, their
husbands (or ex-husbands), or even their peers have to say. Just
as it is the adolescent's greatest challenge to separate from the
crowd—to learn to think of oneself as an *I* instead of a *we*—on
the road to rediscovery, a woman truly becomes a Player: she
begins to stand on her own and trust her instincts and judgment.

• *She figures out what* she *needs and wants out of life and then starts
to pursue her own dreams.* As a wife she had promised to honor
and obey, and to be a true helpmate. "Stand by Your Man," the
popular country-and-western tune told her. On the road to
rediscovery, she finally actualizes her *own* potential. Betty Duprey
wasn't getting what she needed in her marriage; all that mattered
was her husband. "I was part of *his* development, and I didn't
want him to fail." But after her divorce, Betty was on her own,
no longer obliged to support anyone else or to be subordinate.
"I was finally able to take care of me."

In circling back and rekindling interests they surrendered to
the cause of marriage and motherhood, our would-be Players
also connect with parts of themselves forsaken long ago. Anne
Garner took a writing course, reviving a childhood dream. A few
months later she moved out. She was fifty years old, still a wife
in legal terms, but she had run away from home and from a
thirty-year marriage. Anne was finally able to luxuriate in her
own company, doing what she loved, writing poetry and watching
old movies. "I sat on the floor and ate peanut butter sandwiches
off paper plates." She laughs, recalling what it was like to be alone
in her new apartment for the first time. "It was a tiny studio, but
it was *mine*. It was every fantasy I ever had—and the first time I
was able to express myself."

Anne cluttered her new apartment with thrift-shop treasures
and covered the walls with photos and pictures. "Things were
hanging everywhere—wind chimes, mobiles, plants. And candles—I *love* candles. It was very sixties [a time Anne missed out
on]. I even had blue satin sheets! It was a fun time—I thought I
was hot shit!"

Players: Starring in Their Own Lives

Seven years after her divorce, Paula Oslow talks from the vantage point of a Slow Motion who traveled the road to rediscovery and became a Player: "I was like the teenager who needed to leave home. But I came to realize that the dissatisfaction was within myself." After her divorce, Paula dove into a whirl of social activity. "I jumped into my first affair—with my boss. But I learned real quick that the answer was not another man but for me to get to know myself.

"I feel like I'm living my third life now. My first was until I was seventeen—I was raised on a farm and rode horseback every day. My second, from seventeen to forty, was as a married suburban housewife, doing all the traditional things. Then I gradually started to change, but I didn't know how it would manifest itself. After the divorce, when I got my own apartment, I had this feeling of a kid starting out. I finally began to feel that I, Paula, was living my own life, and I've never been sorry. My third life has been to find out who I am and to be an activist, a political person out in the world."

In Players' lives, the videotape machine keeps running. They know how to connect with other people without losing themselves. Players are autonomous and independent; they don't see themselves as the appendage of a parent or a husband. They are in touch with their own needs and do whatever is necessary to meet them. They don't have to be rebellious, like Rewinders, because they feel *entitled* to their growth, rather than feeling guilty, as so many women report. Like Paula Oslow, however, most of our women became Players *after* they were divorced. From our interviews, we estimate that no more than five percent were able to define themselves in the context of marriage.

Though Players are rare in our sample, Melanie Spade, a novelist who describes her protagonists as "powerful women," is a noteworthy exception. Like most girls of her time, Melanie wanted to get married, but on *her* terms. "I wanted it all—the white picket fence *and* the great career; I didn't care much about children."

Born and bred in New York City, the only child of affluent parents who applauded her talents, Melanie had parents who defied the mainstream message. "My mother said you're not only going to college, you're going to a *good* college." Melanie's parents also allowed her to travel after graduation. "I got out of high school in January, and because I had been skipped, I was only sixteen. I wanted to see the south, and I had time to kill before I enrolled in college. I had a father who would let me do these things."

Melanie describes herself and her friends, as "the beginning of women getting off their asses!" Not surprisingly, she became a significant mover and shaker in the early women's movement. "I protested on the steps of The Plaza hotel when they refused to let unaccompanied women into The Oak Bar." Her first marriage fell apart because she was moving up the corporate ladder in advertising. "I was going somewhere; he was going nowhere. He didn't have a direction." After her divorce, Melanie felt "as free as a bird!"

Why were so few women in the study Players? Some Players probably never married in the first place, like Katharine Hepburn, whose well-publicized thoughts on marriage, careers, and children make it clear that she believed it was impossible to have what she wanted *and* a family as well. Other Players are undoubtedly *still* married and may never get divorced, because they have mates who also have strong identities and with whom they share a mutual respect for each other's growth.

Most important, getting married and being a Player meant defying tradition. A study conducted by the Mellon Foundation in 1956, which polled a group of Vassar graduates, concluded that women were mainly interested in becoming housewives. Any commitment to outside goals or careers was rare. Those who were considering a career said they would stop when they married and had a family. It was as if being a Pauser was implied in the marriage vows!

Whether times have changed or not is debatable. Certainly, for women who married two or three decades ago, there was virtually no support for a Player's path. Young women who were able to buck the culture and achieve a strong sense of self early in life in spite of it had to have unusually supportive parents (like Melanie Spade's parents), as well as some encouraging mentors along the way.

Interestingly, during their interviews, several women referred to their girlhood selves as "tomboys"—quite a pejorative for those exhorted to be "little ladies." They were high achievers in school, good in science and math, masterful athletes, talented writers and speakers, leaders in school activities. We might have called them Players! But few of these women considered becoming lawyers, politicians, doctors, or engineers. If they harbored such subversive ideas, their dreams fell by the wayside. Their accomplishments were rarely applauded, they had no role models, and the workplace itself was limiting and resistant.

Young women were often guided onto home ec or vocational tracks in high school. After all, they were "just girls." Some even chose that route themselves. Betty Duprey recalls, "In school I was part of a group of young women who were always table-talking about our trousseaus. We were the young, going-to-be-engaged set, always about to be married. I gave up the academic course, because I was going steady." Betty was fourteen at the time. Three years later, she was married.

Remarkably, a clear before and after picture appears in the way many of our women talked about themselves as young teens and then as wives. Their emerging identities were obviously suppressed. Many of the best and the brightest were boxed into a corner, forced to negate their personal desires. Debby Black remembers:

At ten and eleven, I was outgoing, gregarious. I loved to have fun. I did very well in school with very little effort, but I always felt I was being held back. My parents were amenable to my exploring, but they used to put restrictions on me, and I fought them.

But then the adventurous Debby hit her teenage years.

I became an un-tomboy at the age of twelve. I was told by my best friend—a boy who was the leader of the gang—that I was too old to be that way. He told me I couldn't play hardball anymore [*an apt metaphor!*]. Other things were changing too. When I graduated from elementary school, I had received an academic award in math. Then I hit ninth grade and my confidence in my math ability went right down the hill.

This phenomenon has also been observed by psychologist Carol Gilligan, who notes that preadolescent girls go through "a moment of resistance," when they begin to see that their confidence and strength is not what society expects of them, so they learn to hide what they know and censor their thoughts.

Listen to Anne Garner talk about her earliest years:

> My father was a lawyer, a poet, an author, a statesman, and a politician. Before my teen years, I was writing a children's column for a local newspaper. I was writing poetry and short stories at the age of seven, so I knew I would be in that field.

We hear a different Anne entirely when, later in the interview, she talks about graduating from high school:

> I went on to business school because I was *fit to do nothing* [emphasis ours]—no skill in the world. Since my father was a lawyer, I took legal stenography.

Why did Anne, the talented writer, the high-achieving teenager who made it through high school by the time she was sixteen downshift her ambition so drastically? "I had such an affinity for law, but there weren't that many options. I had to take what they gave me."

The Pie Factor

Interestingly, certain women who chose careers and *look* like Players on the outside, *feel* the same inside as some of the more sheltered women in the study. Like Janet Cummings, a forty-seven-year-old attorney divorced after a twenty-year marriage: "Even though I knew I could support myself financially, the same divorced-woman tapes were going through my head when Bernard and I split up," she admits, "because the most significant factor was being over forty. You clearly understand what your limitations are at that age. When you're younger, you think, 'I'll fix this' or 'I'll do that,' but now you're forced to deal with reality in a greater way than you had in earlier years."

Janet's insights about herself crystallize an important point: just because a woman works outside the home or has an impressive career, doesn't mean that she has her developmental life in order. She is not necessarily a full-fledged Player. In some instances, in fact, the professional veneer is a false facade, masking work that needs to be done inside.

A New York City debutante whose father was a prominent surgeon, Janet grew up thinking, "I'd marry a broker and move to the suburbs. That's what you did when you got married." She dated in high school but "never got too involved." Janet married in 1970, after college and late in comparison to her girlfriends. "I was twenty-five—almost an old maid." She laughs, remembering how her mother "worried" about her. She describes her husband, Bernard, a man ten years her senior: "He required me to make no emotional commitment and made none himself."

Two years after she got married, Janet was working as an administrator at a social welfare agency. Constantly frustrated because she "had to teach first-level associate lawyers about tax law," she decided to go to law school herself. "Bernard thought it was a great idea. He never seemed anything but supportive."

Their first daughter was born in the middle of law school, and their son arrived when she started work at a law firm. Bernard was always there to take up the slack. "I had to work many weekends and nights, and he took care of the kids. I could never have had a career but for his willingness," she admits.

At first glance, this seems a perfect Player's marriage. In time, however, Bernard's "emotional incapability" began to eat away at Janet. "We were always cordial, in fairly close communication about the children, but we were spending less and less time with each other. I felt Bernard was literally incapable of involving anyone in his life. It's not that *he* changed," she stresses, "but at some point *I* began to notice."

Undoubtedly, that point coincided with her half-sister's attempted suicide in 1981. Though Janet first sneered at the allegations of incest that prompted the suicide, a few years later Janet began to have flashbacks about her own sexual abuse, recalling events long buried in her psyche. But not until she initiated her separation in 1990 did "the other person" inside her begin to emerge.

"One day I was sitting at the word processor, and there was something on the screen I didn't write. Another time, I was in a trial, making a summation. And I had no idea what was going on in court."

Now Janet understands that when she *dissociates,* the wounded child inside her takes over. Janet explains, "There have always been two people: The up-front me has always been extremely capable. She obviously kept me going all these years. The other person—a completely shattered, frightened individual—is totally dependent. I'm now trying to understand how we get them back together."

Janet's case may seem extreme; however, many women—by some estimates, as many as one in three—are dealing with some form of sexual abuse today. Certainly, other of our interviewees volunteered stories of childhood abuse, as well.

More important, Janet's story dramatizes a very important developmental principle. We call it our developmental-pie theory. Imagine identity as a pie divided into three equal pieces:

- social autonomy (understanding who you are)
- emotional integration (understanding what you feel)
- personal responsibility (understanding that you alone are accountable for your own welfare)

To become a whole person, one must work on all three pieces of the pie. In Janet Cummings's case, she unconsciously chose a husband who wouldn't challenge the part of her that was locked away as a result of so many years of sexual abuse. Even though it was her half-sister's crisis that first precipitated memories of Janet's abuse, it was the trauma of her separation and divorce that destroyed her once impenetrable defense system. "I was unconsciously racing to get away from it all those years," confesses Janet, who is now in intensive psychotherapy to deal with the demons of her childhood.

Today, picking up the painful pieces of her life, she fears, "It will be years before I sort it all out." At the same time she is hopeful because at least now she is dealing with *all* of herself. And, on most days she feels ready for it. "There must be something more than the kind of emotional deprivation I had for the last twenty years. I assume that at some point I will come to peace with who I am."

For other divorced women in the study also, "coming to peace" means concentrating on the emotional slice of the developmental pie, as Janet Cummings is doing now. Gwenn Banning, for example, worked as a nurse throughout her marriage. She, too, looked like a Player in many respects. But her husband, Steve— a job-hopper eternally in search of a vocation—was Gwenn's real career. She constantly bolstered his ego and tried to help him find himself. Gwenn admits, "I thought I would grow old with this man. I even specialized in the cardiovascular unit, because heart disease ran in his family, and I figured one day he'd have a heart attack, and I'd have to take care of him."

When it came to money, Gwenn—like the vast majority of women in the study—was also a Pauser. "Steve handled everything. I would give him my paycheck, and he would give me whatever I needed. That didn't bother me at all. I wasn't aware of any financial problems."

When Steve's mismanagement of their finances got so out of hand that he was about to declare bankruptcy, Gwenn said, "No. I'll work more hours, we'll cut back on expenses, and we'll borrow from whoever we can. I didn't want to mess up our credit."

Gwenn lived her life for her husband. She rushed in to save him because she believed her job was to support him, in this case literally, even if that meant working sixteen-hour days during her ninth month of pregnancy (it would be their second child). Was she resentful about cleaning up a mess that she had had absolutely no part in creating? "No, I loved him."

Gwenn's world crashed when Steve left. Then, because she had no idea of what *she* felt after decades of concentrating on her husband's feelings, Gwenn had to circle back to fill in the major gaps in her emotional development and finally begin to take responsibility for herself. Because she was a Pauser, not the Player she appeared to be, she moved very slowly at first. "I tried to learn to balance my checkbook after he left. I couldn't, so I photocopied everything and mailed it to Steve who was then in South Carolina and asked him to do it!"

Every woman has a different developmental task to accomplish after divorce. Some must look at the social piece of the pie, finding the *I* in the mirror; others need to focus on the emotional piece, so that they understand what they're feeling; and most must reckon with the personal-responsibility piece, which includes learning to take care of themselves and support themselves financially.

In the end, divorce often impels women to "grow up." Anita

Parsons, separated for six years, divorced for three, says of her female friends, "We can laugh about it now." And what happens when she and her divorced companions compare notes about their ex-husbands? "What always comes up is how self-centered they were—like little boys." At the same time, Anita, who married at twenty "to get away from my parents," admits, "I guess I was like a little girl in the marriage too. I definitely feel more grown up now. I do a lot of things that I would have never done when I was married."

While their "traditional" husbands were busy racking up outside achievements, counting on their wives to maintain the relationships and to tell them what they were feeling, women like Anita and her friends often counted on their husbands to define them and to take care of them. Katharine Hepburn articulates these women's perspective in the 1955 movie *The Rainmaker:* "I want a man who can look into the mirror and tell me who he is—a man who can look into my eyes and tell me who I am!"

Some theorists maintain that men's and women's development are different—men grow through their activities and women through their connections. But this study points to social conditioning as the real culprit in marital distress. Neither "little boys" nor "little girls"—that is, men and women cordoned off by society into strictly defined roles—have the developmental tools to negotiate lasting relationships. To be a whole human being, one needs to nurture both independence *and* the ability to be "in relationship." Otherwise, both genders are cheated of at least one piece of the developmental pie.

In *The Second Sex*, Simone de Beauvoir affirms D. H. Lawrence's view of sexual love, paraphrasing, ". . . marriage should be a combining of two whole, independent existences, not a retreat, an annexation, a flight, a remedy." Especially for women married two or three decades ago, traditional marriage was often precisely what de Beauvoir warned it should not be: "a unit, a closed cell." Twenty or thirty years later, it is no wonder that the participants in the "Divorce Over 40" study flounder when it comes to dealing with the world of accomplishment and financial independence. Not so incidentally, their husbands—men who are uneasy when it comes to communicating or articulating their feelings—for their part, were denied the emotional piece of the pie!

2

Emotional Survival: Riding the Roller Coaster of Divorce

Anne is dead, the phone is cold
Grease congealed on the stove
Laundry is molding in the hamper
Ashtrays overflowing
Flowers withering in their vases
Grimy towels, mismatched socks
Soap operas drone on without her
The freezer needs defrosting.
Any more TV dinners in there?
The cat keeps searching for her.
Are we out of butter again?
Damn it, Anne! Why did you have to go?

—"Obituary for Anne," by Anne Garner

The Emotional Landscape of Divorce: Three Snapshots

The death of a long-term marriage is never a simple matter. In addition to experiencing external changes—new living arrangements, new family configurations, new relationships, new roles—divorced women have to honor their internal changes as well, an infinitely more difficult, and enduring, task. However, there is no such thing as a typical reaction to divorce. No two women are the same, nor are their stories, as these "snapshots" of that first moment of impact illustrate.

◊ Shortly after her twenty-fifth wedding anniversary, Gail Leperk's husband, George, finally went into an alcoholic rehabilitation facility. By then, Gail had suffered through years of his verbal abuse and volatile temper. "He was braining me. Alcohol was never the problem—everything else was."

Over the years, Gail, ever the loving, patient, understanding wife and mother, had been to seven different counselors, always

66

thinking it was *her* fault. "Sex was his number one complaint. There was not enough, or it was not good enough. It was always me—I was cold, frigid. He always put me down. And I accepted it." By her own admission, as a married woman Gail was totally dependent on George; she did nothing on her own.

"Even though things were getting worse and worse, I thought that we would work things out. I loved the good that I saw in him," she maintains. "He busted his gut for us, and he tried hard to be a good father. I thought we could make it work. That kept me motivated. I thought I was doing God's will."

Unfortunately, when George Leperk finally faced up to his alcoholism, he also met another woman. It was his second affair, as far as Gail knew; he met her in the hospital. "He had told me about the other one. Said he *needed* it." Only six months had gone by, and Gail was again confronted with George's infidelity. "I was in such shock! I said, 'That's it!' Intellectually, I knew I wanted the divorce the day I found out about the second affair. Emotionally, it took me a much longer time." During those next few months, a barrage of feelings pounded Gail. She felt "Shocked, abandoned, alone, full of self-pity, thrown out into the world, outraged. I was hurt. I cried a lot."

◊ When Evelyn Dorrin's thirty-four-year marriage ended, at first she plunged into "emotional hysteria," as she called it. She then flipped into being relieved and rational, all in the course of twenty-four hours! Evelyn, who characterizes herself as a late bloomer, was nevertheless ahead of her time in certain respects. In 1954, when her first son was born, she insisted that her husband change diapers ("I wasn't going to be home every single night"). Once the kids were in school, Evelyn worked; in the seventies, she was a member of a consciousness-raising group. (Even though she has moved several times since then, she never threw away her dog-eared copy of that first issue of *Ms.*, a memento of her early feminist stirrings!)

Looking back, however, Evelyn admits that for a long time her marriage was lifeless. "My children were away at college. He would come home, and we would have nothing to say to each other. There was just something missing." Finally, Evelyn, said to him, "Herb, there is something wrong, and I think you want to live alone."

Much to Evelyn's horror, a month later her husband took her up on her offer. He moved out. "I suppose it was mid-life crisis," suggests Evelyn, echoing the sentiments of so many women in the study whose husbands left, they said, "to find themselves," which was often a euphemism for taking up with a younger woman.

Evelyn was at once shocked, enraged, frightened—and hopeful. Her emotions kept changing, day to day, sometimes in the course of several hours. "There were nights when I would look in the mirror and I would say, 'Well, what are you going to do now, dummy? You're alone!' And then other days, I'd say, 'You know, maybe I needed a spark in my life. Maybe it's a good idea that he moved out for a few months. Maybe he'll want to come back; maybe he won't.' And then I'd think, 'And maybe *I* won't want him back!' " Some days, even in the face of utter despair, Evelyn also felt free for the first time in her life.

◊ "Oh, that initial shock of recognition!" exclaims Anne Garner, a fugitive from a thirty-year marriage, recalling her first night alone in a tiny sublet apartment. She was fifty years old and the mother of five step-ladder children—aged twenty-six, twenty-five, twenty-four, twenty-one, and eighteen. Only the youngest was still living at home when Anne moved out. For several years, she and her husband had been sleeping in separate beds, in separate bedrooms, living separate lives. "When I left, he didn't even notice that I was gone!"

Buddy Garner was an usher at Anne's brother's wedding, when she, a seventeen-year-old bridesmaid, spotted him across the aisle. Though she once worshipped Buddy and thought she "couldn't live without him," over the years Anne discovered that she and her five-years-older husband were worlds apart. Buddy never finished high school; Anne always wanted to go back to college.

"He didn't understand me," she notes, recalling the time she quoted a prayer to Buddy that connoted what *she* wanted from their relationship: "May your marriage be such a oneness that when one of you cries the other tastes salt." Buddy's answer was: "Anne, I don't even taste my own tears, how am I supposed to know what yours are like?"

In the early seventies Anne, a devout Catholic, was given

permission by her priest to go on the Pill. "I had gotten pregnant too many times," she explains—six children in nine years, one stillborn. She also developed recurrent phlebitis and had to have the swollen varicose veins in both legs removed.

"At that point, I figured God was pleased with us; we had five lovely children. It was my turn to enjoy the good married life. I remember thinking I could finally have sex whenever I wanted to! But my husband was not prepared for me. He said, 'This is wonderful. Where were you when I needed you ten years ago?'

" 'Having your children,' I answered. He told me he didn't want me anymore. He became impotent—physically or psychologically, who knows? It was a dirty joke! There I was forty years old, and he stops sleeping with me! He felt that he couldn't handle my demands, and I hadn't even started yet! I knew he wasn't going to change."

Gradually, Anne began to pave a road to her own independence, working for the PTA, the Rosary Society, and the American Cancer Society. Eventually she also went back to college to work on her writing, a talent she had abandoned at the altar. When her professor announced to the group that he was taking a sabbatical and wanted to sublet his apartment, Anne seized the opportunity.

"My first night alone it was raining—damp and nasty. The bed hadn't come yet. I had no lamps, no chairs; the apartment was filthy—and you know what it's like to clean someone else's mess! I sat there in the dark and thought, 'What have you done with your life? You're sitting here on the floor. You left a beautiful house with eight rooms.' I was scared. I had never been in an apartment before. I heard every little click, every creak.

"It was my first attempt out of the nest. I had never been alone. It was just frightening—not the way I had imagined it would be. But I also remember going to work on a high. I had decided, 'If God gives me ten minutes, ten weeks, ten years, I'm going to make something of my life.' I had lots of conflicting emotions. Part of me said, 'What have I done?' and the other part, 'I'm glad I did it!' "

There are no road maps for the emotional landscape of divorce. We can report the statistics that relate to women's feelings; for example, the study documents that, initially, seventy-two percent of women feel angry. However, statistics describe groups; divorce happens to individuals.

A composite of factors colors a woman's initial reaction to her divorce: What was the climate of her marriage before it ended? Was there any communication? Was the woman getting her needs met at all? Was she able to see and process various clues, or did she wear blinders during her marriage, which would render divorce more of a shock, and therefore make it difficult for her to accept the fact that her life, her status, her relationships, would undergo a profound transformation?

Divorce is about change; and change is the hallmark of adult development. Because the experience of change is so highly individualized, *the developmental picture is a critical factor in understanding the rediscovery process after divorce.* For it is emotional pain that, quite literally, sets in motion the wheels of growth and change, and it is "where a woman is," in developmental terms, that determines how she *reacts* to the disequilibrium caused by this wrenching crisis of identity.

On the surface it appears that *tangible* events or circumstances precipitate the feelings associated with divorce. Gail Leperk felt betrayed because of her husband's infidelity; Anne Garner felt dismissed by a husband who, after thirty years of marriage, "didn't even notice" when she moved out; Evelyn Dorrin felt angered and saddened by the lack of communication in her marriage. But such events were also challenges that, in turn, inspired these women to look beyond the marital identities that were being stripped away from them. To survive and to separate from their families, both literally and figuratively, they had to change their old, more or less dependent selves into new, autonomous selves.

Hence, each woman feels the emotions connected with the events of her divorce, but she also feels the pain and terror of her own transformation. Ultimately, her emotional recovery from divorce depends on how ready, willing, and able she is to undergo such an awesome process of growth, and how much she has already begun to develop a separate sense of identity.

For example, Evelyn Dorrin, a Slow Motion, chalked off her husband's departure to a "mid-life crisis." Evelyn was unprepared for Herb's leaving; she was unnerved by it. For all she knew, her husband, like Gail Leperk's, might have been having an affair. But by that point in her marriage, Evelyn had already begun to carve out her own world. She didn't need her husband to define her the way Pauser Gail Leperk did. Being more independent and therefore further along the road to rediscovery, Evelyn was therefore more receptive to change than Gail.

A woman's stage of development influences *how* she deals with the events that temporarily derail her life after divorce, and, conversely, divorce affects her development. If a woman has a sense of who she is and what she feels, she will naturally be better equipped to express her feelings, which is a prerequisite for getting her life back on track.

Emotional Clustering

Researchers commonly cite a set of core emotions that women experience throughout the divorce and rediscovery process: shock, anger, fear, loneliness, and relief. However, the "Divorce Over 40" study illuminated a new insight: a woman anticipating separation or in the throes of divorce may not feel *any* of those emotions. Or, she feels many of them simultaneously. As our three snapshots at the beginning of this chapter portray, instead of isolating particular emotions, women experience what we call emotional clustering.

At times one emotion, such as shock or anger, may predominate, but for the most part, emotions are experienced in concert, not as disconnected events. Humiliation, embarrassment, and guilt often mingle with betrayal, anger, and sadness, offset by a dash of exhilaration and relief—not an easy "cocktail" for most women to swallow.

Lorraine Feldman's diary of the early days of her divorce offers a vivid picture of emotional clustering. Still reeling from the initial shock, Lorraine wrote this entry shortly after hearing about her husband's betrayal:

> The tears again—how does one stop the tears? The tears that did
>   not come at first . . . they took time . . . and it took time for
>   the numbness, the shock, the pain to settle in.
> The tears come for yesterday.
> They come for today; they come for tomorrow.

71

The tears come for the children, not little ones, but ones who have
always known a family—a mother and a father—as many
children of today have not.
The tears come for self-pity.
The tears come for comfort—
Your comfort comes from your lover.
My comfort comes from my tears.
I will survive, as so many others have.
I will cry many more tears, but I will survive!

Not surprisingly, emotional clustering sometimes brings surges
of conflicting feelings. This is a crucial point, because so many
women say they feel "crazy" during the divorce process. How can
a woman "feel distraught and frightened one minute and start
whistling and laughing out loud the next," as Lorraine Feldman
describes it?

The women in the study confirm the phenomenon of emotional
clustering, and their experience underscores its importance.
Women do not experience "stages" of divorce on a set schedule.
Different feelings come and go; you can't predict how strongly
they will be felt, how long they will last, or when they will crop
up.

The truth is, in divorce, emotions rise and fall; antithetical
feelings are experienced simultaneously. Consider how different
Anne Garner's first few weeks of separation were from either
Gail Leperk's or Evelyn Dorrin's! No wonder divorce is so often
referred to as a roller coaster—unpredictable and frightening.
The ride often feels as if it will be never-ending!

"When you're in the middle of it, it's horrible," agrees fifty-
three-year-old Vera Castro, who divorced seven years ago. "It's
such a terrible, negative, down experience. It's like there's never
going to be sunshine."

Understandably, emotions can frequently diminish or reappear
at critical transition points: Gail Leperk's shock and humiliation
when she first learned of her husband's affair; Anne Garner's
loneliness and fear the first night she spent in her new apartment.

Some emotions will prevail during the entire process of separation and divorce, *or* they will not be felt at all, *or* they will recur
many years after the marriage ends. Emotions are *not* necessarily
dissolved or "worked through," nor is a complete catharsis always

a prerequisite to healing. In fact, the stories women tell demonstrate that even after therapy and a lot of hard work, certain feelings, especially anger, can emerge, reappear, and persist years after the fact.

Joann Cress, for example, is happily established in her new life, five years after her divorce. She has transformed herself into a spirited, take-charge Player who meets life on life's terms. She has a good job, a loving male companion whom she has been with for four years, a solid relationship with her grown sons, and, most important, "I have my life back." Still, she reports, when she saw her ex-husband at her son's wedding recently, "I didn't want *him* sitting in my pew. I know it was a dumb thing. I couldn't believe how angry I felt when I saw him. Still!"

Because women can be so different in developmental terms, their emotional clusters won't be the same—even in similar scenarios. For example, Ellen Garland, like Gail Leperk, was also married to an abusive alcoholic. He had gone into treatment and was a sober member of Alcoholics Anonymous for several years before the marriage ended, but like Gail's husband, he continued to cheat on his wife. And for a long time, Ellen also "took" it.

But Ellen Garland was a Slow Motion. Unlike Gail, who was a typical Pauser, Ellen didn't put all her emotional eggs into her husband's basket. Though she put up with Roger's philandering, watched him siphon their money into his separate bank accounts, agreed to sign papers that gave him increasing financial control, and, for a long time, wasn't strong enough to face up to her husband, once she heard the message of the women's movement in the early seventies, she slowly changed her life, taking small definitive steps to make her existence more palatable.

Ellen went to work, got involved in a church group, made new friends. To deal with Roger's alcoholism and to better understand his condition after he got sober, she continued to go to Al-Anon, a support group based on AA's twelve-step philosophy, for anyone affected by a family member's drinking. She became increasingly disgusted with his controlling, sometimes abusive behavior, and at one point she even moved into a separate bedroom. "But I still didn't know how to say no to him," she admits.

One night when Roger pressured her into having sex, Ellen couldn't refuse, so she took a drink to bolster her confidence. One drink led to another, and the next morning—to her horror—she found herself back in her husband's bed. "That was it! No more. If I can't stand up to him, I've got to get out," she decided.

Wives of alcoholics typically "walk on eggshells and glass." Because they were on different developmental paths during their marriages, however, Ellen Garland and Gail Leperk had to traverse different emotional landscapes in divorce. Consequently, their emotional clusters were dissimilar too. Ellen knew she felt angry and betrayed; in fact, the combination of emotions helped propel her out the door. In contrast, Gail remarks, "My anger didn't surface 'til later—it took me months to feel it. I was still in denial."

Being a Slow Motion who, at least in the beginning, embraced the stand-by-your-man credo, Ellen recalls how ambivalent she felt packing the last few precious knickknacks during her final days as Mrs. Garland. "We were in the dining room, and I was crying and at the same time telling him how to do the laundry because I knew he didn't know how to take care of himself." Nonetheless, Ellen, who had begun to take steps toward independence, was neither shocked when her marriage died nor frightened to be on her own. In fact, she says, "I remember a feeling of euphoria when I found a place of my own to move into."

The Leavers and the Left

One might think that Gail and Ellen reacted so differently because one woman was the leaver and the other one was left. Indeed, researchers commonly cite different emotions experienced by the leavers, who allegedly feel guilty and anguished, and the left, who feel rejected, angry, disillusioned, misused. However, the study suggests that, at least in the case of women exiting long-term marriages, who did the leaving or who got left doesn't affect a woman's adjustment to her new life as much as where she is developmentally.

Consider the journeys of Anne Garner and Lorraine Feldman, who trekked their emotional landscapes with very different perspectives. Four years after their marriages ended, both women became Players via completely different routes. As their stories illustrate, over the first two to four years, the lines between the leavers and the left are blurred.

Anne Garner *appeared* to be the leaver. It was she who walked out on her husband. Secretly, however, she also expected Buddy to care. "I thought he was going to come after me, and we would have these great moonlight suppers on the terrace with the ocean roaring." It never happened. "He never even knew I was gone. I would go home at lunchtime—to empty ashtrays, throw in a load of laundry, and go over the mail. Eventually, I didn't want anything from him—except to be left alone." But for a long time, Anne admits, "I still thought I might go back."

She never got the chance. When her sublet lease was up, Anne's husband told her to keep the apartment. Anne may have physically left her marriage, but years before, Buddy had abandoned her emotionally. Then he confirmed it. Ironically, Anne admits, she hadn't intended to sever the marital umbilical cord entirely.

Anne finally started to concentrate on herself, instead of trying to figure out whether Buddy Garner still wanted her. Over the next two years she spent a good deal of time "licking her wounds." Sometimes the loneliness was excruciating. "Everyone abandoned me—my mother, my father, my kids. I was an embarrassment. In my family, you don't run away from a marriage."

Doing more than soothing a bruised ego, Anne began to look deep within herself. "I watched old movies, took long, thoughtful walks on the beaches, and wrote lousy poetry." The various poems from that period are revealing and undoubtedly reflect Anne's mood swings. Her tongue-in-cheek "Obituary for Anne," which appears at the beginning of this chapter, is far different in tone from the somber "Requiem."

Why does it take so long to die?
Why must we creep and crawl through tunneled days and nights
    long after all such comforts are gone
    long after our soul's faint cries
    long after the echo of remembered ecstasies fade?
Can't we just close the door
    on touching and feeling
    on external expectations
    and resign ourselves to oblivion?

Leaving her house was only the beginning of Anne's long-overdue separation from her family. "As a child, I never even had my own bed! When I was little, I slept with my brother; when I got older, I shared a bed with my aunt—and then with my husband. I never had the feeling of being totally alone. That was definitely the turning point in my life—even more than becoming a mother. For the first time, *I felt like I had control of my own life.* My family couldn't understand it when I told them, 'I'm trying to find myself,' but that's exactly what I was doing!"

At the outset, Lorraine Feldman—one who was left—seems to have little in common with Anne Garner. Devastated and humiliated when her husband began to live openly with another woman, Lorraine never imagined leaving her husband. She wrote this entry in her diary about a month after he stopped coming home:

> God—Please help me. I'm scared.
> I go through periods where I'm on top of the world. I'll make it.
>   I'll come through stronger and better than I was.
> But then I have weeks when I am out and out scared.
> I wake up at night or in the morning, with my leg unconsciously
>   shaking. I haven't done that since high school or college days.
> Dear Lord—Please let me make it. I know I will, but I'm scared.

Making matters worse, throughout her twenty-two years of marriage, Lorraine had clung to the perception that she and Marv had a good marriage. "We were the best of friends, equal partners—it was a simple, easy marriage with its ups and downs." For a long time after her husband left, Lorraine continued to be plagued by what she perceived as *her* inability to understand him. She thought it was her job to monitor his emotions. "Marv and I were always talking, but what was inside of him, I don't know. I felt like the princess who was going to unlock whatever pain was inside of him." Lorraine also felt guilty, because she thought that somehow she must have failed.

Lorraine's and many other women's stories resonate with the "princess" theme—the notion that a "good" wife possesses a miraculous power that can even divert divorce. Indoctrinated by a culture that positioned them as caretakers, these women shared an abiding belief during their marriages that they could change their husbands and somehow make it all better. After divorce they discovered that they had to make it better for themselves.

In time Lorraine began to undergo a metamorphosis, by delving into the three pieces of the developmental pie. She increased her hours at work because she needed more money and, she realized, "It was important to keep myself busy." Equally significant, Lorraine also started to see how competent she was and always had been. Typical of Slow Motions who had been unconscious of their growth, she took inventory of what she had stockpiled in the past.

Lorraine never had her own money in marriage; Marvin doled it out piecemeal. He was always generous but always in control. "He would leave twenty, forty dollars on the dresser and say, 'Do you need more?' " When Lorraine worked "for fun" as an aide to the town recreation program, she remembers the triumph of saving several of her five-dollar-an-hour paychecks, enough money to purchase a Seiko watch for a hundred dollars. "I still have that watch—the first thing I ever bought with *my own money!*" Her "little job," as she thought of it then, was a small beginning, but Lorraine still savors that first taste of financial independence.

Lorraine met new people through work; and she also put herself in situations, such as enrolling in a dance class, that enabled her to create a new, single social life. Most important, instead of belaboring Marvin's problems, she began using *I* at the beginning of sentences—as in, "I feel . . ." and "I am . . ." and "I want . . ." Lorraine Feldman finally began to take responsibility for her own life.

Four years later, after Marvin had inched his way out of the house, Lorraine felt much more self-assured. She had begun to know who she was; she even planned trips for herself. Ultimately, it was Lorraine—the one who was supposedly left—who finally told Marvin that *she* wanted out. It was time to move on in her life. "He never asked for a divorce. Who knows if he ever would have?"

Who Am I?

When a woman like Lorraine begins to start her sentences with *I*, she is on her way to becoming a Player, because she is beginning to define herself. Likewise, when Anne Garner sat on the floor and asked herself what she was doing there, she was essentially beginning to answer the most important question of development: "Who am I?"

Divorce is a time of uncertainty and letting go. Initially, at least, many divorced women feel a loss of social stature. Suddenly single, they find themselves alone, which is even more devastating when the loss coincides with the children leaving home and parents getting sick or dying, as it does for so many mid-life women.

"I missed walking into the house after work and having someone say, 'Hi,' and getting a kiss—someone to shoot the breeze with. Not that I did that with my husband—but at least he was a *body* there," forty-year-old Bonnie Lenza, replied after being asked, "What was hardest about being single?"

Even Melanie Spade, forty-five when she divorced, expressed trepidation when she answered that question. A gutsy Player who had traveled extensively before marriage, Melanie's response came as a surprise: "Sleeping alone. At first, I was frightened silly. I even got a roommate for a while, so I wouldn't have to be alone. I finally resorted to keeping the lights on!"

Equally important, women have to come to terms with the fact that many of their old roles have become obsolete—a tremendous source of anguish in the aftermath of divorce. What becomes of the "dutiful and devoted wife" who has no husband, the "caring and competent mother" whose children have left home? All divorced women have to find who they are, but the process is even more taxing for mid-life and older women who are so firmly entrenched in their roles. Understandably, for many such an abrupt about-face leaves them at sea.

Gail Leperk, who "did not have any personal goals for myself" when she married at nineteen, with only a year and a half of college completed, echoes an often-heard refrain among women in the study: Gail's basic motivation as a young wife was "to be the best mother that I could be."

Twenty-five years with a mercurial alcoholic husband "tore down whatever self-confidence I had," reflects Gail. From her vantage point, however, being "Mrs. George Leperk" at least gave her a sense of who she was. The divorce destroyed or, at best, changed each one of her roles: "I came to realize that I was not grieving so much for my husband, but for the whole life-style we had developed."

Though she had truly put herself on hold throughout most of her marriage and she "didn't see myself as a unique person with special abilities," Gail, divorced only a year at the time of her interview, had already begun to make great strides: "Al-Anon was a tremendous support—the people in the program helped me get my head on straight. I was encouraged to let the tears out, and I did. My friends helped me the most by making me realize that I spent all of my energy on my family."

Accordingly, Gail began to focus on herself, rediscovering the woman who was beneath the roles. "I went back to college and took a course, and that made me feel good about myself. I did so well that the next semester I signed up for three! I started thinking that I could have a good life. And things started to get better."

It is not only *her* view of herself that a newly divorced woman has to deal with. Others have their perceptions of who she is too, which affect how *she* feels about her new status. Vera Castro was a Slow Motion during her marriage. Though she led a very active social life, involving herself in local politics, Vera still considered wife and mother her primary roles. She wasn't yet comfortable being just Vera.

"I dealt with tremendous role loss after the divorce. First of all, I wasn't Phil's wife, and being so young when I got married, after twenty-seven years, it was a big void. I found that many women I had associated with in politics looked at me differently." Vera remembers her first postdivorce social event, a cocktail party for a local politician. "I was terrified to go—it was sheer agony. I can remember hyperventilating in the middle of the room!"

For the next social function, Vera asked her twenty-year-old daughter to join her. "It seemed to make everyone around me more comfortable. At least I could be 'Lara's mom'—it was a familiar role." Lara's presence may have put other people more at ease with Vera's new status, but we suspect it was Vera who was most relieved to have her daughter at her side.

From Fearing Loneliness to Enjoying Aloneness

Talking about role loss is not new, but our survey also highlights another developmental dimension that affects postdivorce adjustment: the *degree* of loss. The more invested a woman is in what she *does*—her "secondary" identity—instead of who she *is*—her "primary" identity—the harder it is for her to conceive of herself as a separate person and to be comfortable in her own company.

Pauser Doreen McBride, for example, admitted that she was "like a puppet during my marriage—I did what I was told." Doreen married immediately after high school, she never had any ambition other than marriage, and she was happiest when she was with her children. In short, her identity as a wife and mother was *everything* to her. Naturally, such a profound degree of role loss cast a pall over Doreen's emotional landscape and made the search for a separate identity an elusive and arduous undertaking.

Contrast Doreen with fifty-seven-year-old Sylvia Shaunnesey, a Player, who was not as devoted to the roles society assigned her. Unlike many of her peers, Sylvia expected a fifty-fifty relationship but discovered that her husband was "only willing to give ten percent." Early on in her marriage, Sylvia made a decision: "Talking to him was the worst—and I wasn't going to change who *I* was. So, I had my own job and my own friends. My children were my children, but I don't think they changed me—I wasn't on that track." The fact that Sylvia continued to nourish her own development, never losing herself to marriage or motherhood, made it easier for her to adapt to single life when her husband "snapped," as she put it, and took up with another woman.

Not surprisingly, loneliness and the fear of being alone—feelings expressed by slightly more than half of all women in the first year after divorce—also reflect a woman's place on the developmental continuum. A woman who can't yet see the *I* in the mirror has scant understanding of herself. Unable to express her feelings, she tends to aim her emotions inward. She often gets depressed. No wonder she hates to be alone. She doesn't feel good about herself, so when she's alone, she is constantly in bad company!

However, a very interesting phenomenon occurs as she grows and takes steps to develop a sense of identity and independence: she also begins to develop a greater acceptance of being alone. She begins to like who and what she is and therefore needs to rely less on the validation of others. Instead of feeling detached from herself, she begins to find a source of comfort in her own company.

In fact, according to the survey findings, loneliness and the fear of being alone abate for most women one or two years after divorce. These women discover that *loneliness*—a longing for others—is different from *aloneness*—being alone. A woman who knows who she is and accepts herself is comfortable in her own company. As Evelyn Dorrin puts it, "I'm not involved with anyone in particular. I have lots of female friends. We go out to museums, movies, craft shows. But there are many times I'm just very happy to be with *me*."

Roadblocks to Finding an Identity

Initially, some women are frightened of facing themselves. They *feel* empty, so they think they *are* empty. "After the divorce I realized that I had cut off my feelings for so many years," reports Doreen McBride, who describes herself as an "obedient" wife. "It was mind-boggling to feel so deeply about so many different issues. I now know that for years I refused to see that my marriage was failing. Why was I so afraid and weak?"

Many women ask themselves that same question. The answer lies in their social conditioning and in their individual histories. Expressing emotions, especially anger, is a stunning achievement for mid-life women, most of whom were socialized as little girls to believe that it isn't ladylike to get angry and that feelings, in general, are meant to be kept inside, or denied.

Much has been written about the phenomenon of *denial* in alcoholic families. There's an elephant (alcoholism) in the living room; everyone walks around it—but no one mentions that it's there. Gail Leperk, the ever-patient wife, made excuses for her husband, cleaned him up when he got sick, dragged him to bed after he passed out on the couch, and always pretended that everything was fine, until he finally walked out on her!

A woman in any kind of miserable marriage can do the same thing: justify her husband's behavior, keep up her end of the conversation *and* his, work overtime to bolster his ego—in short, turn herself inside out to be a "good wife."

Betty Duprey stands out as a graphic example of a woman pushed to the limit before her denial broke down. Married at eighteen, from the time she was twenty-one she knew that her husband, Nate, had been unfaithful. "He was fooling around with a bookkeeper in the office." Nate told Betty she was "imagining things," and for years she felt insane. "I would say to myself, 'Oh, my God, there must be something crazy with me.' "

Then, one day Betty discovered "little blood scratches between my thighs." She called her doctor. The diagnosis was short but certainly not sweet: crabs. " 'What is it from?' I asked Nate, and he came back at me with, 'Well, who have *you* been with?' Is that the lowest? After all those years of my being dumb, lipstick on his collar, coming home at all hours. And, can you believe it? I was always worried about *him!*" Her back to the wall, Betty finally threw her philandering husband out.

Many women inadvertently replicate their childhood dramas in their marriages. For example, Gail Leperk now realizes that her father was considered "a heavy drinker"—a euphemism often used to describe alcoholics. When divorce finally forced her to face how she had allowed her husband to treat her, Gail came to understand that George was a carbon copy of her father. During the divorce process, feelings about her father that had been germinating inside Gail for forty years finally came to the surface. To recover from the shock of her divorce, she finally had to begin to separate the pain of the present from her unacknowledged past and to recognize a part of herself that she had never seen.

This mirroring of the past is true not only for women in alcoholic or overtly abusive relationships. Scratch the surface in marriages where a husband subtly denigrates his wife, fails to support her interests or applaud her intellect, and you often find a pattern of denial that dates from childhood.

Caroline Breed, a "good girl" who grew up in the South, remembers how she coped with intense emotions during her marriage: "I'd go in the shower and cry, so that no one would hear me." Given the unique circumstances of her past, Caroline's strategy fits: her mother had attempted to kill herself by drinking a bottle of lye. Caroline was only four when it happened, but the event cast a dark shadow over what Caroline describes as an otherwise idyllic childhood. "My mother got over that—she was a very strong outgoing women," asserts Caroline, "but no one in the family ever acknowledged her attempted suicide."

Talk about an elephant in the living room! The strong family ethic of denial was indelibly stamped on Caroline's psyche: *never talk about your problems, fears, or weaknesses.* Moreover, the brief but tragic event ingrained in Caroline a pervasive fear of abandonment. "I spent most of my life afraid to confront anything."

Suspecting that her past must have influenced her marriage, we theorized, "You probably withstood a lot of emotional mal-treatment, rather than risk abandonment."

"Oh, no, you've got that wrong!" she exclaims. "Not a *lot*. I could withstand *anything!*"

Years later, when her marriage was crumbling, Caroline told a therapist about crying in the shower and fantasizing about her own suicide. The therapist recognized that in order to begin to actualize her full potential—and certainly, to survive the impending divorce—the adult Caroline would have to integrate the parts of her personality that had been too painful to deal with. Like many victims of emotional, physical, or sexual trauma, she had to get in touch with the abused or frightened parts of her unconscious that had arrested her development. Only by recalling how frightened she was as a child when her mother was taken away to the hospital and returned weeks later with "a voice like a man," permanently damaged from the lye, could Caroline learn to soothe the child inside her and begin to free her adult self from those debilitating fears and dependencies.

Women who were literally abused or suffered devastating loss as children are only the tip of the iceberg. In a sense, the vast majority of mid-life women were unwittingly "traumatized," not by any one person in particular, but by the dictates of a patriarchal culture, simply because they are women. Their horizons were restricted, and they were taught early in life to consider themselves the "other sex," if not the "weaker sex." The "good little girls" became "nice ladies," permitted to age chronologically, but never to feel empowered or truly "adult." Understandably, some of our survey respondents even *sound* like trauma victims.

> Terror. The terror was paralyzing. I became a zombie. I felt nothing; I just cried and cried. I was in shock. The fear was so paralyzing, so blinding that I "felt" very young. I was extremely vulnerable, as if my physical body was constantly in danger of shattering. At the same time, I was acutely aware of the loss of any tactile human touch.

Becoming single forces mid-life women to question their ability to survive in the world without the support of a husband or an intact family unit, which for many had been the only way they had ever pictured their lives. "I still feel married after three years. I don't want to be divorced," writes a survey respondent no longer sheltered by the cocoon of her twenty-one-year marriage. She is clearly at a crossroads, but she is afraid to take a different path: "I have too much conflict about being divorced. I worry about what I will feel, and what society in general thinks."

Rhythms of Rediscovery

Rediscovery doesn't happen in a vacuum; everyone around a divorced woman has opinions, often contradictory, about what she should do after divorce. Some friends and confidantes urge her to fill the void quickly by keeping busy and replacing the old with the new. Others caution her to get in touch with her feelings and needs before making any major changes. Added to her own confusion, these mixed messages can be maddening!

Gail Leperk's mother was "very supportive" after her divorce; not so, some of her children, who were teenagers at the time: "My son was supportive; my daughters were not. Their father was very manipulative and twisted everything. They were very confused. They couldn't understand. They wanted me to get on with my life a month after this happened!"

Unquestionably, the "Divorce Over 40" study suggests, women need time to mourn their losses and rediscover themselves. Like the tortoise who wins the race in the familiar fable, a woman who makes a conscious decision to slowly process her hurt and deal with her diverse and often contradictory feelings usually becomes a Player before one who tries to speed through the process.

"Change of any kind scares me and makes me feel depressed, so any changes I can avoid at this time, I will avoid," offers a woman who knows she needs to sort out her emotions and understand who she is before moving on. "So, I am staying in my house until I get through the grieving process and feel in control of my life again."

Explaining her postdivorce rhythm, Gail Leperk also remarks, "Al-Anon taught me to take things one day at a time and that not everything has to be decided in one day. I was gentle with myself. I took my time. I was married for a long time, and I knew that I had many changes to go through. That's also why I only signed up for one college course at first. I wanted to see what it was like and how it would be for me."

When a long-term marriage dissolves, a woman must face the severing of old ties and rise to the challenge of launching new beginnings. While her one-day-at-a-time philosophy understandably encouraged Gail to take it slowly, that's not the whole story. For one thing, the rhythm of rediscovery is affected by circumstances. Not every woman has the "luxury" of riding out a crisis. She must have a means of interim financial support—her own income, an ample divorce settlement, or her family's assistance, if not a "nest egg" that she had the foresight to squirrel away while she was married.

In addition, every woman is influenced by her developmental path:

• *Pausers,* such as Gail, often *can't* move very quickly after divorce—clearly a benefit, as long as they don't remain frozen. Kathryn Mason, a die-hard Pauser, was still wearing her wedding band almost a year after her divorce. She certainly wasn't plunging into rediscovery at top speed!

• *Slow Motions* are, by nature, cautious and careful. How evenly a particular Slow Motion paces herself after divorce depends on what her life was like before, how much of her self she has already identified, and how ready she is for change.

By the time her marriage ended, for example, Annette Winwood was relieved. "It was as if little pieces of it were being lopped off, bit by bit," Annette explains. "He would come home and go to bed with me and face the wall. There was no sex; he was desperately unhappy—and yet he refused to talk about it. I was in agony." The marriage ended in stages. At one point, Annette sensed her husband was having an affair. "I'd come out of the shower, and he was talking on the phone. You can *just tell* from a man's voice."

For a long time, Annette didn't want the marriage to end, but her husband finally walked out on her. "He left me a note." Annette's husband had finally chosen the other, younger, woman over her. But by then she had accepted that there was no hope of reconciliation, and she was glad that it was finally over. Slow Motions such as Annette often perceive divorce as an opportunity to explore their newfound freedom, a chance to start over. After years of putting everyone else first, they bask in the first rays of solitude, on their own for the first time and no longer restricted by parents or a husband.

• *Rewinders* tend to act more like the fabled hare. On one hand, because they begin to sample freedom while still inside the cocoon, moving in new circles and meeting people who don't automatically see them as someone's wife or mother, they tend to adapt more easily to single life. On the other hand, they haven't necessarily found their identities; they may just be rebellious. A few even refer to themselves as "spoiled brats"!

Rewinders are often quick to bury the past by engulfing themselves in a whirlwind of change, which is usually a poor form of adaptation after divorce. They plunge into new relationships, change jobs, and alter their life-styles, leaving themselves little time for reflection. Rewinders want what they want when they want it; they have no patience for process. Like teenagers, who change situations as a way of coping with their feelings, Rewinders reason, often unconsciously, that a new boyfriend, a different job, or a new home will magically make the hurt go away. In retrospect many years later, they tend to mourn these hasty decisions.

Typical of a Rewinder in the last several years of her marriage, Lisa Frazier began to throw herself into her own life with a vengeance, putting so much distance between herself and Dave that when she finally had an extramarital affair, she had little reservation about ending the marriage—or about selling her house, an impulsive move whose consequences still plague her, ten years later.

Her situation is not uncommon. It often takes a Rewinder many years to cut through the bold exterior and the colorful bravado to meet the frightened teenager inside her. Irene Presto, who is now forty-six, was separated for ten years before she actually got divorced. She was a woman who relished the experimental seventies and was jealous of girlfriends who cheated on their husbands with seeming aplomb. When her husband left her, Irene spent the next decade arguing with him over a financial settlement, dealing with her then teenage children, and trying to make up for lost time. Especially in the early years, she sowed more than her share of wild oats. Irene doesn't necessarily regret anything she did. However, now she realizes, "I wasted time not getting my act together. But there was a part of me that was busy playing all those years, getting even with him.

In retrospect, Irene sees that she didn't really want a divorce as much as she longed for a sense of freedom. But it took her a long time to see that having her freedom didn't necessarily mean she was on her own. "You know, my husband always told me I'd find someone who'd fuck me but never support me. Now I realize what I really wanted: someone to fuck me while *he* supported me!"

Rewinders bypass an important prerequisite for changing their lives in the present: they don't give themselves a chance to come to terms with the past. "I cut myself off from any reminders of my marriage. I could not assert my rights to see the children, so I didn't pursue a consistent relationship with them," remarks a woman who never thought through the consequences of her actions. "I immediately developed a whole new world of school, job, and female friends, along with a new intimate partner. Now I realize it was all too sudden."

• *Players* instinctively know it is better to give themselves time. To a large extent, these are women who are in circumstances that don't force them to make decisions under pressure. Many already have good jobs or enough money to see themselves through the crisis period, so they don't immediately have to go out to work for the first time or make sudden changes. They don't have to vacate the marital home instantly, or if they do, they feel comfortable in their new homes—not as if they suffered a major loss in life-style. These women clearly feel a greater level of control over their lives by taking things slowly.

Not all Players are necessarily so levelheaded after divorce, however. "I don't think you should sit home and brood. You don't have to be in love with every man you date, but you should get out," advises Melanie Spade, who did a bit of wild-oat sowing after her first marriage ended. "Divorce is a terrible blow to your ego. You go mad for a while. You want to be out every single night. I had the opportunity to do that, and I did. I went wild!"

Two or three months later Melanie met a wealthy older man. "He thought I was wonderful, and he was wonderful to me. It made me feel good about myself again. It was the best medicine!"

The above descriptions notwithstanding, we hasten to add that divorced women sometimes aren't always true to type. Melanie Spade acted more like a Rewinder immediately after her divorce. That's because adult development is a fluid, ongoing process, a series of inclines and plateaus and, sometimes, a slipping back.

In the search for her identity, any woman can look for herself in the wrong place or reach a dead end. Becoming frightened by her newfound independence, a woman may trolley back and forth between dependency and growth. She's likely to say things such as, "I'm not myself anymore," or "I don't know who I am," because she's feeling the confusion and pain of rediscovery.

New Beginnings—or False Starts?

Granted, it's tough to be immersed in the arduous process of redefining oneself and, at the same time, to be a single woman in a Noah's Ark world. "People do things *together*," insists a survey respondent. "In the beginning, I hated couples in church and in the community because I had lost my partner." Because she had the good sense to seek professional counsel, however, this woman's picture brightened considerably. "I came to understand all the pain that kept getting triggered—to begin to understand my pain as growth. And then I could continue being my independent self after being so dependent on someone else's life."

Developing a new identity requires time, but some women try to take a shortcut, hoping to make themselves "whole again" by diving into a new relationship. These women usually don't trust themselves enough to work through the feelings of self-doubt and to face their fears about being alone. They secretly hope that a rebound relationship will take care of them. "I jumped into relationships too quickly. And whenever I dated someone, I immediately became monogamous. I should have played the field," laments a woman who realizes in retrospect that she was too insecure not to have a man in her life.

Some women are aware of the pitfalls of new long-term commitments but are powerless, or too frightened, to avoid them. "I am probably making a mistake looking for a new relationship, instead of learning to accept myself alone, but I prefer married life," confesses another survey respondent. "Because of that, I've allowed myself to become attached in a situation which can only lead to further heartbreak."

Regrettably, women who bypass that wrenching period of self-examination are often attracted to men with exactly the same qualities as their ex-husbands. And worse still, they may get involved with men who are married or on the rebound from their own divorces, men who are also developmentally stuck in the past. No wonder six out of ten second marriages end in divorce!

The point is, a woman must define *herself* before developing a relationship with a significant other. After Bonnie Lenza divorced her husband of ten years, loneliness propelled her quickly into a second marriage. If her first marriage was premature because she was only eighteen, her second was premature because she wasn't much older than that developmentally. It, too, fell apart, four years later.

Bonnie learned her lesson the second time around. "I was always a needy person and needed a man; now I don't. I've come to terms with that. I'm at a point now where I realize that I'm going to be by myself. I can now channel all my energies into my career and be the best I can be. I'm not going to settle for less."

How long should a woman wait before establishing new intimate ties? Like healing, it is different for each individual. The best judge is inside yourself, if you take the time to listen. As this five-year veteran of divorce points out, "It takes about three or four years after divorce to regain your self-esteem and realize your worth. Sometimes women miss that opportunity before remarrying."

The recommendation to "regain your self-esteem and realize your worth" says it all; women who meet this challenge establish a new sense of inner freedom. Emotionally, once they have gained their perspective, most women see divorce as a positive step forward. For many it is the first time that they dare to ask themselves what they want out of life and then to actually pursue their dreams.

Though the emotional landscape of divorce can make for an arduous journey, eighty-four percent of the women in the "Divorce Over 40" study break away from long-entrenched roles and self-perceptions. They become more confident and develop a willingness to meet new or unexpected challenges. And they are able to make decisions and choices that are true reflections of their inner selves. In short, these women grow up and, quite literally, "find themselves."

3

Dollars and Nonsense: Why Women Are Unequal Opponents on the Battlefields of Divorce

"Take some more tea," the March Hare said to Alice,
very earnestly.
"I've had nothing yet," Alice replied in an offended tone:
"so I can't take more."
"You mean you can't take *less*," said the Hatter: "it's
very easy to take *more* than nothing."

—Lewis Carroll, *Alice's Adventures in Wonderland*

Phyllis in Wonderland

"I had to go on welfare!" says Phyllis May, in disbelief. "I lost absolutely everything." Divorce plunged Phyllis May into her worst nightmare. As a married woman, she lived with her husband and two daughters in a moneyed suburb of St. Louis; they owned seven cars, three of them the Corvettes her husband, Lenny, collected. Together, the couple also owned a multi-million-dollar cosmetic manufacturing business.

"How was I going to survive and keep my house? He told me he would pay my bills, and that I would never have to work. But he defaulted on every aspect of money."

Despite her lavish previous life-style, Phyllis May's most pressing and painful concern after divorce is a universal one: money. A striking 88 percent of women worry about money in the first year after divorce. Five years later, nearly seven out of ten women still cite money as a major source of concern. Interestingly, *managing* money is not as distressing an issue; only two out of five express this concern. It's having *less* money that torments most women.

They have good reason to be apprehensive: The "Divorce Over

90

40" study documents that more than half of all women report difficulty keeping up payments on their home, making repairs, paying utility bills; and nearly two out of three lose the family home.

Having farther to fall, the affluent are often among the hardest hit. Phyllis May's $750,000 house went into foreclosure. Several of the cars were repossessed. And there were weeks when Phyllis and her children lived without electricity. Unlike many women, Phyllis was at least aware of their assets. "I knew exactly what was in the checkbooks, exactly what was in the businesses."

Still, she was no match for her husband—a scenario that is replicated time and again in other women's stories, regardless of their income levels. Rather than let Phyllis share in the proceeds, Lenny May purposely ran the business into the ground. In violation of a signed agreement that precluded him from liquidating assets before the divorce was finalized and without her knowledge, he managed to sell the building that housed the office and factory and bilked her out of the profit.

"I had no choice but to go on welfare. I had to feed my kids, so I couldn't be proud," insists Phyllis, recalling the long lines, the endless waiting, the humiliation. "And to think . . . he promised me we'd never have a messy divorce!"

Because her husband had so skillfully manipulated his financial position, Phyllis May was awarded no alimony and only $200 a week child support for her three children. Her husband stopped paying child support within a year—as did the husbands of 56 percent of the women in the study. No wonder almost half report that they have trouble paying for their children's needs!

Attempting to collect back child support, Phyllis returned to court on several occasions. The last time, she recalls, her "money-hungry" attorney didn't even bother to show up, so she appealed on her own behalf. "But that family court judge told me there was nothing he could do. He said if I had to, I should work three or four jobs to support my kids!"

Five years after her last court appearance, Phyllis May's story is amazingly upbeat. Meeting her today, effervescent in her stylish Day-Glo jogging suit, her blond hair coiffed and perfectly tinted, makeup meticulously applied, she still looks the part of the wealthy woman of leisure. It's hard to imagine her needing public assistance.

Fortunately, during her marriage Phyllis had made many acquaintances in the business world. When Lenny first left her, she was humiliated and overwhelmed. But with time and armed with bookkeeping, a skill she had learned in high school, she began networking, contacting the people she had met over the years. "I managed to sell one of his cars; I worked two jobs; and I just kept at it until I could get off welfare." Eventually, she was also able to sell her house and pay off all her debts.

"I've asked myself many times how I did it. Maybe I have this inner strength. Maybe I'm just a survivor!" Any residual bitterness Phyllis feels is aimed at "the system and how women are treated" and at her lawyer, who, in the end, was $30,000 richer.

Not one to seek sympathy for herself, Phyllis accurately observes that other women whose husbands leave them are at a far greater disadvantage than she was: "I know some women who don't even know how to write a résumé or fill out a job application. I didn't find going back to work difficult; I found the *pay scale* very difficult."

Indeed, despite her years of struggle, Phyllis May was better off than many of her counterparts in Financial Wonderland—the place where women, by dint of their "roles," are taught never to bother with money. These women emerge from their marriages devoid of any kind of financial training or knowledge; hence they have scant ammunition on the economic battlefields of divorce: twenty-eight percent don't even know how to write a check, let alone balance a checkbook; sixty-five percent don't understand taxes, nor can they fill out their tax returns; forty-six percent don't know how to apply for credit; fifty-eight percent have never made major financial decisions; and eighty percent have no investment knowledge!

Lenny had the edge on Phyllis during the legal process of divorce because men, especially men of means, are fierce, frequent, and seasoned competitors on the field of financial conquest. Typically, women don't even qualify as novices, particularly if they have limited work experience. When a divorcing couple faces off over the bargaining table to debate the economics of their separation, it's comparable to a tennis game—where only the *man* has a tennis racket and understands the rules. No one but a Mad Hatter would bet on the woman in that match!

In the Dark About Money:
A Developmental Hazard

Pitted against a legal system that doesn't take their needs and rights into account, many women are emotionally shaken and financially destitute in the wake of divorce. In Chapter Nine, we deal with the long-range economic picture, which, for some, continues to be bleak. "I literally sat in the dark for fear of not being able to pay the bills," wrote one survey respondent, inadvertently using an apropos metaphor, since so many women are "in the dark" about money.

This is a cautionary tale for all women—for single women, divorced women, married women, and their daughters. It's not just the system that deprives women of "green power." It's their culturally ingrained attitudes toward money. Addressing the issue, journalist Jane Bryant Quinn notes in a 1991 column in *Newsweek:* "Despite the gains of the last quarter century, many women still cling to the belief that handling money is a man's job, derived from intrinsic knowledge that women simply do not possess. As a result, women resist taking responsibility for their financial well-being."

Indeed, if a woman has a developmental Achilles' heel, it is usually a self-limiting outlook on money. Remember that identity development is like a pie divided into three pieces: social autonomy (knowing who you are), emotional integration (understanding what you feel), and—here's the part that's unwittingly overlooked by many women—personal responsibility (understanding that you alone are accountable for your own welfare). Even if a women defines a separate identity for herself socially and emotionally, she can't complete the process of growing up if she doesn't fully accept the burden of taking care of herself financially. In essence, an important part of her identity remains out of reach.

The first time a boy of twelve gets paid—for example, for cutting a neighbor's lawn—he immediately becomes enamored with the power of money. In contrast, a girl comes home from her first job—usually a caretaking job, such as baby sitting—less interested in the money she made than how she *felt.* Forty years later, though chronologically grown up and married, that same "little girl" still sees herself as the caretaker, the shaper of relationships, the connector, and sees money as a tool of nurturing, not of power and independence.

Because most women in the study grew up in families that mirrored the societal status quo, this inability to grasp the importance of financial independence and the power of money cuts across developmental categories. Though a Pauser is most likely to keep herself in the dark about money until divorce shines a glaring spotlight on her dire financial reality, Slow Motions Rewinders, and even some Players often wear blinders when it comes to family finances too.

In fact, many women in the study realized only in retrospect that not having access to money and not understanding family finances kept them "in their place" and virtually stripped them of power in their marriages. Confusing cash with caring also caused some of them to maintain delusions about their marriages. They longed for emotional contact from husbands who didn't know how to express their feelings, but they allowed themselves to be comforted by material things instead.

"I thought that meant he cared," says Joann Cress, admitting that when the husband who cheated on her bought her a new bedroom set and a gold and amethyst ring, it soothed her wounds.

A similar refrain occurs in Betty Duprey's story: "He would always buy me something when things got bad," she says, referring to her husband's drinking binges and his dalliances with other women. "He'd tell me, 'If I didn't love you, do you think I would come home to you? Would I want you to have this beautiful home?' I believed that!"

The same psychological defense mechanisms that enable the wife of an alcoholic to overlook liquor on her husband's breath, or enable the wife of a philanderer to ignore lipstick on his collar, prevent women from understanding the importance of money management. "My not taking any steps to learn about finances was a way of denying that anything was wrong in my marriage," admits the now wiser fifty-year-old Paula Oslow.

"I never dreamed that I would have to depend on *my* abilities to get a job, so I never went to school, I never worked for the kind of pay you could live on, and I never saved my own money." Paula knew her marriage was in trouble a good ten years before she left. When she was able to face the prospect of surviving on her own—and delve into the personal-responsibility piece of the pie—she finally walked out on her husband.

Feelings and Finances

The "emotional divorce" is about severing ties, working through negative feelings, and rearranging the family, but the "legal" divorce is purely an economic proposition. Given the deck our culture deals them, many of the women in the "Divorce Over 40" study were unprepared to fight in this arena.

It is particularly revealing, for example, that when women feel shortchanged by their settlements, they may blame it on themselves: forty percent note that a "desire to be fair" outweighed their self-interest. Even in the adversarial stages of divorce, they continued to nurture and look out for their men!

"I learned one thing going through the legal process. It's really money you're discussing. The bottom line is, *what is it you want?*" stresses Peggy Kennedy, who came close to having a breakdown at the end of her marriage to a physically abusive man. "When you scream principle in the lawyer's office, the principle doesn't matter." Not quite so wise when she was going through her own legal process several years ago, Peggy had to pay her husband to end the marriage. "He had a better lawyer. He also had a lot of connections. He was definitely in his own territory."

Women tend to bog down in fear and guilt related to money —especially where the children are concerned. "I felt very vulnerable. I could not feed my children properly. I could not eat or sleep, and when I did sleep, I'd wake up choking, because I felt I forgot to breathe," comments one women.

In fact, a third of the women who are concerned about the loss of financial security are also anxious about their children's reaction to the divorce and their new standard of living. As one puts it, "I did not want to alter my children's life-style as a result of the divorce. It seemed greedy and selfish to expect them to do without because I chose to leave their father."

A woman who feels worried, frightened, guilty, or defenseless does not make a savvy negotiator. Men, on the other hand, who tend to see divorce as a conquest to be won, generally know the rules of the bargaining table and find it easier to protect themselves.

OUR TURN

"I didn't have any experience," concedes Fran Sargent, a free-lance graphic designer. "Elliott was a financial wheeler-dealer—his career was about negotiating; mine wasn't. Sure, he agonized over our splitting up—but he seemed to be able to leave his emotions at home whenever we talked about the settlement!"

What's Equitable About This Distribution?

In the legal sphere, where women are pitted against their husbands *and* an entire male-dominated system, women's insular attitudes about money put them at an even greater disadvantage—despite the supposedly reformed divorce laws of the last several decades.

In the past, divorce was granted on the basis of adultery, desertion, or cruelty; it was always someone's "fault." As such, the "injured" party—usually the long-suffering wife—was awarded alimony (sometimes, for as long as a lifetime) and property; and, unless she was a raving lunatic, she was given custody of the children as well. At the dawn of the liberated Me Decade, however, the California Family Law Act of 1969 began to change all that, ushering in the age of "no-fault" divorce.

As a result of no-fault laws, now enacted in almost every state, marriage has become more like a business partnership. When a marriage is dissolved, the assets are distributed between two partners, increasingly by a process known as equitable distribution. All marital assets (the house, the car, various investments), regardless of whose name they're in, are divided according to a number of so-called objective criteria. The factors considered include, among others, the partners' respective roles in acquiring or earning the assets; each partner's age, previous work history, and future earning capacity; the age of the children; child-care responsibilities; and so on.

In theory, equitable distribution sounds great, and, in fact, many hailed it as a revolutionary concept—at first. As it turns out, the distribution is anything but equitable, and it is rarely beneficial to women. The legal system, which is designed by men, tends to disregard the fact that women, especially older women who haven't built up careers, are *not* equal to their husbands in the realm of finances. Most wives don't have their husbands' capacity to earn money or their ability to maneuver it.

Caroline Breed didn't get much support from the legal system when it came to divvying up marital property in her case. The assets were missing. "He was very secretive," she says of her husband, a big-league businessman who earned a high six-figure salary in one of the major corporations in the Midwest. To no one's surprise except Caroline's, Tom Breed competed in divorce as aggressively as he vied with his adversaries at work and as strategically and energetically as he played touch football with his cronies.

Caroline, mother of three, forty-four years old when her marriage ended in 1986, could neither fathom her husband's duplicity nor could she combat his underhanded tactics at the end of their twenty-six-year marriage. "He had post office boxes out of town, out of state. He was shifting money around. I now realize he spent a great deal of time plotting this, and, in fact, he eventually declared bankruptcy. I got no property. We had oil wells, land, apartments. We had *everything*—and I got none of it!"

No-fault laws—and the attitudes of the men who wrote and now administer them—mirror the culture. They place virtually no value on a woman's contributions. Like many wives, Christine Moss worked with her husband during her marriage for no pay. She not only raised two children, she handled the family's financial dealings over the years, as well. She also comanaged a restaurant and a real estate business with her husband.

"We were pretty successful—a brownstone in the City and a house at the beach." Despite their material bounty, the wedge between them continued to widen, and Christine saw the hand-writing on the wall. So, she also went back to college, a common choice for mid-life women who abandoned education in favor of marriage.

Forty-three and in the midst of the legal process when she was interviewed, Christine's view of what would be equitable is a moderate income, derived from the various businesses, which would ease her transition period after divorce. "It would give me an opportunity to finish school and a little time to get my career going."

However, Christine's lawyer warns that she may not get much, if any, of the profits from her husband's businesses. "Sure, I'm resentful. I'll also be penalized because I went back to school.

Now that I have an education—I need only fifteen credits for
my master's—his attorney assumes I can work. But there are no
teaching jobs out there."

Christine, already knowledgeable about finances, obviously has
done her homework. She has also talked to other women who
have been through the legal maze. "A lot of women past the age
of forty find it very difficult, especially women who have no
training at all, because they get a lump settlement, but nothing
to see them through. If I had remained stupid, maybe I would
get maintenance *and* support!"

The truth is, thanks to divorce "reform," in many states, alimony
is all but a relic of the past. Spousal support, as it is now called,
is hardly ever awarded. More often, the woman is simply awarded
a settlement.

In her widely quoted analysis of equitable distribution, which
was based on a study of divorced couples in California, sociologist
Lenore Weitzman concluded that in the first year after divorce,
on the average, women with minor children experience a seventy-
three percent *decline* in standard of living, while their husbands
increase their standard of living by forty-two percent. Though
some observers are skeptical about Weitzman's data, our study
certainly confirms that the majority of mid-life women's standard
of living plummets after divorce.

The problem with no-fault divorce and equitable distribution
is cultural lag. Many judges now assume that all married women
are employable and capable of being economically self-sufficient,
but some mid-life and older women who emerge from the cocoon
or are pushed out are even worse off than Christine Moss. They
have never worked; they have no education, no skills, no knowledge of finances. No one told them twenty or thirty years ago
that someday they'd need careers, investment portfolios, or
Keough plans; and many are stuck in old-order attitudes.

"I was totally ignorant about our finances," confesses Jackie
Sears, a classic Pauser, still reeling five years after divorce.
"Throughout our marriage, David kept insisting that there was
never enough money. I never questioned his honesty. I just
accepted that we would have to make do with what we had."
Jackie never worked; David never gave her more money than
she absolutely needed, so she couldn't have saved if she had
wanted to. When he walked out, her life suddenly became one

financial calamity after another. The boiler broke and she couldn't afford to fix it; the local utility company threatened to turn off her electricity. "I found out in court that my husband had been earning a six-figure salary!"

In the name of equal treatment, reformed divorce laws "liberate" women like Jackie Sears from the primary source of financial security they once counted on. Often judges require all assets to be liquidated, including the family home, which few women can ever replace. The survey data reflect this dire reality: Sixty-four percent are forced out of the family home.

No wonder most women in the study complain that there is a gap between what they wanted and what they were actually awarded. For example, half of all the women wanted "security for the children," but only twenty-two percent got it; sixty percent wanted secure living arrangements, but sixty-four percent were forced out of the family home; half wanted compensation for the years they put in as wives and mothers, but slightly more than twelve percent saw that factor reflected in their settlement. And where health insurance coverage and/or access to ex-spouses' pensions are concerned, twenty-nine percent wanted part or all of it, but only fifteen percent got any of it.

Thus, divorce often means women have to adjust to a lesser life-style; a third have to find less expensive residences, and a third have to find full-time employment to survive. Even when alimony is awarded, as in Caroline Breed's case, the family income plunges dramatically, from six figures to $12,000 a year. Caroline's settlement was doled out in the form of $1,000-a-month spousal support payments over an eight-year period, which, so far, her husband has paid "religiously."

Caroline was also granted a year's worth of child support, until her twin daughters, her youngest children, turned eighteen. Looking back, Caroline's marital life-style seems like a distant dream. "We had a three-hundred-fifty-thousand-dollar house with a pool and a sauna. We had a maid, a yard man, and a pool man. We even had a jet waiting to take us to a party. It feels like it was in another lifetime."

OUR TURN

Lawyers and Other Strangers

As we have seen, many women are overpowered by their husbands on the financial battlefield. The study documents that the majority of women fail to investigate or uncover important information about finances prior to divorce. For example, seven out of ten don't know whether they're eligible for their husband's health, pension, and social security benefits. Most women also aren't aware that they might be saddled with outstanding bills, and unlike men, who often plot and plan prior to divorce, only twenty-six percent clear up or at least reduce marital debts before beginning divorce proceedings.

The vast majority of women ask no one, not even friends, family, or coworkers, for help. They're embarrassed and afraid to pose questions; they feel ignorant when they hear the answers and ashamed that they don't know more. "I was scared to death," concedes Fran Sargent, whose legal divorce took four years. "No settlement seemed big enough. No amount of money would take care of me—because I couldn't imagine doing this on my own. I kept feeling that someone was taking advantage of me—if not my ex, then my lawyer or his lawyer."

When men hide assets, their wives must commission outsiders to search out real estate holdings, bank accounts, securities, and other assets. In fact, over the past two decades, an industry of specialized, high-cost "experts" has grown up around matrimonial law to perform this task. The more affluent the client, the more complex the finances, in which case, attorneys often command a brigade of real estate agents, accountants, auditors, private investigators, brokers, appraisers, and business specialists. These legions of experts can be expensive and overwhelming, especially to a woman who feels vulnerable and exposed and who has precious little experience in this realm.

Culturally ingrained innocence may color a woman's opinions about the experts she encounters. "Women are just not accustomed to playing with the Big Boys," as one woman's husband told her.

It is also clear that some divorce professionals need lessons in bedside manner. Often they treat female clients with less patience and respect than they accord men. "He was never available" and "He never explained things" are standard criticisms. While not all divorce lawyers are patronizing or cruel, nor all judges unfair, the study is nevertheless peppered with women's dismay and disdain for the manner in which they are treated by the people they encounter in the divorce process.

When Betty Duprey suspected her husband of cheating on her, she consulted a lawyer, who, in turn, referred her to a detective. "That detective began to ask me all kinds of questions about my sex life—what kinds of positions I like," says Betty, still flustered and embarrassed to tell the story even though it happened so many years ago. "I felt violated. Then he told me, 'You know, if you're not satisfying your husband, somebody else probably will. Women like you who are so prim and proper and don't like certain positions, you're going to lose.' "

That may sound like a one-in-a-million occurrence, but it's not. Other women report similarly humiliating scenes: "I went to this lawyer for a while, but the man only wanted to find out about my sex life," recalls Frances Slender. "Then he distorted and exaggerated whatever I said, to build up my case. I got very upset that he was doing this. He got mad and said he couldn't handle me. I had to find another lawyer."

Many women end up feeling that they've been had by a system that's supposed to protect them, and some even feel degraded by the men they hired to champion them. "I was used as a pawn—defined as either the vacuous, virtuous victim by my attorney or the greedy parasite by my husband's attorney," writes a survey respondent. "The game was a savage, ritual contest between two powerful attorneys, who don't want to lose. The game is money."

In retrospect, several interviewees realize that they lacked the self-assurance to rely on their own judgment. Indeed, some reported that they felt like "little girls" during the process. While they knew they had to pay for "expert" advice, at the same time, they didn't trust anyone, not even themselves.

It's not uncommon for women to go to more than one attorney. "I could have put a down payment on a summer house and bought a car with what I paid those lawyers—all three of them," interjects Fran Sargent. "The first one was too slow to act—or so I thought at the time. I fired him. The second, a barracuda who promised to discover Elliott's hidden assets, was, in fact, a greedy bastard who ended up firing *me*—a month before we went to court. In the eleventh hour, I had to pay the third one ten thousand dollars in advance, just to take the case. By then, I had no choice."

Interestingly, some women sought out female lawyers, thinking that having a same-sex attorney would obviate the problem. In general, the odds are probably greater that female attorneys will be more sympathetic, but it won't necessarily be true.

"That's why I went to her," explains Gwenn Banning, whose attorney was a past-president of the National Organization for Women (NOW). "Steve was literally out the door the day my last child went to college," Gwenn says of her husband of twenty years. Shocked and hurt by her husband's abandonment, Gwenn was doubly disillusioned when her female lawyer didn't turn out to be the staunch ally Gwenn had hoped for. "When I asked her to explain things that weren't clear to me, she got angry and impatient. She just wasn't nice to me."

A Player's Guide to Getting Through

Not every woman has a horror story about her divorce. Some interviewees describe very positive relationships with attorneys and other consultants; a small minority sail through the process smoothly and unscathed. Although only two out of five women feel they were awarded "a good settlement," there are lessons to be learned from those who do—and warnings worth heeding from those who don't. Here are ten important points to remember if you're in the throes of negotiating a settlement (see Chapter Nine if you're already past this point and have begun to plan for your future):

Don't blame yourself. Women are the victims of generations of conditioning when it comes to money, and attitudes can't change overnight. More important, it's virtually impossible to make sound decisions and learn financial skills when you're besieged by guilt, fear, and other emotions. So, take time and take care. "Be as patient with yourself as you are with your children, and as respectful toward yourself as you would be to your parents. And don't be ashamed to ask for help," urges one woman, who obviously speaks from experience.

Understand your own finances. When it comes to money matters, the study documents that most women are sorely uninformed.

During marriage, nearly two out of three never discuss finances with their spouses; forty-two percent don't look at tax returns, checkbooks, or financial records. Divorcing, more than half have no idea what kind of property is jointly owned; sixty-two percent don't understand or aren't aware of investments; about a third didn't have a clue about bank and credit accounts.

Many of our survey respondents offer this advice: "Keep a budget. Keep a list of everything. Know where every penny is going. Try to stay away from credit cards," one woman writes. "Do it in steps. Save as much of your money as you can," offers another, adding a familiar refrain: "With me, I did not fight when we were dividing things up."

Value your contribution to the marriage. "I'm going to fight for his police department pension. It's worth fifteen hundred dollars a month—and I deserve it," says Christine Moss, who seems to have a good handle on what's rightfully hers. Given most women's cultural mindset, it's understandable that so many fail to grasp that husbands' bank accounts, proceeds from businesses, or pensions contain *their* money too. Women don't value their role in home management or their part in maintaining family welfare, because society doesn't. It's expected; it's what women *do*.

Paula Oslow actually turned down her husband's offer for half of his $35,000 pension. "I told him I didn't want it. In hindsight, I would have said, 'Yes, I *deserve* half of the retirement, because I maintained the home while you went out to work.' I also would have negotiated to be kept on his insurance policy until such time as I'm working and have my own coverage."

Don't be passive in the legal process—do your homework. No matter how good your lawyer is, he or she is an outsider. Also, an informed and active client makes a good professional even more competent. Kate McKinley was pleased with her divorce settlement—but that wasn't simply because she had a good lawyer. She was careful not to relegate too much responsibility to him. A Player throughout her marriage, Kate claims that before marriage and kids, she had a good sense of her own identity. Not surprisingly, she also reports, "I had a great rapport with my attorney."

Kate did her homework. "I was responsible for all the finances during our marriage, so I knew the value of everything. I worked up a settlement agreement, and my lawyers agreed to it. We only had to do a little negotiating. I got everything I wanted. But it was fair. My ex got what he wanted also."

Bonnie Lenza regrets not taking a more active stance when it came to determining the value of their custom-built house—a considerable asset. "I never got an appraiser; he got three, who were friends of his, so the appraisal was very low. I did get half, but I should have gotten my own appraiser."

At least Bonnie learned from her first mistake. She and her husband owned another piece of property jointly with his parents. "I wouldn't agree with that appraisal. He got very mad, but I held on and ended up a little better on that." With hindsight, Bonnie says, "If I had taken some courses in financial planning, I would have been more aware of what was going on."

Learn from women who have been there. "Only a few are truly taken by surprise," observes a very perceptive survey respondent. "When the end comes, and if the woman asks for the divorce, she really should prepare ahead. Find out all the rules and regulations in divorce. Decide what *you* want and stick to it!"

Karen Marshall was one who "knew." She recalls the point in her marriage when she began moving further and further away from her husband, who disapproved of her increasing independence. "If I was interested in anything outside the home, this was a threat to everything Saul believed a wife should be." Her husband's attitude didn't stop Karen from catching up on her education. At first she only took classes at random, but eventually she started pursuing a degree.

"I was taking a course on women and the law and got into a discussion with Saul about divorce. He said that if he wanted a divorce, he would split everything down the middle. 'And what if *I* wanted the divorce?' I asked him. He told me he wouldn't give me a penny! At that point I started putting away money for myself."

Some might be appalled by such a Machiavellian approach, but Karen's sentiments and tactics are highly recommended by the divorced women in the study. "I did something that I encourage every woman to do: have money that he doesn't know about. Sock it away somewhere!" urges Melanie Spade, who says she didn't sink financially after her divorce because she followed her own advice. "I had saved about ten thousand dollars, which, in

1968, was a good amount of money. He didn't know that I had it. He thought he was leaving me with nothing."

Clearly, women who arm themselves with information and play an active role during the divorce process are infinitely better off than those who act like ostriches about finances. "It was just a matter of time," confesses Elizabeth Harkness, who was married to an alcoholic for thirty-eight years. "I had become very knowledgeable over the years because he had been in the hospital two or three times and I had to take over for months, doing everything," says Elizabeth, sixty-eight. "I knew what we had and where things were. It took me a little bit of time to find everything, but by the time I was ready to pack it in, I had done my homework very well.

Christine Moss swung into action the minute her husband asked for a divorce. Having heard from other divorced women what she's up against, Christine, now in the thick of negotiations, is not leaving anything to chance. "I'm very clever. I have the master key to my husband's office. He writes everything down on paper because he can't remember anything. I've even steamed open envelopes to find things out."

Don't settle too fast. Many of the women in the study warn other women not to rush into their divorces. "Refuse to divorce until you have negotiated a good settlement agreement. Don't be pushed into anything because you're feeling unhappy, tired of it all, and want to end the unpleasantness." Another advises: "Get your thoughts together and have specific goals. Let your head rule, not your emotions. It may sound coldhearted, but women need to prepare themselves for divorce."

Gisella Morgan, who was married to a very wealthy doctor, admits, "I ended up with one hundred dollars a week and the house—because I didn't want to fight." About half of the women who, in retrospect, believe they "settled too quickly" did so because they wanted to end the pain, about a third did so because they wanted to cease dealing with an angry or difficult spouse, and a quarter did so because they lacked enough information to ferret out their husband's assets.

Many regret their haste even years later. "Every once in a while it's like a toothache—a little twinge," admits Anne Garner. "He has a beautiful home in Florida—I've seen pictures—a motorcycle, cars. . . . He had no financial worries. You see, he has a pension I didn't ask for. At the time it didn't seem important, and it seemed like his money."

Try mediation, if possible, as a first resort. "We went through divorce mediation, and with the help of a very intelligent mediator, we wrote our own separation agreement," explains Lena Entemann, whose experience was definitely the exception. Hardly a widespread practice in the past, divorce mediation seems to be coming into its own in this decade. The idea is that the mediator is on neither spouse's side and that by defining the issues of both custody and money, the mediator merely assists both parties in a discussion of their respective needs. Mediation is done in an environment that is not as emotionally charged as a lawyer's office, but mediation isn't binding; a final agreement must be written up by a lawyer and approved by the court.

Some couples can't work out their differences in mediation, but if they are able to, mediation can be a less expensive, less combative alternative. Lena, a reading specialist, is an advocate of mediation, but she also believes that her divorce went so smoothly because, "I always assumed that I have a very salable profession. I also inherited a small amount of money when my father died, so I didn't feel financially threatened. But I still have to be careful. I'm not lavishly rich."

Work on generating an income and becoming financially independent, no matter what's happening with your legal divorce. Thinking that she had to keep a low financial profile—advice given by many matrimonial lawyers who want their female clients to appear needy in the court's eyes—Fran Sargent, a Rewinder, barely made any money while she was going through her divorce. The legal process became her "job."

"That delayed my process and prolonged my delusion that a 'good settlement' would take care of me. This is hindsight, but I know now that the amount of money I got wouldn't have changed dramatically if I had been earning money while I was going through the legal process. And I probably wouldn't be in as much debt today if I had started taking responsibility for myself earlier!"

In contrast, Alice Hampton, a Slow Motion, had already begun to work on her financial independence, that third piece of the developmental pie, when her husband walked out on her. The

Hamptons were married for a long time after the life had been squeezed out of their relationship. During the final three years of the marriage, Jack steadfastly refused to acknowledge his extramarital affair, though his infidelity seemed all too clear to Alice. Instead, he systematically cut Alice out of his life. "Suddenly, he decided I shouldn't participate in the business anymore. I had nothing to do, so I got a job as a receptionist—for fifteen thousand dollars a year. It turned out to be a blessing in disguise."

Within a short time, Alice practically tripled her initial receptionist's salary, and, not so incidentally, she became a more able participant in the divorce proceedings as well. "I found out that our property in the mountains was in foreclosure. He wanted to buy it from me, but I refused to take an IOU from him. I knew it wouldn't be worth anything. I took him to court and had the house put up for sale. If I had waited for him, he would have lost the property."

Alice got seventy-five percent of the proceeds, which she parlayed into sound investments. "I didn't do very well, but at least I got *something*. I bought an apartment, which I rent out, and I have a few IRAs." Though she was trounced emotionally, Alice made herself accountable for her own future.

Move ahead in your life, even if you think you got a raw deal. The journey is different for everyone. It took Rewinder Irene Presto ten years. "For a long time, I blamed it on my attorney," she explains. "I felt that he absolutely drew this case out unnecessarily. He created more animosity than existed to begin with and it lasted for ten years—sixty thousand dollars later!"

Rewinders in the study, mistaking rebellion for independence, often have a hard time owning their part in delaying the legal divorce and taking financial responsibility for themselves. A few years ago, Irene finally realized, "My ten-year divorce was an abomination—absolutely horrible—but in retrospect, I guess I allowed it to happen too. Even though I felt financially I didn't get what I wanted—I'm sure everyone feels that way—I finally settled. I had grown enough, and I was able to take care of myself. It was time to end this and get on with my life."

Likewise, Fran Sargent now understands that she kept refusing to agree to a settlement because she was frightened. "Despite the promise of a windfall share of our marital assets, I kept missing the point: *I* had to take care of me—and to do that, I needed an income. Finally, I bit the bullet and got serious about working, but it took me a while."

Besides generating income, working is an elixir that helps many women get on with their lives. "What helped me cope was that I had already been a working person. I had to get up every morning and I had to function on my job from nine to five," notes Evelyn Dorrin whose husband's "mid-life crisis" precipitated their divorce after thirty years of marriage. The marital assets were split in half, and Evelyn was able to buy an apartment with her share. "I'd *rather* work three days a week at this point in my life," she admits, "but I have to work five."

Put your economic problems in perspective. Many women in the study comment that, because of their postdivorce finances, they have to work past retirement, but those who leave their bitterness behind are ahead of the game. As Evelyn Dorrin puts it, "I know that this is the way it is—and that's fine."

Whether a woman starts out as a Pauser, a Slow Motion, a Rewinder, or even a Player, she is far along the road to rediscovery when she can get on with her life—despite her fears, despite her anger, despite the fact that she thinks she's gotten an unfair settlement.

Caroline Breed is no longer bitter or shocked about her new, severely reduced life-style because she has finally found herself; and she is, at last, courageous enough to stand on her own. "That was a major change—from being taken care of to taking care of myself. For all the things I had done, and all the honors I had, when my husband left me, I didn't know how to fill out my license-tag renewal. I remember sitting there and looking at it and feeling like an absolute fool," says Caroline. "But I made it my business to learn, and now I teach financial management. I'm very motivated, because I want to help other women learn how to take care of themselves."

Paula Oslow's standard of living declined severely after divorce, but she, too, gained *herself.* "Emotionally, I never wanted alimony because something in me said it was really important to make the break economically." Ten years later, Paula knows her instinct was correct. "I *still* would not want alimony—for my own personal development it was important for me to be financially independent."

Reminiscent of so many other women in the study, Jody Burke, initially feared "being a bag lady" after divorce. She was just beginning to go back to college and had no concrete plans for employment when her husband walked out on her. But today Jody, who finished college, earned her degree, and is now self-supporting, realizes, "The first twenty-one years I lived with my parents; the next twenty-two years I lived in my husband's home—and now I'm being *me!*"

Statistically, the survey confirms that distress about money drops with increasing distance from the divorce experience. We suspect that's because with time a woman gains confidence in her ability to take care of herself, regardless of the level of her income. Survivors like Jody manage to put their economic problems in perspective, as part of the overall challenge of forging a new identity. Jody, for example, points out that her financial settlement is "adequate," but only if she lives in Arizona, which was not her first choice. She would have much preferred to return to the East Coast, but the cost of living there was prohibitive on her new budget.

After divorce, women discover that one door closes, but others open. Instead of dwelling on what they can't have, women like Jody look at what they've gained. They reach down deep inside themselves and draw from untapped emotional reserves and newfound social strengths. They develop management skills, learn the facts of economic life that they have previously ignored, and take risks that will help them grow. No longer in Wonderland, they are finally getting to that last slice of the pie.

4

Letting Go:
How They Cleared
the Path to Rediscovery

I pushed myself to overcome loneliness and self-pity by taking risks and challenging myself. I would walk into a room of people alone, plan weekend activities by myself. I conceived one new thing every day to look forward to. I tackled one huge emotional problem at a time. I searched for inner peace and strength in nearly every encounter—getting to know what stuff I was really made of. I realized my long-term goal was to be a survivor—to give the best example I could as my gift to my children.

—Survey Respondent, on "letting go"

Inside, Outside, Upside Down

A picture book Fran Sargent used to read to her kids sums up what she called her "letting go" process. *"Inside, Outside, Upside Down* was its title. It was one of those Berenstain Bears books. That's how I felt for at least the first three years after we separated. In the beginning especially, I liked being on the outside—feeling free, doing things, tasting life. But sometimes I was really out there!" she says, laughing.

"I knew I had to concentrate on my insides too—to understand what the change meant to me and to figure out where I was going—as a single woman. A friend suggested writing down my feelings, but that was hard. Quite honestly, it scared the shit out of me! That's when I felt upside down!"

Fran, a Rewinder, admits her insights are clearer in retrospect. "When I was in it, I wasn't so aware of what was happening. It certainly didn't feel like a *process*," she asserts, drawing quotation marks in the air to emphasize the word. "It certainly didn't feel *good.* Some of my so-called coping tactics—you know, drugs, sex, and rock and roll—helped me avoid looking at what was underneath my behavior. It was easier to brave the doorman at Studio 54 than to face myself!"

Though they traveled different developmental routes from Fran Sargent and had postdivorce life-styles far away from the bright lights of New York City, many of the women in the "Divorce Over 40" study certainly identify with her inside-outside-upside-down feelings. In interviews and in comments on their questionnaires, they described their outside work: *external* ventures, such as support groups, employment, hobbies, sports, volunteering, and other activities that enabled them to meet new people. They also talked about their inside achievements: *internal* efforts to explore their psyches and soothe their souls, through psychotherapy, journal-keeping, meditation, spiritual pursuits, spending time alone for the first time.

Sometimes the inside-outside-upside-down dance is two steps forward, one step back. A woman may be incredibly fearful and lonely when she first steps onto the floor and sees the array of options and unknowns that life suddenly presents. Her rhythm isn't quite in sync with the music. The orchestra in her head is playing a funeral dirge, while everyone else seems to be dancing to an upbeat tempo. But pain can be a powerful motivator. It spurs her to keep trying, to learn new steps. She reaches outward and looks inward for the first time in her life, transmuting what at first felt like a curse into a blessing. She begins to feel and respond to the beat, gets in step, takes a few leaps here and there, and, in the end, lands right side up.

Not all women succeed. Much depends on their developmental path. Players, who know that growth happens inside *and* out, are generally most able to respond to the shifting tempo. At the other extreme, Pausers, whose identities are tied up in their roles, are most reticent. Some Pausers can only cling tenaciously to past rhythms. Hovering on the perimeter, they never dare to join their sisters on the dance floor, who are moving on with their lives. Slow Motions who have already begun to dance, perhaps taking only small, tentative steps, are sometimes unaware of their movements. But they keep dancing, gradually building their self-esteem. And Rewinders can be wild dancers, strutting their stuff on the dance floor for all to see—but they often forget to watch themselves in the mirror!

OUR TURN

Looking Into the Mirror

"I had to stop hiding from myself. I had to take responsibility for where my life was going," Fran Sargent concedes. Her initial reluctance is typical of Rewinders. "Once I faced the fact that I needed to make a living and began to hustle some free-lance work, I took myself more seriously as a graphic artist, and that started making me feel better about myself." Even more important, because it required inside work, Fran also began to take an honest look at her fast-lane life-style. She owned up to being a substance abuser, joined Alcoholics Anonymous, and started seeing a therapist. "It helped me to stop running from myself."

A woman can let go of the past only when she begins to gain a sense of herself in the present. Ultimately, every woman who gets divorced must learn to take risks and to plunge into self-exploration, a key element in the rediscovery process. She has to work on both her "insides" *and* her "outsides." The two are interdependent. By itself, taking an action such as joining a support group is meaningless if an internalized sense of self is not developed. At the same time, one can't possibly forge a sense of identity without taking actions in the outside world. Especially after a long-term marriage where a mate has been one's only reflection, contact with other people helps a woman see herself from new perspectives.

When Slow Motion Nancy Rolfing went back to nursing school—a goal abandoned nearly twenty years earlier—her classmates, mostly women in their thirties and forties, provided an important mirror. "We constantly talked about the trouble at home, how domineering our husbands were. They treated us like children!" she explains. "We all felt undervalued. None of us were getting support for our success. Our husbands didn't want us to do anything that didn't directly benefit them."

The more independence Nancy sought, however, the more overbearing her husband became. He blatantly had affairs with other women, he was emotionally abusive, and, finally one night, in a fit of rage, he raped Nancy. Thinking there was no other way out, she took a bottle of sleeping pills.

"As I was getting sleepy, I panicked. I didn't really want to die." Nancy called a friend for help, and after several days in intensive care, she decided that her marriage was not worth saving, but her life was. "It had gone too far. He apologized for raping me, but I knew I had to leave. He wasn't going to change." Nancy also grants, "School and the other women in my life saved me."

Caroline Breed's first experience with this kind of positive "mirroring" was with her therapist. "I wish everyone could have a therapist like him! He saw me in a very different light than I saw myself. And what he reflected back stunned me. He saw a very competent person who had a lot to offer and who ought to go for it. It wasn't the mirror I had been looking at." Shortly thereafter, Caroline, a Slow Motion who had just turned thirty-nine, summoned the courage to go back to college, which was a dream she had abandoned years before.

The first day on campus, Caroline worried. Would her mind even work after all those years away from school? Would she be able to keep up? Would she fit in? In a sea of blue jeans, her neatly pressed linen slacks virtually broadcast her age. But her enthusiasm soon overwhelmed her fears. "I was a freshman and felt like a bride. I was scared and excited. I had never expressed my disappointment about not finishing school to anyone, but I had always dreamed of it!"

Caroline not only kept up, she surpassed many of the traditional students, as well as her own expectations, which is characteristic of the majority of mid-life and older women who resume their schooling. More to the point, the university setting provided other new mirrors for Caroline, in the form of mentors who applauded her straight-A work. "They encouraged me to go for my PhD. I'll admit, I really got off on that!"

The Risk Takers

Whether it happens while a woman is still married or after her divorce, the inside-outside dance begins with a brave first step—in Nancy Rolfing's case, going to nursing school; in Caroline Breed's, college. Taking a risk acts like an emotional crowbar, prying open the wall of denial that otherwise prevents a woman from exploring herself. For some, the initial step is an outside move; for some, the change is invisible, for it happens on the inside; and for others that first step is a combination of inside and outside changes. In each scenario, the dancing allows a woman to better understand who she is.

Often, over a period of time a woman will take seemingly small steps, which, in her eyes, are tantamount to taking great leaps. Joann Cress cut her hair. "My husband always loved it long, but I wanted short hair—it was easier to take care of. In part, he blamed the failure of our marriage on that haircut. If only I had listened to him and let my hair grow long . . . or, if I really cared about him, I would have let my hair grow—and so on. I told him that I was still the same person with shorter hair. He said I was becoming a women's libber!"

Insignificant as restyling one's hair might seem, it was nevertheless a big first step for Joann. She also listed her name in the phone book ("I didn't know I could do such things!"); she looked for her first job ("I was such a nervous wreck looking through the want ads, the newspaper was shaking!"); she went back to college ("I knew I had no one else to blame if I didn't do well"). With each small step, Joann moved closer to discovering herself and, finally, went out the door. "I became a risk taker, which I had never been before."

Force of habit sometimes works against risk taking. Nancy Rolfing admits, "I used to be afraid to go to the grocery store without Vern's permission!" Having come a long way in her own development since those days by the time she walked out on her husband, she nevertheless remembers having a nervous, knee-jerk reaction around six o'clock every evening during the first few months after the separation. "I'd think, 'Oh, I have to get home. Vern's going to want his dinner.' Then suddenly I'd realize, 'Hey! You can go to McDonald's if you want!' "

Statistically, the study documents that risk takers gain more than they lose from divorce. They develop new skills, start counseling, become closer to family members, seek out new relationships, and appear to have an overall sense of well-being. As the next section shows, women find different ways to take that courageous first step or series of steps.

A Guide to Letting Go

While the following does not represent every possible approach, the suggestions—offered by interviewees and survey respondents in the "Divorce Over 40" study—document their ten most common strategies for letting go after divorce:

Air your problems. Talking about yourself may not seem like a risk to some, but consider Lorraine Feldman's experience: "I was in the closet for a year after Marvin left. People would call and say, 'How's Marv?' and I'd say, 'Oh, fine,' as if he were still living here. Or, if someone called for him, I'd say he wasn't home. Then, I'd hang up, call him at his girlfriend's or at the store—if I could find him—and give him the message." She explains, "It took me a while to tell my parents what was happening. I made a special trip to Florida to tell them in person."

Opening up to others enables women to see themselves in a new light. Indeed, talking was the most frequently mentioned piece of advice offered by the survey respondents. "Hang in there," exhorted one. "Don't retreat into yourself. You will go through a 'death and dying' process, and your emotions will vacillate. Talk to your trusted friends. TALK, TALK, TALK—and vent your feelings."

Recognize that you have your own separate identity. It creeps up slowly for some, but many women actually remember the specific moment when they first felt separate, if only symbolically. Just as Joann Cress listed her own name in the phone book while she was still married, Lorraine Feldman marks the day she received an invitation to a bar mitzvah. "It was addressed to 'Lorraine Feldman and Son.' I was no longer Mrs. Marvin Feldman." An entry in Lorraine's diary, in which she "talks" to the husband who cast her aside for a younger woman, refers to that moment when Lorraine perceived the benefit of separateness:

> It felt good. I can answer for myself. I don't have to ask you again and again whether or not you are coming. I don't have to make excuses. I don't have to remind you to get someone to cover for you in the store. I don't have to be your conscience. I am on my own. I can answer for myself. Yeh!

Do something just for yourself. To women culturally defined by what they do for others, doing something for yourself is a major risk! "I was desperate to do something that I thought *I* deserved to do, wanted to do," said Paula Oslow, explaining how she felt when the parents of the boys in her son's basketball team were invited to accompany the team to a tournament in Hawaii. "My husband declined and said it was foolish and a waste of time. I wanted to go, but he said we didn't have the money." For the first time in twenty-one years, Paula defied her husband. "I took an insurance policy that my parents had started for me when I was a baby, cashed it in, got five hundred dollars, and went with the team.

"While I was in Hawaii, I realized that this was the first time I had been away from this man for more than one day. My life was totally dominated by him. I spent a lot of time in quiet places by the water's edge . . . thinking. When I came back, I knew I was changed." For Paula, her letting-go process began with the risk of defying her husband by taking a trip—an outside pursuit—which gave her the time, space, and courage to look inside herself.

Go to work. Paula Oslow's small changes added up to her taking the greatest risk of all: she left home with $43 in her pocket. Like many of the women who saw their roles mainly as wives and mothers, Paula Oslow, who had done only volunteer work, never dreamed that she would someday need a real job. "It was very scary. I was competing against nineteen-year-olds. I got a job as a waitress. The first few weeks, my stomach churned constantly! Then I found an office job for four dollars an hour, which was better than waitressing."

Eventually, from camping out in a friend's living room, which was her only option when she first left home, Paula's employment led to getting an apartment; the apartment inspired her to buy furniture, and, piece by piece, she began to rebuild her life. "I did not want to maintain a dependent status. I finally began to feel that I—Paula—was living my own life, and I've never been sorry."

Risk takers who change employment, the survey data indicate, are generally more rewarded than are sedentary women who don't take chances. Women who started working before their divorces also report that work is a great emotional stabilizer because it gives them structure and keeps them occupied. A paying job also prevents a woman from becoming a poverty statistic.

Go back to school. School can provide an outlet for creativity and channel for intellect; it is often a proving ground for a new

116

identity. As Joann Cress remarked, it was the first time that success or failure was completely in her own hands. After divorce, forty-one percent of women go back to school in the first year. Some women take only a course or two, or they enroll in a workshop specifically on the legal process or money management, to arm themselves with information or skills or to launch new careers.

Many interviewees also reported that going back to school was the turning point in their marriages. "In high school, I didn't think I was smart; I had problems getting by. I even switched out of the college-preparatory track," explains Karen Marshall, who went back to college at thirty-five. She eventually earned an undergraduate and a master's degree with a straight-A average. A far cry from the insecure teenager who thought she wasn't smart!

Jody Burke's attorney husband, Bill, had moved the family from Philadelphia, where Jody had grown up, to Arizona, where she felt like an outsider. "When my son was in first grade, I was very disappointed with my life. Our situation was typical of a number of couples. The husbands were involved in their work, and the wives were lost."

Jody had agreed to "try" Arizona for only a year, but when the year was up, and she told her husband that she missed the East, Bill reneged on his original promise. "There was only one university in town, only two courses I could take, but in desperation, I read the catalog. I had never wanted to get a degree in education, but I rushed down to sign up. I ran through red lights to get there!"

Jody started part-time for the first three semesters and then switched to full time. Soon, the outside changes began to have a profound effect on her insides. In retrospect, getting out there was the straw that broke her marriage. "I think what was going on was that *I was growing*. I became more aware. For years, every day, Bill and I sat and talked, and it finally dawned on me that all those talks were about him and never about *me* or what *I* was doing."

By the time Jody's marriage ended, she was well on her way to getting her master's degree, and her biggest fear—of becoming a "bag lady"—was mitigated by her newfound skills and confidence.

Take the social plunge. After a divorce, getting out there is as important as getting inside yourself. We discuss dating and becoming involved in love affairs in Chapter Five and making friends in Chapter Six, but we'd be remiss here if we didn't at least mention that a new social life is a pivotal step toward letting go of the past and grabbing hold of the future.

The first time most women step out on their own, it usually feels like a risk. "God! I was like a kid on her first blind date! You'd have thought I had never been out to dinner with anyone before—I was so nervous," jokes Paula Oslow, who would never have dreamed of "straying" during her marriage and found herself "a bit rusty" in the social department after divorce.

Some women are more aggressive and self-assured than others. "I put ads in the personals—just for the fun of going out!" says forty-one-year-old Bonnie Lenza, remembering the early days of her divorce. "I went out with twenty guys just to see what's out there."

Read books and articles that help make sense of your situation and what you're feeling. Books can offer solace and encouragement and, at the same time, validate a woman's feelings. Many self-help books provide a sense of community: other people have been through it, talked about it, so the reader can recognize her own feelings. Reading books may eventually give a woman the courage to be vulnerable with other people as well.

Many women in the study mentioned books and magazines as a means of acquiring information and learning how to cope with their feelings after divorce. During their marriages, reading also gave these women their first taste of feminism (which is why Evelyn Dorrin treasured her copy of *Ms.*), transported them beyond their limited, circumscribed lives, and made them realize that what they were feeling was par for the course.

Like many women devoted to their families, Caroline Breed was extremely isolated during marriage. She cared for her three young children and supported her husband's work, but Caroline had no close friends and nothing of her own to fill the void. Then one day, Caroline was in the easy chair in her bedroom sitting area, her favorite spot, reading Gail Sheehy's best seller of 1976, *Passages:* "I was absolutely, utterly dumbfounded and astounded that I was not very different from anyone else and that I was moving through stages that were very normal. It gave me a thread to hold on to—the idea that this was all going the way that it should. It was like a revelation to me. At that moment, it flooded my mind that my parents, my friends, and everyone around me were on some kind of journey. That book had a really profound effect on me."

Set new goals for yourself. Especially during the one-to-two-year period following divorce, women begin to ask themselves a central question that many never posed during marriage: "What do I want to accomplish *for myself?*" Some take up hobbies, do handiwork around the house, learn a new craft or a sport. Two out of five find that exercise is a wonderful elixir for stress, and getting themselves in better physical condition gives their self-esteem a boost.

"I go to aerobics classes three mornings a week—not bad for a fifty-six-year-old woman!" writes one woman who seems to have done it all after her divorce. "My five sons are proud of me. I learned to paint. I didn't know I could! I did the trim on my house, both bathrooms, carpeted the house myself, and did all the landscaping. Best of all, I hung pictures—my husband didn't like holes in the wall!"

Give to others in ways that enhance your self-image, rather than detract from it. Many women are accustomed to giving of themselves to their husbands and children. Volunteer work, however, is a different kind of giving, a giving back to humanity, as it were. One year post divorce, twenty-two percent of the women in the study find volunteer work to be a wonderful catalyst in the letting-go process. Many work with homeless, sexually abused, or battered women; indeed, divorced women often identify with their plight. Such volunteer efforts can put one's personal problems into perspective and also provide a sense of purpose and fulfillment.

Moving beyond the family and then beyond even one's own needs and concerns is an important developmental marker in mid-life. Women who work for a cause, for no pay or for very little, find that the intrinsic compensation is immeasurable, and it enhances their self-image. "No monetary value can be placed on it," insists one of the survey respondents who works a nine-to-five work week and then volunteers in a hospital on Saturdays. "Giving of one's self is the greatest of all gifts. It doesn't cost us anything, and the rewards are the greatest HIGH of my week!"

In a similar vein, two years after her separation, Paula Oslow went to work for a feminist women's health center. "I went there for a tubal ligation, but with the information they gave me about the procedure, I changed my mind. Instead, I became intrigued by what they were doing. You get paid the same minimum wage, and it's a great sacrifice, but it felt to me that this was where I belonged. The women's movement passed me by. I guess I was always a closet radical!"

Physically separate from your spouse. For many women, only physical separation finally forces them to stand on their own, even though they're the ones who risked walking out the door. The truth is, nothing makes a woman grow up faster than being alone.

For some women, the separation occurs in stages. Marilyn Hauptman first moved out of the bedroom she and her husband shared, down the hall, and into her college-age daughter's room. "I finally ended up living in the basement." But that wasn't far enough. "I didn't want the kids to go through the pain of living in the same household," Marilyn recalls, remembering her husband's terrible verbal abuse.

In Nancy Rolfing's case, she moved out, but her teenage daughter was still at home, so the shock of separation was delayed for a year. Then, her daughter trekked off to college and so did Nancy, who enrolled in a college program that catered to older women returning to school. It took her to a dorm in Massachusetts, more than a thousand miles away from her farm in North Carolina. "My going away to college was both a risk and a final separation," maintains Nancy. "I hadn't made a clean break yet. I needed to get away from him and from everyone in that town who knew me. Otherwise, I probably wouldn't have grown up as much."

Band-Aids Are Not Enough

Some women *appear* to have moved into the world and made independent choices, but their insides don't immediately catch up with their outsides. It is revealing, for instance, that Anne Garner, who left her marriage of thirty years and reveled in her own bachelor apartment, still returned every day at lunchtime to empty her husband's ashtrays and do his laundry. Anne may have left home, but she still hadn't let go. "I did all sorts of fun things for myself in that little apartment," boasts Anne. "I delighted in being so bohemian. But at the same time, I thought he would come after me."

Anne could describe her "very sixties" apartment in detail—the blue silk sheets, the potted plants, the wind chimes. The problem was, at first, she didn't have a sense of who *she* was. Things changed only when she accepted that her relationship was dead: her husband was never going to come for her. She was on her own. Her family, who disapproved of the separation in the first place, shunned her, her children were angry at her, and most of her old friends were gone. "It was a time for licking my wounds. I needed a couple of years to pull in and heal myself."

For Anne, moving out was only a Band-Aid for her unhappiness. In many ways, it simply gave rise to other problems: loneliness, self-doubt, and financial insecurity. Much of the healing—the inside work that led to her finally beginning the rediscovery process—came through her writing. Handing us a slim yellow booklet of the poetry she self-published that year, *Silkworm Spinnings,* she warns, "I always tell people, that's where I was then—not where I am now. I wrote day and night. If you read it, you will see the pain. It was the only way for me to get rid of it." She shares a poem, appropriately entitled "Finale":

> I will never again feel your fingers warm against my cheek
> Nor taste the cherry-blend tobacco clinging to your tongue
> Nor shiver with your breath upon my neck
> Nor feel your beard warmly brush my body
> I stretch my leg and feel only cool smooth sheets
> Where once you lay curled up and crumpled
> Stripped naked, unused to my aloneness, I surrender
> My wantings shift through open fingers to other lands

Walls of denial tend to crumble slowly; they're eaten away by years of derision, abuse, and disappointment. "Much of the trauma I experienced after my divorce was because I could not face the reality of a dissolving marriage," muses Irene Presto, whose twenty-five-year marriage to a philandering husband ended when he finally walked out on her. "I tried to escape from my feelings into total denial. For a long time, I watched as if it were happening to someone else." Eventually, Irene found, it was no longer possible to quell the voices on the other side of that wall, voices that knew all along that something was terribly wrong.

"Although I was not very happy, I had gone from shrink to shrink for years, trying to hold on to the marriage. I came from a background where once you are married, you are married forever," explains Irene. "So, part of me was relieved not to be with him under the same roof. But I was also scared to death. I had never taken care of myself. Someone—my father, my husband—had always been there as a provider. I knew it was a relief not to have the tension and pressure, but . . ."

One day, about a month after her husband left, Irene recalls: "I was driving over the Golden Gate Bridge, crying, listening to music, feeling sorry for myself. My father had passed away, and my husband had left, and here I am—alone. My children are getting older. 'What am I going to do?' " I asked myself.

As the San Francisco skyline loomed before her, Irene saw her father's face. "At that moment, I decided to take my dad's legacy—a wonderful zest for life. From that day forward, that's what I've done." Irene finally faced the reality of her marriage, the years of trying to make up for her husband's frequent absences, their constant disagreements over disciplining the children, his involvement with other women, his lack of support for her personal achievements. "I had gone back to school and gotten a degree in social work. He felt threatened, so he would just lash out at me. I would always try to make nice. I couldn't come home and say, 'Gee, I got a good mark on such and such.' "

Irene was no stay-at-home wife. She had, like Anne Garner, already started working on her outsides. But she never quite grasped that her achievements in school and her other accomplishments were benchmarks of her growth as an individual. The day she decided to embrace her father's legacy, her outside mirrored what she was feeling inside. In various forms, other women had similar epiphanies, moments of truth after which they experienced new resolve to get on with their lives.

Some women's "Band-Aids" are deceptive. These women appear to be bright and competent. They're career women and leaders in the community, but they nevertheless have trouble getting themselves moving after divorce. Fran Sargent recalls, "People couldn't understand why I was so depressed after the divorce. I was a very young forty-one, active; I had a career; my kids were doing well; he wasn't withholding money. Well, I may have *looked* good and talked a good game—but I was petrified," owns Fran, who saw a psychotherapist for about a year after her divorce.

"The therapist made me focus on what I brought to the marriage, and my part in ending it. And I finally admitted my fears about surviving on my own, which was the hardest part, because I liked feeling that I was in control, but I wasn't."

Had her therapist not cracked the shiny veneer that looked so perfect, Fran, who asked for the divorce in the first place, might still be blaming her ex-husband for whatever was wrong in her life. "If everything was his fault, I was totally off the hook. I wouldn't have to look inside myself. But the longer I stayed angry at him and focused all my energy outside myself, the longer I delayed my own healing process."

Seeing a Shrink . . . in Order to Expand

For Fran Sargent, psychotherapy played an important role in peeling off the Band-Aid and exposing the wounds so that she could heal. She is not alone. Among our survey respondents, forty percent sought some form of counseling—psychoanalysis, various types of psychotherapy, marital counseling, spiritual counseling, or group therapy—during the divorce proceedings. Counseling can peel off the blinders and open a woman's eyes, so that she can better understand why the marriage failed—and accept responsibility for her actions.

There are no pure "victims" in divorce, as this survey respondent realizes in retrospect: "At the time of the divorce, my feelings were of pain and rejection, since I was the one who was dumped. To this day I have a difficult time," she owns. "But being in therapy certainly helped me understand my role in the breakup and get rid of the guilt. It also helped me cope."

Even Joann Cress, who had made monumental changes within her marriage, credits a therapist for helping her better understand her situation. "Everyone going through a major change like divorce needs someone impartial to talk to. Many problems that seem insurmountable are not that difficult when broken down into small parts or seen from a different perspective," says Joann, adding an important point: "Sometimes women feel worthless and unloved. They need to do whatever is necessary to rebuild their self-esteem."

Interestingly, while some women tried in vain to drag uncommunicative husbands to therapists prior to divorce, few sought professional help on an individual level while they were married. If a woman did, more often than not, it was to change herself; that, she hoped, would improve her marriage. Husbands often encouraged such thinking. One woman's husband actually said to her, "So why don't you get some counseling so we can straighten out this marriage?" However, using individual counseling to solve a marital problem is like the sound of one hand clapping. A woman cannot effect significant change in her marriage without a husband's cooperation. Some women, typically Pausers armored in their defenses, avoid seeking professional help, especially during marriage, because they're not ready to face reality nor are they willing to hunker down and do the difficult internal work that effective therapy demands. A noteworthy exception is Peggy Kennedy, who suffered endless physical abuse throughout her twenty-year marriage; she finally sought the advice of a therapist when her husband first walked out on her.

"I think individual therapy was the beginning for me. I was thirty-six years old. It wasn't as if I said, 'I've had enough of this marriage.' I was going insane and I didn't know it. The therapist asked me if I was ready to take certain risks. And I really thought my husband had left, so I said, 'Sure.'

"One of my first risks was to say *No,* a word he never heard." Peggy's husband came back, more abusive than ever, but she was somehow ready at that point to hold her ground. "In my heart, I knew all along that life would be better without him. Finally, I was ready to take action." Therapy helped Peggy transform herself from the inside, which, in turn, gave her the strength to change what was happening on the outside.

After a divorce, six out of ten women find therapy to be helpful. Typically, counseling is short-term and occurs within two years post divorce. Elizabeth Harkness, who gave up trying to reform an alcoholic husband after thirty-eight years, now regards post-divorce therapy as her first step in reforming *herself*. "For four months, I was in private counseling and then in a group. It was the best thing I ever did. I recommend it to anybody who can't get her life together. It's a quick way to do it. It helped me with the stress. And it helped me realize I was allowed to have my own life."

Like many women married to alcoholics, Elizabeth was prone to rescuing her husband, even after they split up. "They were threatening to throw him out of the rehab. I didn't want to take him back, but I felt guilty." Her counselor helped Elizabeth realize that this was her husband's problem, not hers. "I was so relieved to be alone and not to have to worry about what he was doing, not to have to ask anybody for permission to go anywhere, not to think about leaving a meal for him or leaving a message—just complete relief! Thanks to that counselor's help, I finally gave myself permission to be *me!*"

Support Groups: "People like Me"

Seeking out others who have "been there" can also be a major breakthrough in healing. "I wanted to know that I was not the only forty-five-year-old going through this," Evelyn Dorrin realized about a month after her husband walked out on her. "So I looked in the yellow pages and called a group called SPAN— Single Parents Action Network. They met in a public school, six women in the group. They were all around my age, maybe a few in their thirties. After hearing *their* stories, mine was really nothing!"

Sixty percent of the women in the study feel formal support groups are instrumental when it comes to obtaining information and emotional support and to gauging where they are in the rediscovery process. It makes sense: if you think you're the only one who has been abandoned for a younger woman, who has had a credit card confiscated because a husband canceled it, or whose children are angry because the family unit is splintered, it's quite a relief to find out that your experiences and your reactions to them are typical. And who is more credible than someone else who has been through it and survived?

It's critical to reiterate that for many of the women in the study, the thought of appearing vulnerable in public is an alien concept. To speak out in a room full of strangers is totally beyond their imagination! Thus, many women had to overcome an ingrained bias against this type of formal support. But for a woman such as Evelyn Dorrin, it was infinitely easier to seek out a support group, because a decade earlier she had experienced the intimate camaraderie of other women in her consciousness-raising group. Evelyn remembers, "Back then we were also five or six women, together for three years or so. It was wonderful—we knew everything about one another."

The most important message of a support group is that it's possible to survive divorce. "Most members have gone through a very similar experience, which has a great impact on bringing you back to reality," writes a woman who joined a support group. "It can lift your spirits and show a woman that she can live through the ordeal of divorce and become an even greater person than she thought she was!" In a community of comrades who share similar experiences, not only does one get help, it is also possible to *give* help, which enables a woman to see how far she herself has come.

Groups such as Parents Without Partners, a national support network for divorced parents, can help a reticent woman dip her toe into the social pool, as well. "I remember the first PWP meeting I attended," comments Doreen McBride. "Walking into that room full of people, I was sure I had made a dreadful mistake. I thought I wasn't dressed appropriately—or maybe I was dressed too well. I was afraid no one would talk to me—or maybe they would—and then what? I almost ran out of there. I thought I'd die! As it turned out, almost every woman I met that night told me she felt exactly the same way the first time." Doreen has since gone to PWP dances and events for parents and children. "I even tried camping for the first time in my life. I couldn't believe it—me, a city girl!"

Anne Garner joined a support group because she felt alone in her writing, and she needed to break the isolation. "I went to a meeting for Divorced and Separated Catholic Writers. There were about twenty people there. I needed more feedback—and I got it."

Al-Anon, a support group for family and friends of alcoholics, which, like other twelve-step programs, is based on the Alcoholics Anonymous philosophy, was also mentioned frequently in questionnaires and interviews. Although Al-Anon is not a program for divorced people per se, many women were married to heavy drinkers or philanderers—sometimes one and the same! Al-Anon often helps a woman to come to terms with how she innocently contributed to his addictions and with the toll on her life that years of her husband's drinking has taken, as well.

"At Al-Anon, I learned that we spouses also all have a disease. He was the alcoholic, but I had been his 'enabler' all those years. I kept *him* going," explains Gail Leperk. "I made excuses for him, and I kept thinking that, by some miracle, everything was going to get better." The miracle, as it turned out, was Al-Anon for Gail and many other women who didn't know how to start a sentence with the word *I*. Gail agrees, "Al-Anon taught me keep the focus on myself—to decide what I needed and wanted, rather than always worrying about him."

As in other types of support groups, women can also broaden their social networks through twelve-step programs. "Naturally, my friends in AA didn't drink, and that helped me redefine what 'fun' was. I didn't know I could have a good time without drugs and alcohol," Fran Sargent explains. "But they also became symbolic of my new life—no connection to my ex—so it felt like I was really moving on."

Awakenings: The Spirituality of Divorce

No two women define their spiritual selves in precisely the same way. Differences aside, an unmistakable theme ran throughout the survey: the notion of employing some form of spirituality to deal with fears related to loneliness, aging, and mortality. Some women refer to God as their protector. Others, who eschew organized religion and the concept of a deity, find solace in New Age mysticism or the twelve-step notion of a Higher Power. All share one important belief: they feel supported by something or someone more powerful than themselves, and it is no longer their husbands or their fathers.

Paradoxically, the process of separation (letting go) and the pursuit of spirituality (feeling connected) go hand in hand. Each propels the other, creating a spiral of growth. The more a woman begins to perceive herself as a separate, autonomous human being, the more she also begins to feel a new sense of calm, as if she is finally safe. And the safer she feels inside, the more she dares to explore on the outside.

Long before their marriage ended, some women in the study embraced a form of spirituality and believed in a power greater than themselves. Divorced, they are buoyed by their faith and by their observance of religious practices. "Learning to do things by myself and dealing with my fears were the hardest parts of the first year," says Anne Garner, a devout Catholic who gave much of her time during marriage to her church and to the Rosary Society. "I think each person has her own way of coping with stress. Mine was keeping busy and facing each day with the faith in God that his hands would see me through whatever lay ahead."

For other women, it wasn't a question of following a particular religion. They prayed, they read inspirational literature, or they simply believed that there was a God out there protecting them. Lorraine Feldman was born Jewish, but she wasn't observant. Still, her ordeal compelled her to "talk" to God in her journal. In this entry, Lorraine seems to be learning that faith—not advice—is a better analgesic for the pain and loneliness deep inside her:

> God, he has sunk so low. Is this what he is really like? My stomach turns sour when I meet him. I am burning out. And God, I have no one to talk to besides you. Sometimes I have such pain inside, and no way of letting it out. I don't need a lecture; I don't need advice; I don't need a scolding. That is not what I need and want now. Just hold my hand, squeeze tightly, and let me know I have a friend. That is all I ask. So simple, and yet so very much.

Gwenn Banning found spirituality in AA and other twelve-step programs. Neither an alcoholic herself nor the wife or child of one, she explains, "Some of my friends who are not alcoholics go to twelve-step programs anyway. I like that life philosophy too."

In the first year, because her insides were far behind her outsides when it came to acceptance, Gwenn went to a retreat for divorced people, sponsored by the Catholic Church but based on the twelve steps. "We went through the steps—beginning with step one, surrender. I had to understand that I was powerless over my husband's behavior," says Gwenn, still pained by his betrayal three years ago. She explains that the steps helped her admit her part in the dissolution of the marriage and to believe that a Higher Power would comfort her. "Some people in AA call their higher power God. Others say it's the spirit of the group. It doesn't matter—as long as you get that *you're* not God!"

Some women never use the word *God* or think of a particular deity, but they still consider themselves spiritual. Many have rejected the religion they grew up with. Instead, they sample a smorgasbord of New Age spiritual pursuits: meditation classes, lectures on Eastern philosophies, visits to psychics and astrologers. Phyllis May personifies an eclectic approach to metaphysics: "I believe that the positions of the sun and moon influence your energy, but so do a lot of factors. I try to keep an open mind—to understand the forces that affect me. I think I've reached the karma in my life—I'm on the right path."

Spiritual awakenings do not necessarily occur in churches or when a person is consciously looking for God. Some people, in fact, believe that trusting one's intuition is the same as tuning in to a Greater Force. "I look at life very spiritually, not religiously," says Lisa Frazier, whose story is ripe with spiritual underpinnings and dotted with "signs" from her spiritual guides.

Married at eighteen, for the first ten years of marriage Lisa was a devoted helpmate, clinging to the American Dream. She busied herself with "beautiful things"—decorating her house, buying antiques, landscaping her home. But her soul went unnourished. "My husband wasn't much of a thinker," says Lisa, at forty-four, a handsome, athletic-looking woman and an engaging conversationalist, full of ideas and excitement. "He had no idea what I was talking about! The things he valued were home and children, sex on Saturday night, and dinner on the table, nothing more. That was enough for him, but it wasn't enough for *me*."

For a long time, Lisa admits, "I used food for whatever ailed me. But my weight went up and down like a yo-yo, and I became even more unhappy." Then she discovered racquetball. When she appeared for her first game as a member of the women's league, she says, "I was shaking, I was scared—I had never tried anything like this in my life." That year Lisa got a trophy: The Worst Player Award. But she loved the game, and she continued to play it—five hours a day—and to get better. Good enough, in fact, to play in a tournament a year later.

"Racquetball showed me that I was capable of doing *something*. Here I was, someone who had never done a sport in her life!" Lisa links her external success with her internal connection. "On a spiritual level, I always felt that my godforce—the force of life that created me—was teaching me through these actions what I was capable of doing. I saw myself go from getting the booby prize of the club to playing in the World Open. And I said, 'Oh, my God! I can do this!' The next thought was, 'I wonder what *else* I can do?' I liked it.

"I really have a very good relationship with my godforce," explains Lisa, reflecting on how her success at racquetball was intertwined with her growing sense of independence. Out of an external exploration, she found her way inside—to her identity and to her soul. The physical (the outside) fed the spiritual (the inside), and each step led to another upward spiral of self-esteem.

"I finally got comfortable with me," says Lisa. "I began to like who I was. I guess you could say I was like they say in the title of that book, *my own best friend!*"

The Joy of Solitude

Lisa Frazier offers another kernel of wisdom: "Divorced women have to believe in themselves, build their inner souls, listen to their feelings, and develop their inner strengths." Within the first two years after divorce, many women begin to follow that advice. In fact, two to four years after divorce, eight out of ten women feel positive about themselves.

As a woman begins to like who and what she is, and to trust the voice of wisdom inside herself, she needs less help from others to bolster and support her identity. Coincidentally and significantly, she is also less frightened by the prospect of being alone. After all, who wouldn't want to spend time alone with a wise, compassionate best friend? Again, the survey data confirm this metamorphosis: forty-five percent of women indicate that living alone is a major concern prior to divorce; two years later, however, seventy-four percent relish their privacy.

Feeling more secure inside themselves, no longer must these women develop diversions to ward off the pain and fear of being alone. "I learned that I was a human being, not a human *doing!*" jests Fran Sargent. "I always busied myself, every minute, with plans, with activities. I never allowed myself time for just me. I was afraid of being lonely if I didn't schedule people and things into my life. Now I realize why: I was afraid of who I would discover in there!"

Nancy Rolfing, who is about to finish her undergraduate work, will soon be on her own for the first time. She wisely observes that the process of rediscovery is long and gradual. "Lightning bolts" don't always mark the way, remarks Nancy. "I feel like I'm still growing up. You know, I'm not sure if I could be with anyone again. I'm making my own decisions now. I love it!"

SECTION 2
Moving On

◇

5

Sex and the Suddenly Single Older Woman: Playing the New Dating Game

In the 1960s, any sex outside marriage was called the "Sexual Revolution," a nonfeminist phrase that simply meant women's increased availability on men's terms. By the end of the seventies, feminism had brought more understanding that real liberation meant the power to make a choice; that sexuality, for women or men, should be neither forbidden or forced.

—Gloria Steinem, "The Way We Were—And Will Be," *Ms.* magazine, 1979, excerpted in *Outrageous Acts and Everyday Rebellions*

Nancy: Thinking About Sex

"We went skinny dipping in the ocean and made love on the beach!" exclaims a dreamy-eyed Nancy Rolfing, replaying the memory of her first affair. "It was real romantic!

"It was also very brief!" adds Nancy, who was forty-five at the time. "Over intersession. I was in Hawaii on an oceanography excursion, and he was one of the researchers." Nancy and her oceanographer investigated the island together, clambering over rocks, traversing beaches, exploring tropical groves. In the company of others, they were like two kids, winking across the table, exchanging furtive glances. Alone, they wondered whether anyone had caught on.

Nancy admits she didn't care. The guy was married; the affair lasted only four days. Yet it was the perfect painkiller for a woman on the rebound whose last sexual experience was rape— her ex-husband's version of lovemaking. "It proved that I was still . . ." She hunts for the right word. "Well, he said I was *good.* And I don't know if he was telling me the truth or not. But what it did for me was affirm the fact that I knew how to make love. I felt attractive . . . wanted."

It had been two years since Nancy walked out on her husband, Vern, a controlling man who had grown even more selfish and abusive as their twenty-four-year marriage wore on. Over time, she not only put up with his affairs, she constantly carried his voice in her head. " 'I wonder what Vern would think,' I'd say to myself."

When Nancy went back to nursing school during the last five years of their marriage, Vern, socialized to expect a stay-at-home wife, was incensed. Increasingly, their life together became a test of wills, especially when it came to sex. If Nancy didn't want to sit on his lap, Vern took it as a sign of insubordination. "He felt I wasn't submissive enough." Nancy, who married Vern when she was twenty, thought this was what it meant to be a wife. Vern was her first and only man, and sex—like everything else—was meant to suit his needs. "I liked it when we did it, but I didn't necessarily want it."

Recalling her moonlit dalliance in Hawaii, Nancy Rolfing knew she had come a long way. "When I was a kid, all I wanted to do was get married. I didn't think about sex. I didn't have a clue about it, in fact. Now I'm more independent. I'm not thinking about marriage. But I think about *sex!*"

Nancy Rolfing's transformation mirrors that of many women in the "Divorce Over 40" study. They married young; most were virgins on their honeymoon; many married their first boyfriend. Emerging from marriage twenty or thirty years later, many were innocents. The idea of sexual fulfillment—getting one's own needs met in the bedroom—was at once shocking, frightening, and ripe with the promise of untapped pleasure.

After a divorce, a woman's sexuality is a barometer of her desirability and an affirmation of change. Interestingly, it also echoes the developmental rhythms of rediscovery. Some women dive into the new dating game, filled with wonder and passion. As it was for Nancy Rolfing, first affairs often open the door to a new self-image; they confirm womanhood. Other women are more cautious, venturing forth timidly, picking men who aren't threatening—"safe" dates that keep them out of the bedroom. But at least they're making the choices and asking for what *they* want, which is a far cry from the messages of their youth.

"Good" Girls Don't Do Sex

Women like Nancy Rolfing grew up in more provincial times —when "real" men and women had strictly prescribed roles. Theirs was the pre-Pill generation, a cohort of "good" girls who were brought up to "save" themselves for their husbands. The road to marriage was not paved with condoms, their mothers warned. Sex was something that you endure, not enjoy.

Indeed, most women in the study internalized strict cultural prohibitions about sex. Nancy Rolfing remembers her first pre-adolescent stirrings at age eleven. "I wanted the boys to like me. I wanted them to ask me out," she admits, but she was also painfully aware of being a "good" girl. Nancy's grandmother, who became her surrogate mother when her mother died, had such a tough time talking to her about the "facts of life," Nancy recalls, "I finally said, 'Oh, it's okay, Grandma. I know all about it from my friend Sally.' Of course, I didn't know anything!

"I guess you could say I dated—we went to the movies. We just held hands. But even in high school, when we started petting, I never let it go beyond." Nancy feared the wrath of her domineering grandfather, the powerful family patriarch who kept everyone in line.

Their families aside, many women also remark that parochial school education set the tone for their sexual behavior and their attitudes toward the opposite sex. "It was horrible . . . petrifying," recalls Joann Cress, forty-eight, who attended a strict Catholic elementary school. "It left its mark. They really put a conscience trip on me."

As she moved beyond the narrow confines of her neighborhood, high school provided new challenges to Joann's sense of morality. "Getting undressed in the girls' locker room was a shock. We were taught to be modest. Listening to other girls talk about what they did with boys made me very afraid. I was very withdrawn."

Caroline Breed, who grew up in North Carolina, has similar memories. She went to a small, exclusive all-girls private school run by nuns who taught their wards that there were only three avenues open to a woman: business, which meant that you were single and celibate; the spiritual life, which also meant that you were single and celibate; or marriage. "So, I saw boys strictly as somebody you married—part of a life decision."

137

Not surprisingly, the dating scene was tightly monitored. Proper Southern ladies-in-training that they were, Caroline and her peers were shielded from the boys. "In eighth grade I remember the boys from the boys' school would walk past our window at school, and the nuns would pull down the shades."

Left with their curiosity, Caroline and her friends tried to fill in the gaps. At their afternoon "teas," someone would invariably produce "one of those little manuals for teenagers—which I'm sure would have offended no one." Typically, they would all crowd into a hidden cloakroom to read it and erupt into fits of giggles.

Like that of many of our women, Caroline's sexual experience, even when she was a junior or senior in high school, was limited to "minimal petting." Sex was clearly reserved for marriage. "The only thing worse than getting pregnant was murdering somebody!"

Girls from more permissive backgrounds were influenced by the tenor of the times, as well. "My father was a heavy drinker. I know he cheated on my mother. And I don't think she was an angel either—although she always tried to come off as one," recalls Fran Sargent, forty-eight. "They weren't particularly strict with me, but I got the message anyway: Be a good girl. Save it. The guy won't respect you if you give away too much."

Some women found a sexual loophole, however, retaining the status of "technical virgins" before marriage. They engaged in all sorts of foreplay, got naked with their boyfriends, even dabbled in oral sex—all fair game as long as the girls didn't allow penetration! "I always had my reputation in the back of my mind," confesses Fran. "Everyone knew which girls were considered 'fast.' Even if you did what they did, you wanted to make sure that no one else found out!" Ironically, at a ten-year college sorority reunion in the mid-seventies—when sex had become "hip"—Fran and a number of her sorority sisters finally confided to one another that they weren't always the "good" girls they had said they were!

Growing up in the forties and fifties, many girls dodged the question of sexuality altogether, by making boys their "buddies." Lorraine Feldman had a brother two years older, a very outgoing, popular fellow, a good athlete. When her brother played basketball in high school, Lorraine was the team's mascot—and the only girl allowed to tag along with the boys. She felt privileged. "I was everybody's friend."

Actually, Lorraine didn't do much dating in high school. When she did, she says, "I had to admire those who took me out—I was *'Ronnie's sister.'* " Undoubtedly, it was safer that way. Sexually, she was not just a "good" girl, she explains. "I was basically backward! When I got to college, I was not into petting and necking. I used to think, 'What would I do if a boy wanted to do *that* with me?' "

Sex in the Cocoon

Sex was a frightening prospect to many women. It was mysterious, taboo, even dangerous, because it led to pregnancy. Hence, once these young women moved into more serious relationships, it was a hop and a skip to the altar, and only then would they jump into bed. Marriage finally made sex permissible. A few women had premarital sex with their boyfriend, but only when an engagement ring was securely in place. Sex was justified, as long as he was The One.

When Joann Cress started dating Tony—an "untouchable" because he was four years older—she knew she wanted to marry him. It was January 1964; she was sixteen, working as a secretary. Always the proverbial "good" girl, Joann says, "I kept my jacket buttoned to the neck, because I thought I'd avoid any problems that way."

One evening in April, Tony uttered the magic word, "I *love* you." A few nights later, sitting on her stoop in Queens, Tony made his move. "I still had a sweater on, and he touched my breast. The sensation that flowed from me was incredible!" Tony was the first person who had ever touched Joann. "Oh . . . that feeling!"

For the next four months Joann kept telling Tony she "wasn't ready" for anything more. But then, they attended a friend's wedding, and Tony uttered magic word number two: "He said he was willing to *marry* me." Joann felt pressured to "go all the way" with Tony; she thought she'd lose him if she didn't.

By July fourth weekend, "I finally decided it had to take place." Joann was petrified, and when it was over, devastated. "The first time was not easy. He was not gentle. I never felt there was any consideration for me [clearly a foreshadowing of the marriage to come]. I remember thinking, 'Why do people do this? *This* is what I waited for?'" Joann cried, and Tony tried to reassure her that it would get better. It never did.

At that point, Joann knew she would *have* to marry Tony. "How could I go with someone else, after I slept with *him?*" It would be another two years before the young couple set their wedding date, by which time she had major misgivings about getting married. As the date drew nearer, she became "mopey, there was no joy, no excited feelings." Joann says that by then she was afraid of her husband-to-be. Even the sexual feelings had dissipated, and their lovemaking had become rote. "Compared to the beginning, the tingling feeling was gone." Joann was only eighteen.

Throughout their marriage, Tony was as selfish and demanding in bed as he was in the rest of their life. Joann's pleasure was never an issue. In fact, it would take another twenty-five years before she found out (by being intimate with another man) that sex could be "completely different," but in those days, she admits, "I thought everyone had sex that way."

Having no basis for comparison and no one with whom to share such unmentionable topics are two refrains that resounded in many women's stories. After "saving themselves" for their husbands, many were sorely disappointed about sex in marriage. Trained to be submissive in the bedroom (and everywhere else), they automatically sublimated their own needs for their husband's. Sex, like money, was considered a "man's thing." It just wasn't ladylike for a woman to want sex. So, whatever sexual feelings these women had, most learned to keep them under wraps.

Ellen Garland speaks for a lot of women when she describes the sex in her marriage: "Our sexual relationship was nondescript. I was just there for *him*. I don't think it was that important to me then. I didn't know any better. I was a virgin when I got married.

"The funny thing is, in those days, I thought my sexual relationship with my husband was good," Ellen adds. "But the affair I had after my divorce was a thousand times better. I realize now that my husband was always selfish—sexually too—but I had nothing to compare him to. This new person was extremely giving. What a difference!"

With the advantage of hindsight, some divorced women remark

that their attitudes about sex were influenced, if not controlled, by the men in their lives. Betty Duprey remembers, "Right before the wedding, we went to his family physician—I'll never forget his name, Dr. Race. He told me that there were three B's to remember: Always be a lady when you are outside, be a *balabosta*—that's the Yiddish word for a good housewife, someone you'd call a superwoman today—but be a bum in bed. I was in conflict. I found myself cringing from that idea, because I thought then that intercourse was dirty. I really wanted sex to be beautiful, but it never was."

Betty, who married at seventeen, learned everything else she knew about sex from her husband, who was the same age and almost as inexperienced as she when they first got married. "I was always there for him when he wanted me. He would say, 'Remember what Dr. Race said. Let's try this position,' and I would say, 'but I don't like this position; it's uncomfortable for me.' He'd remind me again, 'Remember Dr. Race,' and I'd feel that I had to do it because otherwise he would go to other women." By the time she was twenty-one, Betty realized that no matter what she did in bed, her husband had sex with other women, anyway. As in many marriages, the double standard was alive and well.

As a rule, the women in the study emerged from the cocoon with limited sexual histories and often sexually unfulfilled. In their marriages, they were controlled by their husbands, and they didn't realize they were entitled to more or capable of experiencing it. Only about twenty-five percent of our interviewees reported having a good sexual relationship with their husband.

The men, after all, were influenced by the same social and sexual mores. They were often just as ignorant and inhibited about sex, but they had to *act* as if they weren't. It was part of the macho ethic that bound so many men's lives. To be considered a good catch, a man had to earn a living. No one suggested that they had to be good lovers too!

Not surprisingly, the topic of intimacy was rarely addressed by the women in the study. It takes two adults, each having a strong, separate sense of self, to have a truly intimate, committed relationship. However, most of these women and men were developmentally incapable of sustaining intimacy—a psychological interdependency in which the individuals temporarily "give up" themselves in order to be part of a larger unit, be it the couple or the family. Sex can be an example of intimacy, but intimacy can also exist without sex. The problem in many of these marriages was that the sex often existed without the intimacy.

Research has shown that how enduring an intimate sexual relationship will be depends on the value each partner places on the basic friendship. With husbands who seemed to be less interested in their wives' satisfaction than their own, no wonder so many women in the study report having felt empty after sex.

Sex in the Age of Liberation

Of the women in the study, less than five percent of the interviewees had extramarital affairs. One of them, fifty-four-year-old Marsha Lenox, explains that for the first ten years of her marriage, she thought nothing of the fact that she felt so removed from her feelings, sexual or otherwise. One night, at a cocktail party, everything changed.

"One of the men there whom I knew talked to me. I went into the kitchen with him, and one thing led to another, and all of a sudden attention was being paid to me that I was not used to. We kissed and that began a six-year relationship. This was a tremendous awakening for me—that someone would look at me." The affair also made Marsha aware that she had never had an orgasm with her husband nor had she ever discussed it with him.

A few women also embarked upon extramarital relationships that weren't sexual. For some, well-schooled in the culture, even the prospect of having an affair was confusing and painful. Gwenn Banning recalls being a young mother in 1969, nursing her three-month-old son, tears rolling down her face and onto the baby's head. "I felt myself being attracted to men. I hated myself for it. I don't know why it happened, but once I had the security of the relationship with Steve, I guess it freed me. I think it was a delayed adolescence."

As early as her honeymoon, Gwenn confesses, "I fantasized that I was with the administrator at the hospital. I felt a lot of guilt." Over the succeeding years, her fantasy life continued to flourish and to occupy more of her time. "Not affairs, but attractions," she clarifies. "It was a game. I was a good person, so I couldn't sleep with them, but I enjoyed the flirting. I almost did once, but I'm very inhibited." Gwenn grants that she was curious—but the fantasy was always infinitely more satisfying than the real thing.

Gwenn, a Pauser whose Catholic upbringing shines through, is still pained. "I feel that those were very grievous sins." In contrast, for other women in the study, having an emotionally intense platonic relationship, or the mere fantasy of an affair, was far more satisfying. In fact, such ruminations often marked a woman's first taste of the social piece of the developmental pie, enabling her to finally view herself as someone with separate social needs.

Consider Debby Black's experience; talking intimately meant more to her than having sex. She had an "intellectual affair" for two years with her boss. Because she was married, the relationship didn't evolve into a sexual affair until she and Mike split up. "Still, we had such a good time together, particularly because of the conversation." Debby's nonsexual "romance" gave her a mirror that was different from her husband, who seemed more attentive to the TV set.

Whether or not a woman toyed with the idea of extramarital sex during the seventies, the right to sexual satisfaction, along with other feminist messages, sometimes trickled into her consciousness. And many of the women who ventured out of the cocoon while they were married—usually Slow Motions or Rewinders—also became more forthright when it came to sex.

Joann Cress's sex life became better when she began to stand up for herself. By then, a good ten or fifteen years into her marriage, she had gotten a job and gone back to college. "I liked myself better, and I was enjoying myself more. If I was tired, I could now say no. I could now say what I liked and didn't like. And I would stop him from doing things I didn't like."

With the dawning of the so-called sexual revolution, the women in the study were also exposed to music that broadcast explicit, sometimes raunchy, lyrics; some watched R- and X-rated movies or tuned into spicy late-night cable TV; others bought sex manuals and vibrators and dabbled in sex-enhancing drugs and ointments—with husbands' blessings, of course, which helped make trying new positions and other forms of sexual experimentation legitimate.

"During the seventies, I didn't want to miss out on what I heard other people were doing," owns Fran Sargent who, like many Rewinders, became more sexually open and experimental as the years wore on. "It scared me, though, because it went against my upbringing. But I was also curious. And as long as my husband went along with it, I felt safe."

Fran believes that some of the books popular at that time, such as *The Joy of Sex* and Erica Jong's novel *Fear of Flying*, which touted the "zipless fuck" (Jong's term for sex without guilt), inspired her and some of her married friends to experiment sexually and a few to even chance having affairs.

Irene Presto, another sexually experimental Rewinder during marriage, recalls being envious of a more "daring" married friend. "She blatantly did the kind of things that I only fantasized about. She *always* had a young lover!"

Irene recalls asking her therapist why she couldn't be more like her friend. "I was jealous. I wanted to be able to have extramarital affairs too. I always said things like, 'You only have one life to live!' But I couldn't have lived with the guilt. And I was too intimidated—too much a product of my time."

When "Good" Girls Divorce: Dating in the Nineties

Being curious about sex, exploring new positions with a husband, even venturing into extramarital sex while still in the cocoon is safe; being single and starting to date again after a long-term relationship is another matter entirely. Although dating after divorce can do a lot to restore a woman's confidence, for many women who emerge from the cocoon after so many years, dating can also be a menacing prospect, for a number of reasons.

Dating isn't what it used to be. The women in this study stepped out of marriage into a completely different cultural setting from what they had known as girls and young wives. This fact hits hard in the dating department for many mid-life women. Suddenly single, many "good" girls find the brave new world of the eighties and nineties as intimidating as it is exciting. The old rule book is outdated. People no longer talk about "fast" sex—it's about "safe" sex now. No longer taboo, sex is out in the open and a dazzling variety of sexual acts are fair game in the bedroom.

"I wasn't ready for it at first," admits Nancy Rolfing. "I came from a small town, lived on a farm most of my married life, and

I was naive. I was shy. And the idea of talking openly about sex, well . . . it was like learning a foreign language!"

It's not that easy to meet good men. "Male companionship has certainly always been important to me, but it's difficult, because I believe that there are many more quality women out there than men. I have been single ten years. Although I have met some nice male companions, they're scarce!" says Irene Presto, speaking for many mid-life women. Few are comfortable going to singles bars or restaurants; some are afraid they'll run into their own daughters! If anything, they prefer singles clubs or social support groups like Parents Without Partners.

Frances Slender is attractive. She finds it easy to talk with people, but the dating game is still a struggle. Frances tried a singles club. She also answered a few personal ads, and, for safety, she always met her suitors in public places such as restaurants. Her experiences, however, have been disappointing. "The personal ads are blatant lies. They say things just to get your attention."

Alice Hampton would agree. She answered one personal ad in *New York* Magazine. "I met one man whom I thought was single, but he turned out to be married."

Pinched pockets aren't conducive to a social life. It costs money to go out to dinner, run personal ads, or join clubs. And when funds are limited, and the kids need new shoes, divorced women often put their own needs on hold. Few have the luxury of discretionary cash for social events, memberships, or trips—all "respectable" ways of meeting men.

Fran Sargent lost those opportunities after her divorce, which is typical of women who live well-heeled life-styles when married. "Elliott and I were members of a tennis and swim club. He let the family membership lapse and rejoined on his own. I would have liked to continue going—the exercise was good for me, many of my friends were members, and it was a great way to meet new people. But it was out of the question on my budget."

The age gap makes dating difficult for mid-life women. Ageism is rampant on the dating scene, say most divorced women in the study. For one thing, middle-aged men don't like to date middle-aged women. Fran Sargent, who at forty-eight looks a good ten years younger, recounts a party she attended recently. "I was talking to a guy who must have been about my age. We had a lot in common—he was in the printing business, I was in graphics, we were both divorced and had children in college. *I* thought we were getting along very well."

At one point during this engaging conversation, Fran mentioned how old she was. "I figured it wasn't a secret. He knew I had a kid in college. Anyway, I'm proud of how young I look. But I guess he couldn't handle it, because the next thing I knew, he was saying, 'You know, there's a guy here I'd love you to meet.' It was *his father!*"

In a similar vein, Shirley Lane, fifty-two when she divorced, gets angry remembering that people treated her like a social pariah: "I was the poor, frustrated, unfortunate divorcée. The [married] husbands would call me, take me out to dinner, and then to bed. It was all done in secret, of course. I wasn't good enough to be invited to their homes. On the other hand, my ex-husband, who was only a little older, was courted by every eligible woman in town. He was an attractive doctor in his early fifties, and he was invited to everyone's home for dinner!"

But the age gap cuts both ways: middle-aged women don't like to date middle-aged or older men either! Physiologically, a woman in her forties and a man in his twenties have similar testosterone levels, which play a large part in desire. However, having more in common sexually with a younger man may not compensate for what he lacks in life experience and maturity.

Many women find it hard to mediate that delicate balance. "I'm really not interested in guys in their twenties," owns Bonnie Lenza, forty. "I like the age group of over-thirty-fives. They have been through enough life experience that I can relate to."

Fran Sargent also acknowledges, "I'm physically attracted to younger men. I mean, their bodies are in great shape. And it's extremely flattering when a young guy is interested in me." But, says Fran, who has a nineteen-year-old son, it gets tricky when young men start talking about their interests. "Once I was attracted to this guy in his late twenties. His parents were getting a divorce; and he was really upset telling me about it. I realized, this could be *my son* talking! After that, he didn't look so appealing anymore!"

Mid-life women are often nonplussed by older men too. "I think about myself as being in good shape," says a deservedly proud Gisella Morgan, whose youthful appearance belies her sixty-one years. "So many people my age are decrepit looking. I couldn't stand to see a man like that naked!"

Alice Hampton, fifty-two, agrees. "I have a problem finding men the right age. Someone in his late sixties is too old. We don't have the same interests, the same energy level."

Furthermore, when a divorced woman like Alice takes steps toward independence, she gains a sense of inner strength that often distances her from men at either end of the age spectrum. Young men like her spirit and her sense of independence, but are often a mismatch emotionally; and older men, accustomed to being with women schooled in the old tradition, find her threatening. Alice muses, "I had an older man offer me marriage once, but I would have killed him. He's a dear, sweet person, but I was too strong for him."

Dating feels too vulnerable. Vera Castro became active in community politics while she was married. Divorced seven years ago, she now comments, "Community service is easy, but the dating game is hard. I have several good men friends, but I'm still struggling with dating. One of my daughters says I go to lunch with the world, but I have a problem going out after dark!"

Vera reflects, "My daughter is probably right. Sometimes, I think to myself, 'Why doesn't anyone fix me up?' But the truth is, I've never given anyone the inclination to do that. They think that I'm so together and independent that I probably don't need help."

Vera, a vibrant, captivating woman, would rather take herself out of the running than feel the pressure of competing with younger women. Some women are also afraid they'll get involved with the wrong type of man. They reason that if they don't date, they won't make any mistakes.

Dating can evoke an abusive past. At forty-eight, Erica Sanford is first learning what it means to date. The daughter of an alcoholic, she was abused as a child, and her California childhood was filled with violence, secrets, and inappropriate sexuality. Typical of many abused women who reenact their brutal or barren childhoods in their adult relationships, Erica became "terribly dependent on men." She lived with a string of men—usually, alcoholics or drug abusers—and married two of them. "I knew nothing about my own sexuality, so I just went along with theirs.

"When my second husband walked out on me, I was terrified,

and I had to finally face my fear of abandonment. Now a year and a half after the divorce, I'm really able to see how all my relationships were part of my denial system. Sleeping around was my way of avoiding the real, personal issues about who I am."

After years of easily jumping into sexual relationships with men, Erica admits that she is now terrified of dating: she has never done it! "I have to learn to establish friendships with ultrasafe men—men who are married or much younger than I am. That's what I've been working on now, and it's tough. It's scary."

Dating often gravitates to sex! All the foregoing issues aside, in many women's minds, sex looms larger than life when they first begin to date. The thought of getting undressed in front of a stranger, let alone hopping into bed with a new man after twenty or thirty years of a steady, predictable routine—no matter how unsatisfying it was—often makes dating seem like a pretty risky business.

Negotiating the use of condoms can be daunting too. Irene Presto thought of herself as "current," as well as responsible, when she produced a box of Trojans from the top drawer in her night table. "The guy laughed at me," she recalls. "I thought I'd die. Talk about dousing a mood!" Irene's beau, in his late forties, was born of a similarly repressive era, a time when "real men" didn't wear condoms—or worry about AIDS. Sadly, mid-life men—many of whom have been safely tucked away in marriages of their own—are unaware, if not unwilling, when it comes to the etiquette of safe sex.

Fran Sargent met a man at a friend's anniversary party who was also schooled in the fifties. A few dates later, she recollects, "We were getting into some heavy petting at his apartment. And I'm no kid—I knew what it was leading up to. So, I said, 'Wait —do you have anything?' He looked at me blankly, which I took as a 'no.' When I retrieved a package of condoms from my bag, he threw them across the room—as if I had insulted him!" Like Irene, Fran not only passed up sex that evening, she never saw the guy again.

Sex: A Developmental Barometer

What separates the girls from the women when it comes to sex and dating after divorce? Why do some women plunge into love affairs quickly and with seeming abandon, while others take a more careful, cautious route to the bedroom? Once again, we turn to the developmental picture for the answers.

As in other arenas of postdivorce adjustment, a woman's attitudes about sex change as she begins to gain a more independent sense of herself. As she relies more on her own inner strength and is less influenced by the opinions of others, she gains confidence in herself. She begins to appreciate and respect her own judgment. And she really likes herself—despite a few gray hairs, an extra wrinkle here and there, and a bit of unavoidable flab!

In fact, even the way women *talk* about sex changes as they become more self-assured. For example, when the women in the study describe their earliest sexual encounters, they often use childlike euphemisms, referring to a man's penis as "that thing" or intercourse as "doing it." As they begin to talk about the changes in their attitudes, however, some of these same women describe the new men in their lives quite differently: "Boy! was he well hung," or "I discovered that I really liked fucking!"

The truth is, how women feel about sex, and *why* they have sex, are significant barometers of psychological and emotional growth.

• *Pausers* often use their first postdivorce sexual experiences to blot out a sense of failure and rejection. There's nothing like a good rebound love affair to console a loyal, self-sacrificing wife whose husband walks out on her. Her self-esteem has been badly battered, and she needs a powerful tonic to soothe the wounds to her pride.

• Though *Slow Motions* have already begun to take steps forward in their own growth, many are still unsure that they are desirable women when they first divorce. A Slow Motion whose husband initiates the divorce may also use sex to drown out the voices in her head that cry "Failure!" But a new love affair also gives her a testing ground, an occasion to prove herself attractive, and a chance to validate her femininity.

• *Rewinders,* spunky teen-agains that they are, often use sex to rebel against convention. They want to make up for lost time. Although few of the women in the study had extramarital affairs while married, those who did were usually Rewinders. Before or after divorce, Rewinder sex can be wild and impetuous. Like a teenager, a woman in the throes of this kind of affair can make impulsive and even dangerous decisions. The highs are often incredibly high—far surpassing anything experienced by Pausers or Slow Motions, who usually have an easy-does-it attitude about sex and love affairs. But, as with most high-return ventures, the perils are great as well.

• *Players* use sex for companionship and for building intimacy. They are usually aware of what they want from a relationship. If it's just sex, they have no illusions about attaching other meanings to it. On the other hand, if they're interested in building a solid foundation with a man, they consider sex an important part of the package.

These are anything but hard-and-fast "rules." Melanie Spade, a woman who was a Player during her marriage, indulged in Rewinder sex after her divorce—because she discovered the Pill and, as she put it, "went wild for a while." Categories also overlap and run into one another. Still, a woman's initial motivation for having sex—to ease the pain, to lessen insecurity, to rebel, or to build intimacy—can tell you a great deal about where she is in developmental terms. Following are some examples of each type of affair.

Analgesic Sex: Blotting Out the Bad

A love affair was just what the doctor ordered for Lorraine Feldman's bruised ego. In her diary, her transformation is obvious—from her initial reaction to a singles scene she can't abide to her first postdivorce affair. This July entry, posted two years after her husband walked out on her for his younger woman, evidences that, at the outset, Lorraine is barely limping along in her new life:

Second year anniversary—Do I say,
  Happy Second Anniversary, Marv and Cheryl
  Are you both happy?

Do you both have what you want?
I'm not happy.
I'm nothing.
I'm here and I survive.
I just can't become part of the singles scene.
I am who I am.
Now what?

A few months later, friends introduced Lorraine to George, a widower who liked to dance. A good conversationalist himself, he was captivated by Lorraine. Unlike hubby Marvin, new lover George encouraged Lorraine to talk about herself; he liked to hear her ideas about life. In short, George gave Lorraine a crack at center stage, a spot she had always reserved for the men in her life: her dashing but domineering dad, her popular man-about-town brother, her politician husband. Lorraine began to see the world in Technicolor again. This excerpt, from the New Year's Day entry, reflects her metamorphosis and, at the same time, captures the pervasive "good" girl image:

Good morning, 1982!
1981 was a year for maturing. I was kissed, hugged, caressed, and loved. It's amazing how long it takes for the mind and body to adjust to change. I grew up and married in the fifties with the morals and values of the fifties. I never cheated on my husband. I never would have considered it!

A few months later, Lorraine is well on the road to rediscovery. Her first love affair wasn't the only element that helped propel her out of her shell, but the following entry (written on the three-year anniversary of her divorce) indicates that romance was certainly an important ingredient:

I've grown in this year.
I drove with Lauren [her daughter] to Colorado.
I was loved and I loved—not for an eternity but for a moment in time.
But it was good and beautiful. And I was beautiful . . . for the moment I glowed, and it felt good.
A friend reached out. I took his hand . . . and the two of us walked together . . . not for an eternity but for a moment in time.

It was good and it was beautiful. Thank you for my moment in
time with my friend.
We walked together and we were friends.

Lorraine seemed to fall into this first affair; it was a fruit borne
of her social development after divorce. She had joined a dance
group, began to accept blind dates, and spent more hours on her
career, all of which kept her around people. Her first affair
developed organically, out of this new social life.

In contrast, some women have a more calculating attitude
toward their first postdivorce affair. Gwenn Banning, for example,
purposely sought out a new relationship in which she had the
upper hand. "There is a man in my life now," she reported on
her first interview, two years after her divorce. "He's older than
me and a widower. He's not for me, but I did go to bed with
him. He thinks I'm hot shit. I went to bed with him to prove to
myself that I was no longer Steve Banning's wife."

Gwenn is not at peace with her decision, though, which is often
a predicament for women who use sex only to soothe their
wounds. "This man loves me. He wasn't just looking to get laid.
He has a lot of feeling. But I guess I've become more selfish."
Gwenn is not alone. Quite a few women in the study mentioned
putting their needs first in relationships; they want to "turn the
tables." In effect, they're saying to the world, "This time around,
I intend to get what *I* want!"

Reassuring Sex

Joann Cress met Ken, a fellow student in one of her classes,
two years before they began dating. When Ken first began to ask
her out, she resisted the idea that he might be interested in her
as a woman. "I considered him just a friend—nothing more. And
he didn't push me."

One major drawback was Ken's age. He was fifteen years
younger than Joann. At first she refused to call their meetings
dates because she was embarrassed about the age difference, but,
she says, "My friends at work encouraged me." Joann also doubted
that Ken could really be interested in her. "I was sure he would
meet someone younger and do the same thing to me that Tony
had."

For all the many changes she had made while married, Joann nevertheless traversed some rather rocky terrain, coping with the legal side of her divorce and adjusting to life as a single woman. During this time, her support system had literally disappeared: her sister, a close confidante, died suddenly of cancer; a week later, her mother passed away too; and a few months after that, so did her father.

Talk about loss! The final shock was that Joann then learned that in the final years of her marriage, Tony had been having an affair with one of her best friends—an even greater blow to her pride than his earlier indiscretions. "I trusted her. I told her everything. She told him, and then he used it all against me.

"Believe me, I didn't want to jump into *anything* at first," says Joann, laughing. "I was afraid of committing myself, afraid that I'd get burned again. In fact, it would have been fine if I never met another man!" Joann admits, however, that throughout her ordeal, "Ken stuck by my side. I leaned on him, but with only one foot. I refused to let myself fall backward at first."

In retrospect, Joann is grateful that she didn't become sexually involved with Ken until at least a year after they started dating. "It gave us a chance to become friends. And I began, very slowly, to trust him," says Joann. "Ken told me, 'When it happens, it will be right.' He never pushed me. He was very respectful of my fears."

Through her relationship with Ken, Joann began to feel a sense of pride in her womanhood—something she had never felt with Tony. Still, for a long time in the relationship, especially once they became lovers, Joann repeatedly "tested" Ken. "I'd tell him he was out to get as much from me as he could!" But by knowing that he was really there for her sexually ("with my husband I would take a shower afterward"), Joann says, the relationship with Ken helped her grow emotionally too.

Sex as an Act of Rebellion

Lisa Frazier's rebellion began at thirty, when she became obsessed with racquetball. She spent more and more time on the court, becoming so good at the game that she was made captain of the women's traveling team and eventually played with the men as well.

One day, as she pulled into the parking lot of the club, the voice of singer Neil Diamond blasting through the moon roof of her green Dodge van, a good-looking stranger in a red Toyota pulled in beside her. Neil Diamond was one of his favorites too.

Jeff was an air traffic controller, who regaled Lisa with his poetic descriptions of the northern lights. "He said he had to walk away backwards, because he couldn't take his eyes off them. I said to myself, 'This is my kind of guy. He's connected to life!' "

Lisa ended up on the racquetball court with Jeff and, eventually, with him in bed. The new romance drove the final nail into the coffin of her marriage. Furthermore, Lisa imbued the affair with the fantasies of an adolescent. "It wasn't an *affair*," she corrects. "An affair is when I would meet a person and sleep with him with no intentions of anything more serious. We were going to get married."

Typical of Rewinders, Lisa continued to see her lover and his situation through the infatuated eyes of a teenager, long after the relationship soured. She believed that because the torrid romance had swept *her* off her feet, it would also propel Jeff out of his marriage. Love—or at least lust—would conquer all.

Jeff never left his wife, and the affair ended violently. Furious because he wouldn't keep "his half of the bargain," Lisa hurled accusations at Jeff. "He smacked me. Then I pushed him down a flight of steps."

Lisa made all the wrong moves, first by putting all her eggs into a married man's basket, then by rushing into a hasty divorce and selling her house. "I'll never be able to afford a house again."

Instead of nurturing her newfound separateness while she was married, Lisa Frazier dove headfirst into a dead-end extramarital affair. Her sexual rebellion and her romantic delusions certainly helped her get out of an intolerable marriage. Unfortunately, she missed a vital step that goes before jumping into another *we* situation: she never gave herself a chance to get comfortable with being an *I*. Lisa didn't have a clue about the meaning of the word *intimacy*, nor was she truly ready to separate. As is often the case with Rewinders, she simply transferred her dependency to a new man.

Mature Sex: Building Intimacy

Melanie Spade admits to a burst of Rewinder sex right after her divorce. She had a string of one-night stands and then an affair with a married man. For a while that illicit romance afforded her the time and freedom to do what she wanted with her life, because she only saw him two or three nights a week. She knew she wanted something more. The contrast between Melanie's reaction to her married boyfriend and Lisa Frazier's is the difference between a Player and a Rewinder. Melanie had no illusions of a magical future.

"I realized that my married boyfriend wasn't going to get unmarried." That's a Player's observation. A Rewinder denies the truth. For a while her career was the major sustaining element in Melanie's life. "The jobs kept getting better, but I also realized that I wanted to get married again. For a long time, nobody I met was suitable."

Melanie, then in her mid-forties, literally "bumped into" her next husband, at a cocktail party. "Bob was a widower with five children. He was tall and muscular, forty-seven years old." It was not easy for a woman of her independence and confidence to find her emotional equal, so when she did, Melanie set out—very deliberately—to get him.

"He was a very stable man. He had his own business. He invited me out to dinner right on the spot. I had jeans on. He didn't care. He didn't ask me where I wanted to go to eat. He had already picked the place. He just impressed me, because he knew who he was, and he was full of adventure."

The first time they made love, Melanie knew that this was different from her other postdivorce flings. "I wanted him to want me. I used sex in a way I hadn't with other men. With some, I didn't care about the next date. And with my married man, I knew I couldn't let myself get too attached. I always called it for what it was—just good sex. But with Bob, I realized I was going to build on this relationship, make it develop into something more enduring."

When a Player contemplates remarriage, she perceives sex as a means to building intimacy. She is able to integrate her physical and emotional needs with her lover's. Because she is secure in her own sense of separateness, she can also embrace her partner for his unique qualities, rather than trying to compete with or change him.

Kate McKinley, forty-five, met Richard, forty-three, who was also divorced, about six months after her marriage ended. "A friend of mine dragged me to this March of Dimes fund-raiser, and I spotted him across the room, sitting with another guy." Kate knew what she wanted, and she set out to get it. "I just went over and started talking to him."

Having married her first husband when she was twenty-two, Kate was very inexperienced sexually. "I was a virgin—and I think that had a lot to do with why I married him. The first time we made love, I thought, 'Hey! This is fun,' so I got married. What I didn't realize was you could do this with other people too!"

After Kate's divorce, she went out on a few dates, but she still hadn't slept with another man by the time she met Richard. "I guess you could call it Machiavellian, but I knew I could end up with Richard, and I wanted more experience." So, Kate propositioned an old high-school beau: "Let's just do it for old time's sake." She also had a one-night stand with another man. She had no illusions about her motives; she wasn't trying to drown out any memories or prove anything to herself. "I knew I wasn't interested in either of them—I was just curious about sex."

With Richard, the sex itself was different. "We talked more. We were more intimate emotionally than I ever was with my husband, even though I had known Richard for only a few weeks. My husband used to feel inadequate when I told him what I liked and didn't like. But Richard and I were able to talk about sex."

Kate highlights a fascinating paradox that, we suspect, separates a mature sexual relationship from one motivated by pain, insecurity, or rebellion: "We played with sex! We could fool around. We didn't take it all so seriously, but, at the same time, it was definitely more serious, more intense."

Women Loving Women

Even though it was not explicitly asked on the "Divorce Over 40" questionnaire, five percent of the survey respondents volunteered that they were in sexual relationships with women. Since comments such as the following were unsolicited, the actual number of women in similar circumstances may be even higher:

"With the prospect of remarriage—or good male companionship—very limited, I feel women should be free to consider lesbian relationships as a source of personal intimacy," offers Helena, a psychiatrist in her fifties. "I have a lesbian partner of eight years and have found great satisfaction and comfort in this relationship—more intimacy, more sexual foreplay, and more freedom to be myself than in my marriage."

Because of societal constraints, many women are undoubtedly closeted in their sexual preferences and some personally conflicted as well. One woman in the study admits, "I'm afraid of what my ex-husband would do, and I worry what my children and family would say about my being sexually involved with a woman."

Her fears are unquestionably well-founded. In fact, such misgivings might also be a deterrent to women who even *contemplate* the comfort of a postdivorce relationship with another woman, and the comments of interviewees indicate that at least some hetereosexual women do. Gwenn Banning, who counts many lesbians among the friends she made after her divorce, remarks that she "wished" she were attracted to women. Likewise, Helga Gross comments, "I think it would be so much easier."

Lesbians and bisexuals are not a monolithic group. In a 1991 report on human diversity published by the American Psychological Association, the authors point out that sexual orientation is "more complex than either *homosexual* or *heterosexual*," because it encompasses so many dimensions, including how one identifies oneself, behavior, fantasies, emotional attachments. The report points out that a person can be *homophilic*—love a same-sex partner—without being *lesbian* or *gay*, terms which imply a life-style, or without necessarily acting on erotic feelings; and a person can be *homosexual*—have sex with a same-sex partner—without embracing a gay life-style or self-identification. The women in our study evidence such a range of behavior: Some identify themselves as "lesbians" when they get divorced, while others indicate that their relationships with other women aren't necessarily "sexual," but they consider themselves to be "intimate" with other women.

"I always had very close women friends in my life, and I felt

connected to them in a different way than to my husband. I think
I had emotional affairs with women long before I had a sexual
experience," explains one woman.

Another says, "I had a brief affair with a woman after my
divorce. I have always thought of myself as bisexual, and my
husband knew that, so he wasn't surprised when I told him, but
I don't think he was thrilled about it. My son, who is eighteen,
doesn't know. I've been celibate for the past two years, but I
definitely think I'd choose a woman if I were to get into another
relationship."

"I hate labels. I'm not sure what I am," writes a third, who is
recently divorced, "but I feel most comfortable being around
women right now."

Regardless of how these women see or think of themselves,
freedom of choice is the issue. Especially as women approach mid-
life, a time of reflection and reordering of priorities, many become
more tenacious about their right to opt for life-styles that are
mutually respectful and affirming. Most assuredly, some women
find that with other women.

There is evidence too that although mid-life mothers are
understandably skittish about disclosing a change of sexual orientation to their children, such honesty has a positive effect on
the parent-child bond. "I was very fearful about what my children
would think of me," admits a survey respondent. "But when I
finally admitted to my teenage children that I loved Sarah in a
way that, at one time in my life, I only thought I could love a
man, to my surprise, they were very understanding. It actually
strengthened our relationship."

Women who are in lesbian relationships often report that the
sex is more satisfying and the intimacy more affirming. "It was
like being with myself!" one woman comments after a recent first
affair with another woman.

Whether a woman finds happiness with a man or a woman,
perhaps a comment offered by this woman best sums up a basic
axiom: "There is no guarantee of happiness ever after with *either*
sex. I've been in both kinds of long-term relationships. Now I'm
living with a woman, and it's definitely the best relationship I've
ever had. But that's not because she's a woman. It's because I've
grown up since my divorce!"

Sex or Intimacy: What Do Women Miss
—and What Do They Want?

Whatever their reasons for having sex, or whomever they have it with, what divorced women miss most is a warm body. After years of sleeping with the same person, being held and touched, they long for physical closeness. "I have had problems with sleeping for many years after the divorce," writes one woman. "I have an extra pillow that I hold on to, to give me the sense of holding on to my husband's body."

In some cases, the physical and emotional void can propel a woman back into the arms of her ex. A few months after they separated, Helga Gross remembers, she met her husband for coffee to discuss the terms of the divorce—and ended up in bed with him. "I needed to do that, to know that it was over. It was terrible—the sex—but I'm glad it happened."

Which do women miss the most after divorce—emotional intimacy or physical sex? The survey data indicate that the two are entwined in most women's minds. Three-fourths of the divorced women who lament the loss of a sexual relationship also miss close companionship and intimacy. In contrast, of women who were not concerned about the loss of a sexual relationship, only twenty-nine percent missed intimacy.

Clearly, because of their early conditioning, for most women the physical is strongly tied to the emotional. However, they also miss sex purely for physical gratification. This is especially true of women who have had fulfilling sexual experiences in marriage and/or women who have had at least one postdivorce affair that awakened their nascent sexuality.

Often, women who were not orgasmic in their twenties are finally able to achieve orgasm in their forties. That's because female hormone levels decrease in mid-life, giving more power to testosterone, which, in turn, can increase a woman's sex drive. Moreover, because of revised attitudes toward sex, many women feel freer and more entitled to sexual fulfillment after divorce. And once they've tasted a bit of the sexual freedom they missed out on during marriage, their appetites increase. In the study, in fact, a third of the women between forty and forty-nine experience more sexual enjoyment after divorce.

Many women settle for sex without the intimacy. In Ellen Gar-

159

land's case, for example, her lover was a married man—a theme we heard in several interviews. She regained a sense of herself as a sexual being through the affair, but the relationship could go just so far. "I knew that I could never really have him, but it was marvelous." Ellen doesn't regret anything. "It was worth it. I was eighteen again!"

A few divorced women knowingly target married men as potential lovers—as a guarantee that they'll never have to deal with true intimacy. In other instances, falling for a married man is a cruel trick of fate. "I can't believe I fell in love with a married man!" exclaims Lorraine Feldman, in one of several follow-up interviews. She has been dating a man from her dance group. Lorraine, who doesn't see remarriage on the horizon, is nevertheless content with the relationship, even with its limitations. It gives her a chance to have her own separate time. But she also has mixed feelings. "His wife is who I was ten years ago. I see her hanging on to an empty marriage just the way I did."

Many divorced women in their forties and fifties find themselves grappling with similar moral dilemmas. "Sure, sex is important to me—but sex with a married man—for me is out of the question," says Amy Brown, divorced ten years, who draws a sharp line for herself. "Even though there is a change in attitudes regarding extramarital sex, each woman has to develop her own philosophy regarding sex after becoming single again.

"Some women think nothing of dating married men," grants Amy. "I feel comfortable only dating men who would be likely candidates for remarriage. But I'm reluctant to settle when I really have not found anyone who is special."

At the other extreme, some women reconcile themselves to intimacy without the sex. Anne Garner, who had six kids (one of which was stillborn), spent much of her married life as a "baby machine," only to discover that at forty, when her body was healed from the ravages of six difficult childbirths and longing for sex, her husband no longer wanted her. After walking out on her husband and setting up her own apartment, Anne met a wonderful man in her writing group. Ben fed her mind and bolstered her ego. "He thought that I was the brightest woman he had ever met. He opened up the world for me, taking me to the opera and various cultural events in the City."

Anne has been seeing Ben for nine years. "He broadened my

life tremendously. We travel together, and he loves me and my children. There is only one thing wrong: he's thirteen years older, and we do not have a physical relationship. I am right back where I started from!"

At the same time, Anne, who is now sixty-two, asserts, "There's a deepening of a relationship when those other things don't get in the way. We have a tremendous oneness, acceptance. I know Ben loves me for who I am, not for what I can do for him. I've only gotten that from three people—the God that I believe in, my father, and Ben. Not that sex wouldn't be nice, but intimacy, to me, is the highest commodity."

Evelyn Dorrin is also satisfied with the platonic relationship she developed with an old high-school friend. "He always wanted to be my protector. We go out to dinner, but there have never been any sexual overtones. This is my social life—and I've accepted it this way. If I wanted to meet someone, I would have to work at it, and I am not willing to work at it!"

Whether they opt for sex or intimacy, or hold out for both in their relationships, the women in the study certainly don't confuse either with remarriage. While some say a steady relationship would be "nice," the data indicate that almost half of all women vote no to remarriage. The main reason is personal freedom. Many women are protective of their newly discovered independence; they don't want to deal with other women's children; and they fear turning into permanent nursemaids, especially where older men are concerned. Rather than chance getting into another caretaking or controlling relationship, they prefer to put their energies elsewhere.

The interviews mimic the data, which also indicate that the further a woman gets from the actual divorce event, the less concerned she is about living alone, and consequently, she is less inclined to feel a need to remarry. "Dating and even remarriage meant more to me when I was first divorced," reflects Karen Marshall, who divorced in 1980. "But now I'm not interested. I feel independent—and I like it!" A sign on Karen's office door reads, "I wouldn't marry God if he asked me."

When push comes to shove, many divorced women, especially the younger women in our sample, between the ages of forty and forty-nine, fear they'll make a mistake by remarrying, so they choose personal growth rather than risk becoming passive or dependent again. An overwhelming percentage—eighty-four percent—of divorced women experience feelings of achievement after divorce and feel free to be who they are, many for the first time in their lives. They're content with themselves, whether they're busy holding down a job or furthering careers, involved in the community or enjoying children and grandchildren, in or out of relationships.

"Remarriage is not really something that I think much about. It would be nice to have somebody to cuddle with," says Lena Entemann, who adopted two young Chilean children when she was fifty and got divorced a few years later, "but I don't ever think I'd want to cohabit."

Christine Moss, forty-three, recently divorced after a twenty-four-year marriage, has been seeing "a nice guy" since her breakup, but remarriage is not in the cards. "It's good for my ego—how he feels about me. But with all this stuff being dumped on me from the divorce, I can't see getting involved again." Christine is busy sorting out her life and her kids' adjustment to the divorce—they're fifteen and seventeen—and she has just so much room on her plate. "I kind of like the way I live right now. This guy I see only comes in on weekends—and that's fine!"

What would make a woman change her mind about remarriage? Our findings indicate that the promise of financial security entices some. Forty percent of the younger women in the study consider money a good reason to remarry; fewer older women feel that way, presumably because their finances are often bolstered by pensions or government benefits. Over half would remarry for sexual intimacy or to have someone to grow older with. However, all admit that finding the right person is easier said than done—especially the second time around. Because they don't want to lose what they've gained, these mid-life women tend to be much more selective.

Maggie Prince, who has had a number of affairs since her divorce, runs down a checklist of qualities she's seeking in a man: "Someone who can communicate—express an opinion, make decisions, express his thoughts and feelings, whether good or bad. Someone who has an interest in my children." A tall order, but one that many women would happily secure if they could.

Maggie, who tends bar and meets many men in the course of a day, is realistic and resolute about her independence. "I'm not interested in another bad relationship. I'd rather be miserable alone than miserable and married!" she quips, adding, "Life is too short to be unhappy. I may not have a man on my arm, and I may not have a lot of money, but I'm happier than I was when I was married."

So what about a social life? "There just aren't a lot of great men out there," Maggie laments. "But I go out a lot after work, with the same circle of friends. We all hang out together—as friends."

Maggie Prince is not alone. Thus, it's understandable that when it comes to their social life, the vast majority of divorced women place the greatest value on friendship.

6

You've Got to Have Friends:
Why Women Are Women's
Best Friends

The extent to which females [chimpanzees in the Tai National Forest]
bond with one another influences how much they are dominated by males.
It's one of the important ways for females, who are smaller than males,
to balance the physical gap.

—Barbara Smuts, psychology and anthropology professor,
University of Michigan

Miz Florrie and Her Friends

"If this had happened to me two years ago, I would have been
devastated," drawls Florence Hacker, an elegant, winsome blond
with more than a hint of down-home Alabama in her voice. At
the time of the interview, her husband of thirty-one years was
living in a local motel with a twenty-eight-year-old cocktail waitress
("She's a year younger than my oldest daughter!"), and "Miz
Florrie," as her friends call her, was thriving on the kindness of
a cadre of concerned women who were determined to see her
survive.

"I just never thought this would happen to me," laments a
mournful Florrie, who just turned fifty. Since her husband left
four months ago, Florrie's friends have gathered around her like
a pack of mother hens. Every day they call to check on her; every
night, she eats dinner with one, if not all, of them. They take her
to the movies; they invite her to card games; they share solace
and suggestions; mostly, they provide a collective shoulder to cry
on. "These women have been just wonderful. They don't want
me to be alone."

In many ways, the story of Miz Florrie's marriage and divorce
—and the support from the women in her life—is typical of
hundreds of other women in the study, albeit with a Southern

flavor. A fifties "good girl," born Florence Pierce, she grew up in a small town in Georgia. In 1959, after winning a local beauty contest and then going on to become runner-up in a statewide pageant, at nineteen Florence married Earl Hacker, a handsome hometown boy. She immediately settled into the roles of doting wife and nurturing mother. By the time she was twenty, Florrie had a beautiful home and her first child, a daughter. When her second daughter arrived two years later, she thought she had everything she ever wanted.

Nine years ago, because their girls were no longer living at home, the Hackers left Georgia and relocated to a tiny oceanfront community in Texas. Earl was happy, but the move plunged Florrie, a stay-at-home wife, into isolation.

"I didn't make many new women friends when I first came here. It was very hard." Only when Florrie began to get involved in the community, did she start to meet the locals. She worked with other women on the planning board and the town's beautification committee, and, in time, a few of the women also became sometime bridge buddies, but Florrie didn't consider herself "really close" to any of them.

When Earl walked out, however, Florence realized that making friends was a matter of survival. "I had always been a pretty private person until this happened. Subconsciously, I think I knew I had to open up. I probably would have died if I didn't." Florrie remembers the walk on the beach when she finally confided to one of her friends, a woman whose cousin had recently gotten divorced. "I immediately felt that she understood me." Since that day, Florrie has felt her friends' support wash over her and sustain her through the "darkest nights."

She sums it up: "Just knowing that they think I'm a worthwhile person, that most likely it wasn't my fault, that I shouldn't be blaming myself for what happened, that I have nothing to be ashamed of—" She pauses, on the edge of tears, her voice cracking. ". . . and the fact that they all care for me, that makes all the difference."

Only four months into her divorce, Florence Hacker is well on her way to survival, because she's a woman who has always been willing to face problems when they emerge and because she is allowing herself to be cared for by other women. A significant aspect of her recovery—as it is for eighty percent of women in the study—is that she already grasps the importance of female friends.

When Florrie feels stuck, her friends help ground and center her and give her concrete suggestions. When she is filled with anxiety and desperately afraid of the future, her friends bolster her self-esteem. And when she is blind to reality, her friends provide a mirror. Florrie admits that the women in her life perceive her in a way that—even on her best days—she just can't.

"I think they see me as attractive, fairly intelligent, and level-headed. They see what I've done with my home," remarks Florrie, who has never worked at a paying job. "I guess my friends see more possibilities for me than I can actually see for myself! I hope they're right!"

Friendship and Growth

The idea that a nurturing friendship can go a long way toward easing the pain of loss or cushioning hardship is certainly not new. Other researchers have shed light on the importance of social bonds as a buffer against life stresses—economic reverses; the illness or death of a spouse, child, or parent; or any kind of major change that causes upheaval, such as going back to school or changing professions. Moreover, numerous medical researchers have linked having close friendships to better immune functioning, lower levels of cholesterol, more hopeful prognoses after bouts with cancer, and lower death rates among heart patients. As one researcher concluded, "Having someone to talk to is very powerful medicine."

Some psychologists and sociologists have also looked specifically at married women's friendships, concluding that close friends and confidantes can actually brace and strengthen the marital bond. Women friends often provide a dimension of emotional support that husbands don't.

In the "Divorce Over 40" study, friendship also emerged as a highly significant factor related to women's social relationships after divorce—an important social and emotional ingredient in the developmental pie. Women who lacked friendships after divorce were adversely affected in a number of arenas, from making time for themselves to pursuing employment to caring for their children. In short, friendship can mean the difference between an expeditious adjustment after divorce and continued despair and mourning.

A common misconception is that women have difficulty establishing friendships after divorce due to the stigma attached to the event. The data indicate quite the opposite. Most women do make new friends after divorce—fifty-nine percent by the end of the first year, seventy-two percent in the next two to four years, and after five years a very convincing eighty-four percent develop new friendships.

Most important, the findings highlight that the *nature* of women's friendships changes as well. Of course, women have more time to pursue friendships when they are single, but the survey shows that most women also *make* more time for their friends and characterize their friendships as closer after divorce. The reason is clear: As women more clearly define their identities, they feel more comfortable being intimate and thus are more open to establishing new friendships. In addition, psychological growth can spiral upward thanks to friendships. That is, the more a woman exposes herself to her friends, the more she is able to see into her own inner core—and theirs. This is an important first step in building intimacy.

For some women, intimate friendships are established *only* after divorce. It's understandable: everything in our culture teaches young girls to make boys—and then their husbands—their first priority. Therefore, even women who had friends in childhood report a dramatic change around puberty, when an interest in romance and the opposite sex tends to relegate girlhood friendships to last place. Suddenly, best friends are viewed as adversaries, "competition" in the battle to win a husband.

Caroline Breed attended an all-girls' school and had many girlfriends as a child and well into her teens. Marriage at nineteen changed all that. Early on, she and Tom moved to Minnesota, beginning a period she calls "the wilderness years." Though Caroline says she was "really good at handling being alone," she was socially quarantined. Tom, at least, had some friends at work; but Caroline didn't work outside the home. "I had the cleanest house in the state!"

Her isolation was a theme that ran through other women's stories as well. "It pulled me much closer to him and made me very dependent on him for my social and emotional needs," she says. The next twenty years were punctuated by a series of residential moves, always to advance Tom's career—a situation that certainly wasn't conducive to Caroline's developing meaningful relationships outside the marriage.

When women are cut off from their friends—by circumstance or their own volition—they are also cut off from themselves. This process parallels the developmental phenomenon discussed in Chapter One, that "moment of resistance" (psychologist Carol Gilligan's term) when a young girl begins to see that confidence and strength are not what society expects of her, so she learns to hide what she knows and censor her thoughts. By dissociating herself from other females, a young woman loses a valuable mirror. Her innermost thoughts are obscured, her identity subverted.

In Caroline Breed's case, it took more than half a lifetime for her to rediscover the value of friendship. When she returned to college at the age of thirty-nine, she was finally in one place long enough to make friends. And for the first time since she was a teenager, she allowed herself to open up. Equally important, as she began to discover her identity, she also could take the blinders off and begin to see how enmeshed she was with Tom. Even though he resented her new relationships, she realized that not only were her friends a constant source of intellectual stimulation and validation, they also provided a vital lifeline to her emerging self. Their support transformed her. "I really found my place. I became a different person."

Lisa Frazier also relished married life at first, but eventually, "the homemaker life-style" left her feeling empty. She joined a consciousness-raising group. She also started going to meetings of Overeater's Anonymous, where she met Barbara, whose example and influence would ultimately change her life. Lisa was impressed by what Barbara had done on her own—accomplishments Lisa never experienced as a sheltered, sternly disciplined young girl, such as going to college, living on her own, managing her own budget. "I learned a lot from Barb."

One day when Barbara had to cancel a lunch date because of a prior commitment she had forgotten, Lisa reacted like the hurt teenager (in developmental terms) that she was. "I was so disappointed I cried!" Barbara, who evidently understood what was happening, told Lisa that she had become too reliant upon her. Barbara felt suffocated. In effect, Lisa had transferred dependencies from her husband to Barbara.

Lisa remembers, "Barb told me, 'I know just what you need. You've got to get more *involved* in life.'" Lisa knew her friend was "onto something," as Lisa put it. The "something" turned out to be racquetball, which boosted Lisa's confidence and helped her discover who she was.

If the socialization process doesn't entirely dampen the possibilities for friendships during a woman's adolescence, the institution of marriage certainly helps. When Joann Cress was eighteen and first married, Tony was in the navy; they lived in a mobile home in a trailer park near the base. Tony didn't want her to work, and since Joann "didn't get satisfaction from doing the laundry and cleaning," she got pregnant. But even after her first son was born, she felt isolated and overwhelmed.

A shy kid in high school, Joann was a loner who always felt "on the fringe"—a phrase many women use to describe themselves as teenagers. Hence, early in her marriage, when she began to socialize with the other navy wives, her relationships were developmentally very "young." The women on the base were the friends Joann had never made as a young adolescent. "We'd laugh, share—I really leaned on them."

By comparison, her husband was demanding and selfish. Joann began to relish her dates with her female friends more than her time with Tony. "He left for work at two, and then it was okay. I'd hang out with the girls. I was disappointed when their husbands didn't have the same days off."

Still, Joann's sharing could go just so far. Because she was not developmentally ready for intimacy, she couldn't allow herself to be too vulnerable with her new girlfriends. "I made mental notes about their lives. I would listen to them and think, 'That's not what we have in our marriage.' But I never would have dreamed of telling them how I felt."

In part, Joann wouldn't share her feelings because she was taught not to ("never hang your dirty laundry"). But it was more than that. Because she lacked a sense of her own separate identity, Joann also *couldn't* share her feelings; she didn't know what they were! Joann is far different from the way she was twenty-five years ago because she has since worked on the social and emotional pieces of the developmental pie. Looking back, she realizes, "I didn't know I was in so much turmoil for so long."

The Late Bloomers

It took a divorce for Joann Cress to realize the value of friendship. Many of the women in the study—"late bloomers"— traveled a similar path. Because of both their social conditioning as girls and the constraints of the marriage cocoon, they weren't able to nurture friendships with other women during their marriages. They were deprived of an important piece of the developmental pie. Late bloomers avoided or, at best, had very limited friendships. It wasn't until their marriages were in trouble, or they actually divorced and, as a result, "grew up," that these late bloomers permitted themselves to risk true friendship.

The fact is, friendship takes on a new meaning when a woman can no longer cling to a man's arm. In Florence Hacker's case, which is quite typical, when she lived in Georgia with Earl and her daughters, she was friendly only with other married women. Her friends were the wives of Earl's business associates or the mothers of her children's friends.

Florence, as Mrs. Earl Hacker, had many friendships. But they were purely social, and *they were tied into her roles.* When Earl walked out on her and Florrie allowed herself first to divulge the gravity and desperation of her situation to a friend and then to absorb the love and support of other women, she took a first major developmental step toward independence and, paradoxically, toward intimacy as well.

Gwenn Banning, likewise, was once content to be a little girl to her daddylike husband; she isolated herself during her marriage, because her husband was all that she ever wanted. "I never needed women friends when I was younger," she maintains. "Steve and I didn't do a lot of socializing. I would rather spend an evening talking with him than at a party with a lot of other people. I had big needs," she says, and in her mind at that time, only Steve could meet them. "I wanted his attention."

Gwenn rarely went out with female friends on her own, nor did she identify with other women's problems. Four years after her divorce, however, Gwenn has definitely changed her tune and her developmental age. After Steve walked out on her, she cultivated a network of close friends, whom she credits for getting her through the trauma.

"Now I think women are great. They are the source of my support. I have one great friend, Helen, and I tell her, 'Hel, if you were a guy, I'd marry you. . . . I realize how powerful women are now." As her healing process continued, and Gwenn began to stand on her own, she also became a better friend. "At first the support flowed only one way—toward me. Now I'm there for them too."

Erica Sanford admits that she, too, was slow to let herself trust female friends in her married days. "I started making intimate contact with women only in the past few years, especially when my second marriage started falling apart." Erica was emotionally battered and developmentally stunted by a series of abusive relationships with men, two of whom became husbands. Her spirit and sense of identity were crushed over the years. In many respects, she was like a child in her marriages, needy and dependent. She concedes, however, that her female friends really helped her get through the hard times. It was a spiral of growth: as she began to take small baby steps toward standing on her own, she was better able to perceive the value of friendship.

Peggy Kennedy, the victim of a physically abusive marriage, was also afraid to make friends during marriage. "I spoke to no one." Once, when she tried to confide to another married woman how abusive her husband was, the so-called friend's response validated Peggy's apprehension. "When I called her, she said, 'Are you crazy? He's so handsome, he so this and that. He gives you everything!' After that, I figured no one would ever understand, so I stopped trying."

After her divorce, however, Peggy began to expand her vision of herself. Like many women in the study, she then began to choose new kinds of friends, women who supported her independence and who accepted her unconditionally and wholly, not for the roles she played.

Because of the conspiracy of silence around relationship problems, even women in less abusive marriages were reticent to reveal themselves. Jody Burke remembers "going through hell" emotionally in the final years of her twenty-four-year marriage, because she had no one in whom she could confide. "I didn't want to talk to anybody, because I didn't want anyone to have funny feelings about us as a couple, especially if everything was going to work out."

Some women also shied away from female friends during their marriage because of their husband's reactions. When Debby Black joined a consciousness-raising group and she began to open up to other women, Mike resented having to share her attention with others. "All he read of the newspaper was the sports section, and all he watched on TV were football and basketball games. I'd be reading and I'd say, 'I need to talk to somebody,' and he would respond sarcastically, 'Go talk to your girlfriends.' "

Aware of Mike's unspoken fears about her changing the rules of their marriage, Debby tried to "protect" her husband. "I didn't let him know at first. It was easier to keep peace," she admits. Her response was also a reflection of her development: she acted more like a teenager who was doing something behind Daddy's back than a woman with separate needs.

As time went on, however, Debby began to realize she had a right to develop her own sense of identity, and she began to change inside. Her new friends in the consciousness-raising group became increasingly important. "I was frustrated that I could sit for hours and talk to other people about anything. But I had no communication with him."

Early Starters

Some women in the study were able to foster intimate female friendships during their marriages. Since they already cherished the value of friendship by the time their marriages ended, they had a developmental leg up on late bloomers.

"Early starters" develop friendships and other pursuits outside the cocoon; they forge friendships with single as well as married women; they achieve some degree of personal autonomy; and they begin to explore the frightening territory of personal intimacy. When they divorce, early starters have an immediate and readily available support system. Hence, they have an easier time reestablishing a social network than do women whose friendships have been determined exclusively by their marital roles.

"I always believed in networking—even before it came into vogue," boasts Patsy Marconi, who took it upon herself to bring a female friend with her when she showed up for her scheduled interview at the center! "You can accomplish so much more by speaking to people in the same situation. I had a very supportive circle of friends that I could bounce things off of." Like many women whose families are angry at them because of the divorce or disapprove of it, Patsy has found that her friends have come to mean more than her family. "I would go to my friends before my family for emotional support," she insists, echoing the sentiments of the majority of women in the study. "There are just certain things I would never say to my family."

Other women insist that friends *are* family, filling the gaps that parents, husbands, and in-laws leave. "I consider my friends my real family," says Ellen Garland, divorced six years. "Up to this year, I always had a Christmas Eve party for my friends. Now I'm a grandmother, so last year I went to my son's house. My friends were really upset. I'm trying to figure out how to have my party this year—with *everyone.*"

Evelyn Dorrin, who also arrived at her interview with an old friend in tow, explained that as a young girl, she always understood the value of friendship. "You can have a lot of friends and be very social, but *really good friends . . .*" she pauses to emphasize the difference, "I would say only one or two." Evelyn continued to cultivate intimate female friendships during her marriage. "You do—you have to—in order to have another life. I had a few good friends, and they encouraged me to think for myself and to get out. They'd say, 'Hey let's go shopping. Let's do this or that.' "

Christine Moss learned the value of friendship early in life too. "I go back to grammar school with some of my friends." In contrast, her husband, typical of men in our culture whose friendships usually center on business dealings or sports events, had few friends during their twenty-four-year marriage. "Men don't have anyone they can *really* talk to like women do. They don't know how to relinquish their inner feelings."

A tragedy that occurred in 1977, eight years after she was married, reaffirmed Christine's faith in female friendships. "Our daughter was killed in a car accident, and after that it started. He was drinking. He insisted that we move out of our house into the one I'm in now—which I hate.

"With the death of my daughter, I had a lot of support from

my friends, and I cried a lot. It has been twelve years, but, you know, you can get through it." Christine, who matured through her awful tragedy, also knows that if she can survive the loss of a child, she can survive the loss of her marriage, especially with the continued support of her friends.

"I have many women friends that I can call, that I can do things with," says Christine. Clearly, there's nothing like having a good time to soothe the pain of divorce and to ease the transition to single life. Christine's distress is mitigated by going out to dinner, playing tennis, or catching a movie with friends. Her friends also invite her to parties, include her in Sunday outings, and make family dates that include the kids as well.

Elizabeth Harkness and her alcoholic husband had few couples as friends during their marriage, but she had *her* friends. Socially, husband and wife went their separate ways, he to a bar, she out with her cronies. Her friends were there for her at the end of the marriage too. "I bent the ears of my best friends until they hurt, I'm sure!"

Divorced, Elizabeth had the wherewithal to build a new life: "I found other divorced women and widows who were in the same situation—and got a group going for doing things together." Elizabeth, who was sixty-three when she finally refused to let her alcoholic husband come home, says, "I find my social life very satisfying." Through their interests, Elizabeth and her friends have created a new, shared postdivorce history that balances out the marital memories. Not that they want to forget everything about the past, but it's reassuring for them to know that they can engineer their own good times, rather than dwelling on what they left behind.

Irene Presto, sixteen years younger than Elizabeth, reports similar success. "I have created a large network of friends from different walks of life, which makes my life interesting. I don't know if I'd call it 'family,' " she muses, "but my friends and I do things together. At times we just hang out in front of the fireplace. Lately, because of the recession, we have been tightening our belts. We go to movies, shows, share dinners, and have a wonderful time. Or, we talk about our job-hunting experiences or about new jobs or problems on the job. Our support system is wonderful."

Irene also points out an important long-term benefit of female friendships: "As women go through changes in their lives and especially as they get older, when you have friends, you can share with them and know that you're not alone in whatever changes might be going on in your body and head."

The Magic Elixir

More than family, more than therapy, more than a hefty financial settlement, friendship is a soothing balm throughout the rediscovery process, as well as a training ground for intimacy. Many interviewees and survey respondents describe their female friends as being "on the same wavelength."

Because so many women brought friends to the center, we observed this phenomenon firsthand as well. Irene Presto arrived with two friends, women in their mid forties. One was a widow; the other, Marilyn Hauptman, had just gotten divorced and asked to participate. A few weeks later during her interview, Marilyn revealed very intimate details about her sex life and, unintentionally, testified to her and Irene's friendship as well: "This is something I never told anybody, except you, my shrink—and Irene!"

It's also typical for a woman to report that she cherishes a particular friend who is "going through the same thing." Indeed, divorced women seem to have antennae for other women in similar predicaments. Phyllis May talked about meeting a woman her age who was going through a divorce and feeling an instant bond: "She and I were incredibly close and supportive to one another. We kind of fed off each other. If she had a problem, she could call me and vice versa." If her friend thought Phyllis was okay, it was immensely reassuring to Phyllis. "She was a tower of strength for me. She always said that I was a survivor, and that I could go out there and do it. She pushed me—literally— as I pushed her!"

Phyllis's comments about her friend underscore the importance of identification and mirroring in friendship, as does Fran Sargent's experience: "I could look at the people supporting me, who were bright, high achievers—you know, winners—and, even when I didn't feel so good about me, I figured they saw *something* in me that was worthwhile."

Sometimes the "antenna" principle works unconsciously. For

175

the most part, Lorraine Feldman didn't purposely befriend other divorced women, but they found their way into her life, anyway: "Interestingly enough, except for one or two, all of my friends today are divorced or separated."

Divorced women simply understand each other. Especially in the emotional grip of the legal process, they affirm each other by comparing notes and sharing their similarities, and they empower each other by offering their different views of divorce and their strategies for riding the roller coaster. "My friends were incredible," agrees Anita Parsons, whose husband left without warning the day they were supposed to go to the bank to close on a new house. He left her a note on the kitchen table.

"That morning, he went out the door and said, 'I'll pick you up at ten to five.' I remember having an appointment at the vet that afternoon, and when I came home to pick up the cat, I thought someone had stolen the 1970 Mustang he had restored. It was a collector's item, and it was missing from the garage. The note said something like, 'I've been unhappy for a long time, and I can't go on like this anymore. I can't buy this or any house with you. We don't get along and we have nothing in common.'"

Anita went numb. "I took the cat to the vet! I think it was total denial. There I was, just going through the motions of doing what I was supposed to do. I was embarrassed and humiliated. The next day, I finally told a friend what had happened. Then all my friends just took over for the next several months. They called constantly, invited me places. But more than anything, they *just listened.*"

During a crisis, and on an ongoing basis as well, honest, concerned friends can boost a woman's self-esteem and soothe her fears and anxiety. Kate McKinley also believes that friends helped her get over the emotional hump of her divorce more quickly. "I just let all my feelings come out. I cried, and my friends cried with me!"

Having even just one special friend can determine whether a woman sinks or swims in the emotional aftermath. Gisella Morgan, who maintains, "I didn't cry on people's shoulder," at the same time adds, "I have had one friend for over thirty years. She's always been a very good support."

Good friends listen to what you have to say. They bounce back ideas about future plans, and they offer constructive criticism.

176

They offer unconditional acceptance and support. And they almost always tell you the truth. Gail Leperk, the ex-wife of an alcoholic notes, "My friends changed my thinking and my attitudes. They made me realize that I focused all my attention on my family."

Married Friends: Ties That Unbind

It may sound like a cliché, but divorce really lets women know who their true friends are! Divorce is a major crossroad—a time when friendships are reevaluated—and women discover that there are some friends that they *can* live without. It is understandable that friendships must change. Many are founded only on shared social activities that grew out of marital roles, not out of deeper connections. Furthermore, when divorced women make great developmental strides in the wake of their crisis, it's not uncommon for their married friends to accuse, "You're not acting like yourself!"

Even when old friends are supportive, women must scrutinize the nature of these leftover relationships. Some friends weather the transition; others continue to see the woman as a victim. They pity her, and they may even comfort her. But she is not urged to grow and change.

Clearly, the study suggests that the transition from life in a marriage to life as a single person may be easier for those who start over in the friendship department—a tough assignment at best, tougher still for women who have only couples as friends at the time of the divorce and whose social network centers wholly around marriage and children.

"The hardest part is making new friends," admitted one such woman on her questionnaire. "It became a project to find and make new single friends and to become involved in new activities as a single. Two years later, I am still working on this project. I still have to push myself to find opportunities to socialize."

Even more agonizing, married friends often turn their backs on divorced women, and the blow can devastating. "The most difficult part of the first year after divorce was trying to feel like a whole human being . . . to stop being lonely," writes a survey respondent whose experience is typical. "My social life stopped abruptly. I lacked adult companionship. My relationship with

177

couples ceased; the ladies called, but invitations were no longer extended."

Some married women are threatened by the presence of a newly single woman in their midst, while others disapprove of the divorce altogether. They may even think the woman did something to "deserve" her husband's leaving. And if the woman was the leaver, they may not be able to fathom why she would make such a choice.

"My friends couldn't understand why I couldn't live with someone that easy," says Maggie Prince who never confided her discontent during the marriage. Friends didn't realize that to her, Dean, handsome and personable as he seemed, wasn't "easy"— he was vacant. "As the years went by, I knew that I was just looking at a pretty face with nothing inside."

Reactions of disbelief are particularly common in affluent communities. "Everyone said, 'How can you do that, coming out of that big gorgeous house?'" recalls Debby Black, who notes that within her circle, many women were less than supportive when she fled to a local motel. When her enraged husband forbade her to move back in, she ended up in a tiny one-room walk-up with a shared bath.

"To this day, some of them can't believe it. They could not understand. I was giving up on this really wonderful life-style and a husband that adored me. They thought I was crazy!" Their reaction had an impact on Debby, who admits that for a long time, she was torn between their view and her own desire to develop herself. Fortunately, her other friends—women she had met in her consciousness-raising group—provided a balance.

The ultimate task of a divorced woman is to crystallize a positive definition of herself as a single person, which includes developing her own social network. As for keeping one's married friends, that seems more the exception than the rule. However, broken bonds are not always the result of censure. As with other types of crisis situations, friends are often hesitant to intrude, or they simply "don't know what to say."

Misunderstandings or miscommunications can also keep old friends away, as Fran Sargent found out nearly four years after her divorce. She and her husband were longtime residents of a seaside resort community. During the dissolution process, which dragged on for several years, they shared the "marital summer house," as it was described in legal documents.

"Right after we separated, I had the feeling that Elliott was campaigning against me, spreading vicious rumors. I was embarrassed, so I stayed away from everyone. The weekends I went out there, I kept to myself, or I brought other friends out with me—as a kind of social armor," Fran explains. Her visits eventually dwindled; in the end, her husband got the house. "When I went out there to clean out my things, I finally worked up the courage to visit a few of our old couple friends. I guess by then I had healed emotionally to the point where I was ready to hear what they had to say. To my surprise, they told me they missed me and that they were sorry *I* cut them out of my life!"

Another demon was at work in Fran's case as well: when a woman is involved in a lengthy, bitter divorce, it's hard enough to keep her head above water, let alone worry about whose guest list she's on. Psychically drained, many women prefer the "rush" of a new friendship to the possibly painful reality of explaining themselves to old friends and facing rejection. "I could be whoever I wanted with my new friends. I could talk about the divorce or not. I could say things about Elliott, and they didn't know him. It was so much easier."

Fran also admits, "My self-esteem was at an all-time low. I was scared to let people get too close to me. And in retrospect, I guess I knew that my old friends could call me on 'my stuff.' I needed the new relationships at the time, but it was also good to finally reconnect with the past again—in a new way."

Old Friends Lost/New Friends Found

In the face of rejection—real or imagined—it's not surprising that divorced women seek out other single women specifically, especially other divorced women. "I lost my married friends at the time of the divorce. George kept them all," confirms Karen Marshall, whose experience is typical. "My friends today are friends that I met after the divorce. They are all single."

Lorraine Feldman also represents the norm: "I have only one or two friends that I'm still close to who were couple friends while I was married. Other friends shied away. A few said, 'Why don't you and your son come over for dinner?' but it was very few."

Although those who don't are in the minority, not all women lose their married friends. In Florence Hacker's case, her married friends, who are extremely disapproving of Earl's blatant infidelity, have been wonderfully supportive. Alice Hampton was similarly gratified when a married couple told her, "*You* were the draw in our friendship." And Evelyn Dorrin, who brought a married friend along for support at her interview, told us, "Sometimes married friends give you up, but mine didn't. They include me in all their functions."

For the most part, though, the future contains new friends, or at least a renegotiation of old friendships. How does a newly divorced woman go about creating that all-important social network that is vital to her postdivorce survival? The women in the study, sensing that friendship is critical to emotional healing, realized that they had to put themselves on the line. Based on their experiences, here are several approaches:

Admit that you need friends for emotional support. "I've just become a statistic," announced Lorraine Feldman to a woman in her office who had gone through a divorce the year before. A few months earlier, Lorraine had begun to work part-time as a realtor; keeping busy helped her keep her mind off Marvin's betrayal. Typically, she got scant support from most of her old friends; she knew that she had to make new friends. So why not start with another divorced woman?

Ironically, the woman in Lorraine's office had once worked part-time for Marvin, and like most of the people in the small town, she, too, knew about his affair. Her new friend's understanding and her unqualified acceptance of Lorraine's inevitable mood swings helped ease the shame and humiliation. Although Lorraine had many friends in town, here was one who really listened to her and reaffirmed her self-worth.

Start networking. Irene Presto made a business out of it. "One of the things that I have done over the years as single woman has been networking through businesses and then organizing singles parties. I make singles parties at my home for people who I've met through business. I do all the cooking and inviting, and I charge for expenses. It's usually very nice and very comfortable."

Though few women are as entrepreneurial as Irene, who makes

180

money as well as friends, creative networking starts with just one person. After Anita Parsons discovered one divorced woman she could relate to, she says, the two of them then expanded their circle. "We found a group of about eight women who were in the same situation, and we networked. Now we spend at least part of every weekend together."

Make an attempt to extend yourself to old friends. Although you may end up terminating some longtime relationships, don't *assume* that you can't renegotiate a friendship or that married friends don't want a single woman around. A good role model is Christine Moss, who notes, "I maintained my relationships with married friends by continuing to invite them to my home." Christine's friends, in turn, weren't afraid to include her in their plans, and they accepted her new direction in life without judgment.

Ask for hands-on help. Some friends will take care of the kids when you're going to a lawyer's office or a doctor's appointment, pinch hit in an emergency, or ride to your rescue—just when your wick is about to burn too short. Other friends provide a bed or a couch or a sleeping bag on the living room floor; they'll loan you their car or make offers of money; they'll give you objects of clothing or pieces of furniture stored in their basements. Anything is possible—if you ask. Just don't assume that people can read your mind.

Get involved—and get out there. Volunteer activities, health clubs, art exhibitions, book readings, schools, and, of course, jobs can put you face-to-face with new people. "When I'm bored and have nothing to do, I go back to part-time work," agrees Elizabeth Harkness who, even at sixty-eight, says she has "no trouble meeting people." That's because Elizabeth gets herself out there —into social situations. Many other women reported meeting new people when they went back to college to earn a degree; even taking a single class can provide a new social setting and the possibility of meeting new people.

Join a support group. Look in the yellow pages of your phone book. That's where Evelyn Dorrin found one. She became friends with the six women she met there, although about four years after her divorce, she says, "I outgrew them, or maybe they outgrew me, but it was time to leave."

Ellen Garland tried a national support group, Parents Without Partners, which offers its members educational programs and social events. "It wasn't for me, although I did make some friends there. I also had my friends from Al-Anon."

Of the various types of support groups, in fact, women's support groups and twelve-step programs (AA and Al-Anon and others based on the twelve steps of Alcoholics Anonymous) are mentioned most frequently by survey respondents and interviewees as a potential source of new friends. Lena Entemann covered both bases. "I only had two friends who were aware of what was going on at the end of my marriage," recognizes Lena. "But since that time, I've picked up a lot of steam, and now I have a larger network of friends. I stopped drinking. I went to Alcoholics Anonymous, and I joined a women's group. I'm very open to people now. I'm not afraid to trust."

Ask for information and guidance. Go to divorce resource centers where there are professional counselors who can help you. You'll not only get fresh ideas about legal matters and finances, you might meet other people who have been through it too.

Sometimes a push in the right direction is all that you need to get yourself out of a rut. "I didn't know how to get a lawyer, or in what town I should look for one—because we had just moved," admits Anita Parsons. "A woman I met at the community center knew of one in the neighborhood and said he was good, so I contacted him."

Karen Marshall, who now works as a counselor at a divorce information center, is encouraged by a trend she has observed among women. "More seem to be coming in for information and referrals these days. Sometimes a woman comes in who doesn't want a divorce, but she's being pressured—by a husband, her family, her friends. I tell her it's advantageous to gather information anyway, learn anything you can about finances in the home, about your husband's work. That kind of information is strength and power."

Toxic Friendship

Paradoxically, as much as the study confirms the importance of friendship, it also points out its limitations. An articulate survey respondent summarized one of the potential problems. "Friends are invaluable during a divorce and their support is needed. But," she cautions, "don't take every friend's advice literally. It's not necessarily the right way for you. So many have suggestions, but they really don't understand legal proceedings or finances, and you can go crazy deciding which advice is right!"

Some friends offer advice in their own interest or from their particular vantage point, and women must make sure their suggestions jibe with their own values. The more a woman knows who she is, the better able she will be to field friends' advice. A happy medium is achieved in a relationship when you can listen to a friend and then make your own decisions. As Florence Hacker puts it, "I do value other people's ideas, but I also have a mind of my own."

Another problem is that friends sometimes unwittingly twist the emotional knife, even when they think they're being kind. Florence Hacker's friends often report Earl's whereabouts to her—that they saw him in this restaurant or in that store, remarking that his new girlfriend is always at his side. "That hurts," admits Florrie. "They don't mean to—they think they're being helpful, or making me more aware so I'll take action, but it still hurts."

Fran Sargent adds that friends' input about her ex was both disturbing and confusing. "All of a sudden, they all hated him. He was selfish; he was boring; he was rude." Fran says she knows that her friends' intentions were good, but they probably didn't think through the implications of what they were saying. "Hey! I was married to that guy for a long time. He was the father of my children. They were indirectly insulting me! I was so relieved when another divorced woman told me the same thing had happened to her. It gave me the strength to ask people to keep their thoughts on my ex to themselves!"

Sometimes friends can be draining, as well. And some women, are magnets for people in need. Frances Slender, for example, was a pro at caretaking by the end of her twenty-three-year marriage to an alcoholic. She seems to be following a similar pattern in her postdivorce relationships. "The trouble is," she admits, "the friends that I am attracting are the kind that, as long as I'm doing all the giving, they are there."

In the final analysis, the two greatest toxins in friendship are blame and dependency, both of which usually stem from unmet childhood needs. We suspect that Frances unwittingly attracts people who mirror her own dependency issues. Deep down inside, she is frightened; perhaps her ego is still badly bruised from the divorce. Developmentally, she is not ready for the kind of intimacy that a more mature friendship brings—one in which *both* parties bring strength and independence to the relationship. Rather, she assumes the role of caretaker, as she did in marriage. It *looks* as if she's in charge, but her own needs still go unmet. Then, when her friends let her down—as they inevitably will— Frances can blame *them* for her unhappiness.

Frances and women like her have to learn to establish boundaries, and "just say no" when a friendship makes them feel worse, not better. Rather than blame the other person, they have to look inside themselves and admit to their own dependencies. Otherwise, they will continue to choose people who unwittingly help them perpetuate their old caretaking roles and keep their blinders on.

Friendship as an Anchor

While some women think of friends as family and some even substitute friends for family, the data from our survey show a striking similarity between women who make time for their family and women who make time for their friends. The data confirm that friendship is just as important as family, a source of succor and solace under stress. Thus, if you have *both* a supportive, loving extended family in your life when you get divorced, as well as great friends—which about four out of ten women do— all the better. But even if you just have friends, the effect is overwhelmingly positive.

Close friends are there for emergencies, for celebrations, and for the everyday times as well. Thinking about her future, Jody Burke says, "I pictured this wonderful community of women living together and interacting and throwing together a meal here or there."

Friendship is an anchor, and the intimacy cultivated in friendship is reflected in other relationships as well. The study reveals some fascinating correlations. Of women who feel supported by friends, for example, most note improved relationships with their kids; and they don't feel torn between the needs of their children and the demands of their ex-spouses. In contrast, almost half of the women who lacked support from their friends express concern about their children.

All of these findings are evidence that friendship speeds the developmental process—and a lack of friendship retards it. Women with networks of friends to support them have more time for work, more freedom, and make more time for themselves, as well. Of those who lack friends, a substantial seventy-one percent miss having a regular companion for social events, and six out of ten are concerned about meeting men and dating. These women are also more likely to have financial worries than their counterparts who have friends!

Nancy Rolfing, a fugitive from a stifling and restrictive marriage who "discovered" female friendships later in life, speaks for a lot of women when she says, "Now my friendships come first." Nancy, who divorced five years ago and two years later, at age forty-seven, earned a scholarship to get her undergraduate degree, recently graduated from a small Ivy League college in New England.

"Next to my having kids, coming here was the greatest thing I ever did for myself," claims Nancy. She attributes her growth and happiness as much to her friendships as to the educational program, which is specifically geared to older women returning to school (one of several such programs throughout the country). Recently, Nancy began dating a man she met on campus. She's thrilled with her new love life, but she also keeps it in perspective. "I'm sure the women would laugh at me if they heard this, since I'm never around lately, but my friends still mean more to me. They came before he was in the picture."

And what if she broke a date with her new beau to be with her buddies?—which she might. "Oh, he realizes how important my friends are," insists Nancy. "He'd better—because he'd be out the door if he ever tried to get me to choose between them and him!"

185

7

The Old Gray Mare:
She Ain't What We
Thought She Was

The heyday of women's life is the shady side of fifty, when the vital forces
heretofore expended in other ways are garnered in the brain . . .

—Elizabeth Cady Stanton

The Mind-Body Connection

"Divorce really shocks the system," says one survey respondent
succinctly. The mind can wreak havoc on the body. So often the
woman who feels that life is a "pain in the neck," or the one who
acts as if she's "carrying the weight of the world on her shoulders,"
also has the neck ache or shoulder pain to prove it! In divorce,
especially, women's bodies can be vanquished by their minds. In
her diary, Lorraine Feldman offers a very physical description of
her feelings.

> Can you understand what it is to be rejected . . . total utter
> rejection? There are just so many times a person can get punched
> in the stomach, slapped in the face, pushed to the ground, stepped
> on, mashed into the dirt. There are just so many times a person
> can get treated like shit. There are just so many times that a person
> can be twisted and turned and disregarded like rubbish.

With feelings such as those flooding them, it is easy to compre-
hend why so many women suffer from stress-induced health
conditions during the divorce process. Drastic weight fluctua-
tions, insomnia, infections, headaches, backaches, and ulcers are
most common. Often, women in the study reported a Chinese-
restaurant combination of those ailments.

"For several weeks after my husband told me he wanted a
separation, I had difficulty sleeping and completely lost my

186

appetite," recounts Sylvia Shaunnesey, whose husband came home one day, put a lawyer's card on the table, and informed her that he wanted to end their thirty-five-year marriage. "Naturally, I was hysterical. I lost seventy to eighty pounds. I looked like a walking skeleton. In the meantime, I was run over by a car and ended up in intensive care!"

A woman's psychological functioning is seriously affected by divorce, making her a prime candidate for not only accidents but a host of emotional problems, as well. Some women can't concentrate, become forgetful, or have trouble making decisions. "I had insomnia along with migraine headaches, hypertension, and my blood pressure would fluctuate," says Phyllis May. "I was also nervous—sometimes I felt hyper and could work myself to death, and then other days I would feel depressed and could hardly move."

Other women report full-blown panic attacks, deep depressions, even suicidal thoughts. "I had stress-related anxiety attacks, akin to agoraphobia. They were debilitating, because I never knew when they would grip me," recounts a survey respondent who developed a fear of the outside world. She refused to seek counseling at first, but her body kept sending distress signals. "I also suffered from pneumonia and other respiratory ailments, which I never had before."

Many women are doubly anxious because they fear that minor ailments might lead to major illness, which, as Karen Marshall's story proves, sometimes happens.

Karen Marshall: Discovering the Big Me

Karen Marshall was forty-seven when she found a lump in her breast. "Of course, I connect the breast cancer to my divorce! The link had to do with the enormous amount of emotional stress I had been under, my worries about finances." When her breast was removed, it seemed like a cruel cosmic joke, the realization of her worst nightmare, especially because her life seemed to be getting back on track at that point.

For twenty-five years, she had kept everything bottled up, deep inside her. "My husband and I had a classic marriage. He screamed all the time, and I *never* screamed. Not even during the divorce did I let the anger come out." Karen, the mother of three, explains that her husband gave her a weekly allowance from a suitcase stored in the cellar—"as if I were one of the children."

She was divorced three years and was well into her rediscovery process by the time she was diagnosed with breast cancer. But, she wondered, could she survive a *mastectomy?* Even though her income was still erratic ("I was doing anything I could to make money"), Karen had grown tremendously through her adversity. She had almost finished her master's degree—a dream that had begun during her marriage. And she was happily involved in a great relationship with a new man.

When she went into the hospital, Karen recalls, "My daughter thought I was never going to come out of there alive." Secretly, Karen harbored the same fear. But in her hospital bed, she underwent a major transformation.

"I stepped back, and I got outside of myself. I looked down and saw a woman lying in bed—alone, backed against the wall, very small. And I knew she was someone who looked like me," explains Karen. "But at that moment I suddenly realized that I was a bigger person, and I was going to help that little person pull through."

After the operation, Karen did everything she possibly could to help herself. "I went on a macrobiotic diet, I took vitamins, I did healing meditations, and I used visualization techniques. And I had never done anything like that before," she clarifies. "Throughout the process, I went to women *for* support and I found women *to* support."

Karen, who still does volunteer work for Reach to Recovery, an organization that counsels postmastectomy patients, says of her own battle against cancer, "I fought from within, and now I help other women know that they can go on with their lives. I help them find their inner resources."

As it did in Karen's case, illness can illuminate a woman's developmental struggle! Having begun to forge her own identity, Karen was also able to fight her disease. The "big" Karen who stood outside herself was truly the survivor, a Player, who, in turn, empowered the "little" Karen to go on with her life.

Would—or could—Karen have waged such a battle if she had still been married? Having been the quintessential caretaker during marriage, Karen admits that she might not have been able to give as much nurturing to herself. "It's impossible to say, of course. But I'll tell you one thing. My daughter, who was seventeen at the time, found it difficult when I had the breast cancer, because in order to fight the disease, I neglected her and everyone else," grants Karen. "I think if I was married, my husband wouldn't have let me do that to him or the children."

Karen Marshall: Round Two

Despite her remarkable recuperation, life continued to throw curves at Karen. The man she was seeing around that time, whom she describes as "the love of my life," left her for a woman half her age. She was fifty-one. It was a devastating blow, admits Karen, "But this time I wasn't going to hold back my feelings. I was angry and very vindictive."

Still, Karen did not fall apart.

Most telling, four years later, when she found out that she would have to have a hysterectomy, Karen says, "I didn't feel frightened. I felt strong. I had financial independence since I was working steadily. And I was different inside of me than when I had the breast cancer."

It has been five years since Karen's last operation. She's hopeful about her future. "I may not live forever, but I believe I've added years to my life."

There's no man in Karen's life these days, "but that's perfectly okay with me," she says. She's not bitter, she adds. Rather, she is strong and independent and sure of who she is. As director of a divorce information center for a local chapter of NOW, she serves as a powerful example to women who seek her help.

In Sickness and in Health

Two life-threatening physical illnesses transformed Karen Marshall. The first illness made her realize how both years of stifling her emotions during her marriage and the stress of her divorce had affected her. The second illness enabled her to see how far she had come. Her story is a testament to courage and a woman's ability to survive the hard knocks of divorce, and it debunks many of the myths of health and aging.

Karen Marshall is not alone. Based on our survey, more than

seventy-five percent of the women have stress-related health problems during or after the divorce. The good news is that five years following divorce, eighty-four percent have rediscovered themselves and recovered. Their physical and emotional wounds have begun to heal, they feel positive about themselves, and they have gained a sense of control over their lives. Looking back, many realize that it was a physical malady that first made them aware of the emotional work they needed to do.

That there is a mind-body connection is not news. In study after study, medical researchers have documented that stress taxes everyone's health. Divorce is a major life transition, so it's not surprising that with it comes anxiety, pressure, and health problems. However, for divorcing and divorced women, in particular, it is their ailing body that enables them to finally grasp the gravity of their emotional state.

Remember that these were women who classically put themselves last. Throughout her marriage, the typical woman in the study never allowed herself to address her own concerns, least of all her health. Promising to be there "in sickness and in health," she never believed the marital vows were reciprocal. After all, "in sickness," a woman couldn't fulfill the roles of perfect wife and mother.

Thus, while the study documents the predictable—that the stress of divorce can precipitate health problems—a startling finding also surfaced: a majority of the women experienced some stress-related health problems *before* beginning the divorce process. Had these women "listened" to their bodies, they might have been able to take better care of themselves.

Caroline Breed: Disregarding the Signs

From the early years of her marriage, Caroline Breed's body kept trying to "talk" to her. Even in her early twenties, she had recurrent stomachaches and headaches. "My doctor at the time —paternalistic man that he was—recommended that my husband get me involved in a sport." So, the young couple started playing badminton. "My husband is a workaholic. He badminton'd me to death every night. I liked it, though. For a while, all my frustrations were taken out on the badminton court."

Years later, however, Caroline's physical self was still mimicking her inner turmoil. She developed an ulcer. A doctor prescribed medicine that cured the physical symptoms; he also implied that her emotional state might be affecting her body. Still, he did little to encourage her to find out the *source* of her problems. "He told me to stop worrying so much—to get out and get my mind off whatever was bothering me. But I don't think I knew what was bothering me," she admits.

Caroline tried to lose herself in her volunteer work, but she continued to feel empty and alienated in her life and in her marriage. Nothing was enough to stave off the depression, nor the flood of feelings it induced. Conditioned early in life never to show her emotions, Caroline was also filled with childhood shame connected to her mother's suicide attempt, as this poignant reminiscence exemplifies:

"I'd go in the shower and cry so that no one would hear me. I wanted to die. I remember hearing that if you cut your wrists vertically, it was more effective. They couldn't stitch it up as well."

One day, Caroline read a magazine article about depression, and she suddenly realized that she was having the same symptoms—loss of appetite, fatigue, forgetfulness, insomnia. "I didn't know that depression was clinical or something that's treatable."

Like many women in the study, Caroline thought the failing marriage and her reaction to it was "her problem." The ulcers eating away at the pit of her stomach were evidence of how she had twisted herself inside out to please Tom, feeding his ego at the expense of her own.

Joann Cress: "I Thought Something Was Wrong with Me"

Many women were also plagued by feelings of insecurity as young wives. Joann Cress never thought she was good enough. After the birth of her first child—a year into her marriage—she focused on her weight and on making herself better: better looking, more supportive, a better mother.

Joann felt stranded after the baby was born; Tony refused to let her drive their car, even though she also had a license. "He used to tell me it was 'easier' if he did the food shopping on the way home from work." Tony had found a way to keep Joann literally in her place.

191

Tony's aggressive, controlling personality was apparent in the bedroom, as well. "He wasn't rough in the physical sense, but his sex drive was rough because it was for him. What made *him* feel good was what counted."

Desperate and increasingly disillusioned, Joann tried to fill her emptiness with food—a common coping mechanism for women in the study. Frustrated, she would eat and then diet frantically to lose the weight—a pattern that continued over the course of her twenty-one-year marriage. "I'd get heavy; I'd get upset about it; then I'd diet; and then I'd regain the weight." Joann tried all sorts of diets; she also took diet pills on a number of occasions. "It got so that whenever I went to Dr. Schacter, my gynecologist, he'd say, 'Are you here for your spring cleaning?' That was his way of saying he knew I wanted to shed some pounds."

Interestingly, Joann describes her gynecologist as "the first man I had confidence in. He always made me feel as if I was his only patient." This offhanded comment is a striking testament to Joann's emotional neediness. Like many women, she longed for male validation, which emotionally distant fathers and husbands were incapable of giving. Joann admits that whenever she had an appointment to see Dr. Schacter, "I'd buy a whole new outfit!"

In the back of her mind, Joann thought, "I'm going to lose weight, and Tony won't ever want to look at another woman." Weight Watchers was her most successful regimen. "I lost forty pounds—and do you know what Tony said?" asks Joann rhetorically. " 'What a waste, because you're not going to keep it off!' I had done something that I thought would please him, but he always made me feel terrible—no matter what I did!"

Around 1984, three years before her marriage ended, Joann consulted her doctor again. "I thought something was wrong with me. Maybe I had a tumor. I didn't want to be physical with Tony anymore." But when Joann described her symptoms— fatigue, headaches, a loss of sexual desire, anxiety, depression— Dr. Schacter asked how things were at home. "I just said, 'Fine,' which is how I answered anyone who asked."

After a CAT scan uncovered no physical problems, says Joann, "Dr. Schacter suggested I have counseling. Maybe I was having PMS or maybe there was really something wrong that I wasn't facing."

It's worth mentioning that Joann was more fortunate than

other women who turn to their doctors during a marital crisis or in the throes of divorce. Research shows that physicians rarely offer emotional support to such women, nor do they generally funnel their female patients into therapists' office. If anything, doctors "console" women by writing prescriptions: though women equal roughly half the population, a number of studies over the last decade have shown that they consume a disproportionately large share of all tranquilizers and antidepressants.

Dutifully, Joann made an appointment with the therapist Dr. Schacter recommended. "The counseling lasted about six sessions. The therapist couldn't get me to admit that the problems I described in our marriage—like Tony not being supportive or problems in our sex life—weren't my fault. I was in such denial."

Women Under Siege

Like many of the women we met, Caroline and Joann were under attack. During their marriages, their minds and bodies were in revolt. Only after divorce did they realize the connection between their emotional devastation and their adverse health. In Joann's case, for example, three years later, when she announced to Tony, "I am strong enough to stand on my own—and I don't need you," she also called the therapist. "I told him what had been going on, and he was very impressed. He told me that I had done a complete turnabout. I finally knew what my anger and my depression were about." Joann's physical health has been fine since then.

In much the same way, it took years of stomach pain and depression before Caroline Breed sought professional help and divorced Tom. She still gets choked up when she remembers telling her therapist how she cried in the shower. The therapist realized that Caroline had never dealt with the devastating fears she experienced as a child. She had felt abandoned when her mother was hospitalized for depression following the suicide attempt. So, the therapist led Caroline through a technique in which Caroline sat opposite an empty chair representing a part of herself—the vulnerable child who didn't understand what was happening and, more important, was never able to express what she felt.

"I talked to the child in me who was so sad and inconsolable in the shower," says Caroline, recalling how she finally allowed herself to get in touch with that frightened little girl. "I put my arms around her and comforted her. It was a very emotional moment for me. Today, I am able to comfort myself."

Women and Depression, a 1990 report compiled by an American Psychological Association task force, reviewed studies related to women and depression. As a whole, research confirms that an unhappy marriage is "a grave risk to a woman's mental health." Because women so often feel isolated in their roles, lonely, and frustrated by the lack of communication with their husbands, the task force concluded, "unhappily married women experience more depressive symptoms than either happily married or unmarried women."

The APA report's conclusions are certainly buttressed by the stories told by our women—escapees of unhappy marriages. Reading between the lines, we were able to identify several significant themes that help explain why so many women fail to act on early warning signals related to their physical and mental health.

• Women tend to feel guilty about being sick, as if it were something they bring upon themselves or a sort of personal failing. Rather than look at trouble in the marriage, they look for trouble in *themselves.*

• Many women refuse to "give in" to physical symptoms, diminishing or denying all but the most blatant conditions—in much the same way that they have denied the reality of their marital situations or their need to empower themselves financially. Too often, it takes a severe health crisis, like Karen Marshall's breast cancer, for a woman to be able to justify paying attention to her health and finally taking care of herself.

• Some women use self-destructive coping strategies. Most common are overeating, binging, and crash dieting, sometimes coupled with smoking, which for some women counters the urge to eat. Others use alcohol or drugs, be they prescription drugs or so-called "recreational" drugs, to "take the edge off." Naturally, such habits will aggravate an already tenuous physical and emotional state. Moreover, while the addiction captures a woman's attention and keeps the focus off her marriage, it often makes her feel even more powerless over the events in her life.

Getting in Touch

How does divorce finally trigger an awareness of reality? The answer, once again, lies in the developmental picture. As a woman travels the road to rediscovery and begins to get in touch with her identity, she is able to allow herself the personal care and nurturing she needs. Aches and pains that were once denied can be attended to. Feelings that were submerged and transformed into illness can be expressed, and the link between the psychic and the physical is revealed.

Given some distance from the crisis, women in the study often connect health problems to poor self-image, a lack of emotional support, and feelings of loneliness. "In the marriage and after the divorce, my condition was caused by a lack of emotional support from my family, friends, and society in general," remarks Anne Garner.

However, in the wake of divorce, the pain can be transformative. "I was under great stress before the divorce, which affected my digestive system," reports a survey respondent. "I lost twenty-six pounds. When he left, that's when I started taking care of myself. I finally sought counseling." And sometimes it's the other way around: divorce transforms the pain. "My health has improved! My arthritis is much better," writes a jubilant fifty-year-old divorcée who answered the questionnaire. "My doctor mentioned stress being a major factor years ago, but I never believed that was possible. Now my body knows I'm happier."

Physical pain is a double-edged sword: On the one hand, it is frightening, because it makes women feel that they don't have control. On the other hand, illness substantiates their inner pain. After being in long-term marriages in which they tended to deny so much of themselves, divorce gives many women their first opportunity to validate their reality, to explore who they are, to cherish newfound identities, to heal old wounds, and, ultimately, to take care of themselves.

Lorraine Feldman's diary says it all. In a mock letter to her philandering husband, she asserts her determination to move beyond the feelings of rejection, to gain a life—and an identity —of her own.

A boxer who is beaten one punch too many will die. But I do not intend to die. I have to get out of the ring if I am to live.

And a few paragraphs later, she also affirms the Lorraine who has begun to develop.

Everyone who has been created is important and should realize her worth. No person should be subjected to what you have subjected me. I am a person, I am whole, I am important, I have worth. I am real, I have feelings, I am alive and warm and beautiful.

Taking Care: A User's Guide

Physical and emotional pain spur psychological growth, which enables divorced women to respond to health problems and deal with conditions that may have festered for decades. Five years after divorce, more than three-quarters of the women in the study no longer experience health problems. These women chose a variety of routes to health and happiness. Each strategy enables a woman to feel a sense of control over circumstances and events that had once made her feel so out of control. Indeed, the mere fact that she makes a conscious, aggressive choice to help herself is, in and of itself, healing.

Professional help. As has been stated, seeing a doctor when you have a medical problem or a psychotherapist for emotional troubles, might seem like an obvious step; however, women often ignore their physical or emotional symptoms—until divorce forces them to take action. "I ate all the time and gained weight, even though I swam a mile three to five times a week to cope with my stress. Finally, I turned to a counselor for my physical and mental health," writes a typical respondent. ("Seeing a Shrink . . . in Order to Expand," pages 123–25, describes how women availed themselves of psychotherapy during marriage and after divorce.)

Healthy diet and exercise. Christine Moss, forty-three, divorced only nine months and still under a great deal of stress when we met her, admits that at first she took sleeping pills for her insomnia. "But I found out that I can't take them, so I've been exercising, and that has helped even more."

"I could not sleep, because my mind would not stop! I couldn't eat—I lost twenty pounds in three weeks," remembers Irene Presto, forty-six, echoing not only Christine's experience but that of the vast majority in the study, whose maladaptive coping strategies hurt them physically and plunged them into deeper emotional despair, until they began to take care of themselves. "I feel physically good now. I do the best with what I have. I exercise, eat healthy foods, and lead a well-balanced life, as far as work and fun."

Vera Castro, forty-six, says "walking a lot" helped her after the divorce. And forty-year-old Bonnie Lenza agrees. "I was tense most of the time, so I went for long walks. I ate wholesome foods and kept on a regular diet. I exercised three times a week. And I took up golf."

Twelve-step programs and other support groups. Lena Entemann not only became "a compulsive eater" after her first divorce, she also led a disastrously self-destructive single life and then flung herself into another marriage. Lena began to drink heavily. "I loved to drink and felt I could conquer anything. A sense of power came over me. Then I'd sleep too much, make excuses and stay home from work." Joining Alcoholics Anonymous after her second divorce changed Lena's life. "I began to associate with successful women who had made it. Now I have a heart and feelings that I'm in touch with. I have a much greater capacity to figure out what I want and how to get it."

AA, Al-Anon, and other twelve-steps groups concentrate specifically on various addictions or disorders—for instance, Overeater's Anonymous helps bulimics, anorexics, and overeaters; Smoker's Anonymous helps nicotine addicts. Other types of support groups can also affect a woman's health indirectly.

Doreen McBride, who became depressed and began to overeat during her divorce, notes that the stress also made her start smoking again. "I knew it was bad for me. But then I joined a support group for divorced women—and eventually, I started feeling better about myself, and I stopped smoking." Doreen's and other women's experiences prove that once a woman starts feeling better about herself, troublesome aches and pains fade away, and there's less need to fall back on bad habits.

Friends. As we pointed out in Chapter Six, this is not the first study to document that the company one keeps has a dramatic impact on physical well-being. Irene Presto recalls, "My friends were wonderful and helped me. I had a core group who were there for me whenever I needed to talk. One suggested keeping a journal. I started writing every day and poured out my inner thoughts and feelings. It helped me recover physically."

Meditation and other "empowerment" techniques. Divorced in "the Age of Aquarius," women can pick and choose from a wealth of New Age techniques. Lisa Frazier meditates every day. "It got me through. I would have to say that if I didn't do that, I probably would have had a nervous breakdown. I'm amazed that I didn't get ill, that I don't have cancer. Meditation is my saving grace." In a similar vein, after her divorce, Fran Sargent took a number of healing workshops and empowerment courses. "I learned to make concrete choices about what I wanted and to visualize those things actually happening. Believe it or not, I discovered that whenever I really held the vision out there, it worked!"

A change of scene. "The guilt over the divorce caused insomnia and stomach problems," writes one survey respondent. Counseling helped her, but so did "moving out of state. It has been eight months since I moved, and I have not had one stomachache or sleepless night since. I feel like a new woman, knowing that he can't get me upset anymore."

It doesn't have to be a permanent move. Lisa Frazier traveled to Arizona as soon as she saved up enough money for the trip. "I went by myself. That really changed my life. The consciousness there gave me a whole different slant on life. I know that's where I'll retire." Lorraine Feldman's Colorado rafting and rock-climbing trip also imbued her with a new level of confidence, and Helga Gross's solo back-packing adventure in the Far East did the same for her. Thus, even a temporary change can lead to a sense of physical and emotional well-being.

A positive attitude. Gisella Morgan, at sixty-one, says she didn't have health problems after her divorce, "because I am the way I am. I love work—I would never not work. And I'm very healthy. After the divorce, I read a book about positive thinking, and that helped me too."

Predictably, changing her attitude can change a woman's physical picture as well. Joann Cress observes that being away from Tony for the first time in over twenty years gave her a different outlook on life. "My life was in turmoil, but I knew it would get

better soon. So, I relaxed. I gained five or ten pounds—big deal!
For the first time, I was nice to *me!*"

The Myth of the Double Whammy: Menopause and Mid-Life Divorce

Oh, no! Divorce *and* menopause? The mere idea terrifies most
women approaching mid-life. In fact, if myths about mid-life
divorce abound, so do illusions about menopause. Prior to the
publication of her book on the subject, Gail Sheehy wrote in a
1991 article for *Vanity Fair,* "The nervousness and uncertainty
one discovers just beneath the surface among even the most
attractive and successful women edging toward fifty are a testament to the power of the taboo that still surround this mysterious
'change of life.' "

In the past, women have tended not to talk about menopause,
not even to each other, although as the Baby Boomers move into
mid-life, menopause, like other *normal* circumstances of aging,
have become a "hot" topic. Secretly, some women worry about it.
Those who are divorced or contemplating divorce may worry
even more. The thought of a change of status along with an
alleged "change of life" is overwhelming. And what if they date
again? Imagine being at a restaurant with a new man—and little
globules of sweat suddenly drip into your soup! Or worse, what
if you're ready for a romantic evening? You're wearing his favorite
perfume, you drop the appropriate hints throughout the evening,
he makes the first move—and suddenly . . . vaginal dryness!

"God, did that scare me when I started seeing John," admits
Nancy Rolfing who embarked on a new love affair five years
following her divorce. "Before that, I thought I might never have
another sexual encounter," she remarks. Reminded of her brief
dalliance in Hawaii with her oceanographer, she explains, "That
was exciting, but it just proved to me that I was still alive. It
didn't mean more than that."

When Nancy started seeing John, however, after a few dates,
she realized, this was a potential *relationship,* not a fast fling. She
also began to think about menopause. "I never gave it much
thought before then. Menopause just meant not having a
period—and that was fine with me! But when John came into
my life, and I read about women having hot flashes, the ups and

downs, the frustration of not being feminine anymore, I suddenly thought, 'Oh, no! I don't want *that* to happen!' We were having such great sex. What if suddenly I got dry?"

No doubt for many women the word *menopause* evokes images of hot flashes, irritability, night sweats, sudden mood swings, palpitations, insomnia, bloating, memory lapses, depression, re-duced sex drive—ironically, many of the symptoms that charac-terize women in the throes of divorce! This brings us to an important finding: The symptoms of menopause mirror the most common physical symptoms of stress felt by divorcing women, whether they're menopausal or not.

Consequently, there is no way to discern whether women who report such symptoms are actually experiencing the onset of menopause or stress—or both. Perhaps a woman is in the early stage of menopause. Equally possible, however, is the fact that she feels more comfortable attributing her physical and emotional symptoms to something concrete; having a "condition" feels more "real" than the vagaries of divorce stress.

Eventually, research may uncover the "truth" about menopause. In the meantime, however, many women will undoubtedly be influenced by half-truths, old wives' tales, and other women's misconceptions about this important physiological change. Here are a few things we do know:

• Menopause is different for every woman. The way a woman experiences menopause depends on her constitution, how she coped with health problems in the past, and how various social stress factors—among them, divorce—affect her. Therefore, it's not possible to provide women with a map of the territory.

• Menopause is a subtle transition, a bodily process that occurs over a time span of several years. It rarely hits like a lightning bolt!

• Age is no longer the sole determinant of menopause, especially now that one-third of American women reach menopause through surgery. Having had complete or partial hysterectomies, some women are jump-started into menopause as early as their thirties.

• Menopause doesn't have to be debilitating. Not all women are symptomatic during the transition. For the women in the "Divorce Over 40" study, *menopause was not a significant issue*. The majority didn't bring it up; if asked, most women downplayed menopause—if they noticed it at all.

"The funny thing was, I didn't even realize I had gone through it," laughs Nancy Rolfing who consulted a medical doctor about her menopausal worries. The doctor ordered an FSH (follicle stimulating hormone) test which measures hormone levels. "I found out that I already had my menopause, and I didn't notice!" And what about Nancy's sex life? "Well, I'm far from dry! It's sure is nice to know that you can be fifty and still have great sex!"

Helga's Story: A Question of Independence, Not Hot Flashes

When she was nearing fifty, Helga Gross began to feel a few minor changes in her body, but, she says, "I had made up my mind that menopause wasn't going to be a big deal—and it wasn't!" Besides, she had other things on her mind—such as her relationship with Robert, twenty-seven, the same age as Gary, the oldest of Helga's three children.

Their relationship had been launched four years before, when Helga found herself sitting next to Robert at a lecture and struck up a conversation. "I was attracted to his Colorado look—the hiking boots, the pony tail, the beard, the disheveled clothes— and he was obviously very bright." It turned out that Robert lived around the corner, so Helga offered him a ride home. When they got there, she asked if he wanted to come in.

"I put on some music, and we smoked a joint, and in a few minutes, I looked at him and said, 'You know what I want to do right now? I want to kiss you.' And I did!" Robert was shocked. "He had this look on his face, and I felt that I had done something that wasn't right," recalls Helga, who then went into the bathroom, looked in the mirror, and said to herself, "Wonderful! You moved to Colorado to find yourself, and now you're picking up little boys!"

Despite his initial intimidation and her temporary embarrassment, a few hours later, Helga and Robert ended up in bed. "When he put his arms around me, I felt like I had come home —to a father or mother that loved me—that's the kind of feeling it was. I was so starved for love after all those years with Harvey." Five weeks later, they were living together. It lasted six years.

Pressed to recall those years, Helga doesn't have a clear idea of what her menopause was like because it coincided with so many other significant happenings in her life. "I was very confused at the time. I had just turned fifty. And when I look back at my journals of that time, every other page says, 'I have to find work.' I knew our relationship was ending. And I knew it was time for me to grow up!" In other words, a few hot flashes here and there were the least of Helga's concerns!

More important and certainly more compelling, says Helga, was her independence. "All of the issues in my life pointed to that. I was going into a depression because I was paralyzed about going out and making my own way in the world. And *that* had nothing to do with menopause!"

Aging: Mixed Messages/Mixed Feelings

Living in an ageist culture may also intensify a woman's fears about menopause. Regarding their attitudes about aging, interestingly, our findings cut both ways, reflecting the stereotypes and challenging the myths.

Elizabeth Harkness embodies this conflict. At sixty-eight, she is one of the oldest interviewees, but her outlook on life is youthful and optimistic. She recently went back to college to get a legal associate's degree. While she doesn't let the idea of graduating from college at seventy stop her, Elizabeth is nevertheless mindful of societal bias. "I don't know if they'll want an old bag working in a law office!"

Regarding the stereotypes, approximately half of the survey respondents are apprehensive about growing older. Like Elizabeth, they are no doubt mindful of the prejudices against older women and of the double standard: Women get "older," but men get "more distinguished." Women look "older," but men look "weathered."

Women also fear growing older *alone*, because society "expects" them to appear on the arm of a man. Of women afraid of growing older alone, more than half bemoan the lack of an intimate relationship, and sixty-nine percent miss having someone with whom they could attend social events.

Finally, many women fear aging because they are afraid of

serious illness. Helga Gross, who just turned sixty and is in excellent health, nevertheless admits, "I'm not afraid of death; I'm afraid of *suffering*—getting cancer."

Lacking the traditional support of an intact family, many women also wonder who would take care of them if they were seriously sick or disabled—especially if they have already been burdened with the care of their own ailing parents, as so many women have. Thus, in one breath Elizabeth Harkness says, "My favorite expression is that 'age is a state of mind.' " But in the next she confesses, "My only fear of getting older is being incapacitated. I took care of my mother the last eight weeks of her life, and God forbid I'll be like that."

Often, such fears are intensified by financial concerns. "This is the time in life when your health starts to go," reflects Anne Garner who recently found a lump on her breast. "It'll be a fast five hundred dollars just to see the specialists and have the examinations. And if I have to have a biopsy, when the smoke clears, it'll cost around five thousand dollars!" Anne at least has health insurance; many women are far less fortunate.

Patsy Marconi, forty-seven, a bookkeeper who lost her job and was on unemployment at the time of her interview, is typical of a number of women who lost their husbands' health plans in the divorce. Too young for Medicare and too poor for private insurance, unless a woman like Patsy finds a job that provides health benefits, she is likely to join the ranks of the chronically uninsured. "I'm starting to think about getting older. I don't want to have to be responsible to anyone, and I don't want to go to my children for anything. Nor do I want to take someone into my home in order to pay the rent. But I'm not as aggressive as I was when I was younger."

Lorraine Feldman, who now depends on a next-door neighbor for emergencies, also fears, "What if my neighbor moved? What if I get sick? Who will be there? I have a very close family network, but no one lives in my immediate vicinity."

Such fears are both pervasive and real. At the same time, however, the data and the interviews also defy the cultural clichés. Take Gisella Morgan, a delicate, elegant, and well-preserved sixty-one-year-old. She greeted us at her charming New York City apartment in a T-shirt, skintight leggings, and thick socks rolled down around her ankles, looking like a teenager ready for the gym. "I don't exercise," she corrects, "but I walk everywhere. I never use transportation."

German-born Gisella was married to a wealthy American doctor, who kept her on a twenty-five-dollar-a-week allowance for eighteen years, while she cooked and cleaned, managed his office and worked outside the home as well. A petite woman, still full of boundless energy, she now lavishes that time and attention on herself. She avoids meat, eats lots of fruits and vegetables, doesn't smoke, and never drinks alcohol.

"I'm not afraid of growing old or growing old alone," says Gisella, long divorced and now managing a tourist service; she personally shepherds groups of foreign businessmen around the City. "I'm going to work until I die!" Thoughtful, Gisella adds, "Let me put it this way: I have no problem growing older—so far. What happens next month—who knows? But I do believe I'm going to stay very healthy." She ponders, "What else can you do? I have friends in AA, who say 'take it one day at a time,' and that's what I do!"

The study also pokes holes in the supposition that older women obsess over their appearance or that they worry about "falling apart." Few of the women we interviewed fit that description. Sure, they talk about changing their appearance cosmetically, but few opt for plastic surgery. They watch their weight, but none diet strenuously. More often, women take up sports, exercise regularly, meditate, and do yoga. They accept the lines and the wisps of gray hair with seeming grace. In addition, the survey findings confirm women's positive perceptions: half of these women experience divorce as a chance for a new life, a third see it as an opportunity to take more time to care for themselves, and almost half are confident enough to date again!

Interestingly, when women are "hung up" on their appearances, it isn't because of aging. More commonly, they are plagued by "ghosts" that have haunted them since their teenage years—a big nose, frizzy hair, a "masculine" build, breasts too little or too large. At one time, many of these women thought that their husbands were the only men who would have them.

Karen Marshall, for example, a frail and sickly child, felt "grateful" to her husband for marrying her in spite of her physical condition. She was nineteen. It is only through divorce that women like Karen are, for the first time in their lives, able to reevaluate themselves—especially their appearance and their femininity. They are truly surprised to find that other men find them attractive and appealing and, most important, treat them with respect.

Listening to our interviewees, in fact, it seems as if women's qualms about age are more often based on societal expectation and conditioning or tied to financial anxieties, rather than reflective of the reality of their individual situations. Marilyn Hauptman speaks for many women when she says, "Forty seven? It scares me. Here I am afraid of being forty-seven—not afraid really—I just don't like the number. I feel better. I feel freer than I ever felt before. I'm never lonely, because I think I really like myself today."

Beating the System: Younger Men

It's not easy to buck the weight of one's culture or to substitute myths of your own for society's less promising scenarios. When songs warn us "The old gray mare, she ain't what she used to be," mid-life, and even moreso the twilight years, don't seem to hold much promise. On the other hand, as we shatter such myths, perhaps more women will emulate the late Margaret Mead, who frequently spoke of a condition she labeled "postmenopausal zest"—a sudden blooming, a burst of energy, a newfound identity, and a new perspective on life that follows a trying period of change.

That description rings true for many of our women—even those who haven't reached menopause! Their growth, if not precipitated by a biological metamorphosis, is nevertheless triggered by a different kind of transition: divorce.

Joann Cress says her family found her postdivorce behavior appalling. "Not only did I file for divorce, but I took up with a priest. Actually," she corrects herself, "Ken was *training* for the priesthood, but he was also fifteen years younger!"

Her family aside, it felt awkward to Joann when she first dated Ken. "I never liked being different." The feelings, she admits, go back to high school, when Joann, the youngest child in a low-income family of five, wore hand-me-downs. Years later, the shy, easily embarrassed teenager was still inside her psyche. "Ken and

205

I would be standing on line at the movies, and people would ask if I was with my son. Remarks like that would go right through me."

In time, as Joann, a Slow Motion, accepted her right to have a loving, mutually respectful relationship, outsiders' comments didn't bother her as much. "When I became more comfortable with it, my family became comfortable too." Documenting her progress, Joann notes that the first year they were together, Christmas cards came in her name only; by the second year, cards were written to both of them.

Joann and Ken have been together five years—and still counting. Ken is sensitive to Joann's feelings; their lovemaking is something she never experienced before and never expected to feel. "It's the way I always dreamed it would be with a man."

Joann no longer confuses love with control. Ken doesn't ask her where she's going or when she'll be home; he trusts her. Asked to compare herself to the girl she once was, Joann refers to the movie *Georgy Girl*. "I would do everything everybody wanted, because I thought that would make them like me. I guess at that time I was a bud. Now I've opened up. Full bloom—and I haven't stopped blooming."

Old Issues/New Priorities

Although they were in the minority, several of the interviewees had younger lovers. "I find that he's more open to change, and he's more accepting of my independence," comments Kate McKinley, whose boyfriend of the last six years is five years younger.

Clearly, some younger men are not as locked into traditional roles as their older counterparts. It may be easier for a woman to "be herself" with a younger man. Still, that's only half the story: especially coming out of a marriage in which she was dependent, the woman has to be willing to change too.

Helga Gross now realizes that, as exhilarating as it was to be with Robert, who was twenty-three years younger, the relationship enabled her to avoid standing on her own. Contrary to her marriage to Harvey, Helga was never "subservient" to Robert; they shared the day-to-day responsibilities of running a home. But as Helga's experience exemplifies, that doesn't necessarily make a woman independent. "We were a very liberated couple, but I became addicted to him. When it came to *my* life and what I wanted to do, I was paralyzed.

"When we'd fight, Robert would say to me, 'You complain because we always do what I want to do, but we don't do what *I* want. It's just that *you never know what you want to do!*' "

Robert was very supportive; he thought Helga could do anything and do it better than anyone else. But, Helga now realizes, "Underneath, he was getting disgusted with the way I sat around. I read books, and I played at taking action, but I did nothing to further my life. Robert saw a dynamic woman who didn't know what to do with her life. I think those issues would have come up with any independent, strong man, regardless of age."

The breakup was slow and painful, spanning a two-year period. Her agony notwithstanding, Robert proved to be an important catalyst in Helga's rediscovery process. The last night they were together, she recalls, "We were taking a bath, and he looked at me and said, 'You're fifty-two—you don't have that much time left. If you don't grow up to be your own person, you're going to turn out to be bitter!' I'll never forget that. I knew he was right—and, the truth is, over the years the closer I got focused on my own life, the more I've liked my freedom.

"All my life, my focus was on having a man. Today I know who *I* am, and that's all that matters. The more I have taken the responsibility to make my life work and to support myself, the more independent I've become. Now I like my freedom to choose."

Helga no longer eyes couples with envy, nor is she bitter. If an astrologer told her that she would never have another relationship, she admits, "There would be a little bit of sadness, but it wouldn't be a major disappointment—much less so than if she predicted that I'd never get my money trip together. That would *really* bother me!"

Nancy Rolfing, only six months into her relationship, echoes similar feelings: "I know I could walk away from John and not be emotionally strangled or feel abandoned if he left me. We have a commitment to each other, and the way he feels about me helps me feel good about myself, but my self-esteem is not totally determined by him. I'm much better about valuing myself than I was five years ago."

Those sentiments fit the majority of the women in the study. Five years after divorce, eighty-four percent experience feelings of achievement and feel free to be themselves and validate their own needs; eight out of ten women said they value their privacy and independence. For these women, divorce is a positive step forward. They are more at peace with themselves and better able to face the prospect of aging and of living without a husband or steady partner than women in the study who, not fully recovered from the aftershock, do not feel in control of their lives.

In short, our findings—and the reports of our interviewees— clearly demonstrate the link between personal growth—finding one's identity—and postdivorce adjustment. The fear of growing older alone or the pang of not having a steady partner wanes as women realize they can make their own decisions, reach out to others in friendship, and find fulfillment in work and other interests. No doubt about it: the old gray mare is *not* what she used to be!

8

Broken Ties/Mended Lives: Dealing with Children and Redefining Family Relationships

My family—their sadness and disappointment was as painful as the divorce. I spent a lot of time and effort trying to convince them that it was the best for all concerned. The children were very confused. They couldn't understand it. But when I look back, I know that as I got stronger and got to know myself better, all of my relationships began to change. I'm sad to say that I've lost some people, but the ones who really count are still in my life.

—Survey respondent, answering, "What was the hardest part of the first year(s) after divorce, and how did you cope with it?"

The Turning Point

The night of her daughter's prom, Phyllis May found a different niche in her life for Lenny, her ex-husband. "I allowed this man back into my life as my friend. We have many family ties—his parents, other relatives—but most of all he will always be the father of my children."

Phyllis describes the three years from the time the divorce proceedings were initiated until the final judgment officially ended their twenty-five-year marriage: "We hadn't been communicating directly. It was all done through the lawyers. In court his lawyer degraded me, forced me to the point of hysteria, and my ex-husband just sat there."

Her three daughters were twenty-three, nineteen, and ten. "We all went through a terribly emotional period, crying all the time." Phyllis worried most about Darlene, the youngest. "Children *need* a father." But, Phyllis explains, Lenny had been "running with a fast crowd," a sexy young thing on his arm, spending money on booze and cocaine—the quintessential portrait of a man in the grip of a mid-life crisis.

209

"Darlene hadn't seen him that much during that time, although she talked to him on the phone She was growing up to be a really pretty young lady—and here she was, going to her first prom. She was wearing this beautiful long gown. She looked gorgeous, so I said to myself, 'Now I'm really going to take a stand.' "

Phyllis phoned her ex-husband, the childhood sweetheart who some thirty years before had taken Phyllis to her first prom. Boldly, she told him, "I want to sit down and talk to you. I have a lot of things I want to discuss." Then Phyllis softened as she admitted her true agenda. "But also," she said hesitantly, "one of the things I really want you to see is your daughter all dressed up in a ball gown."

Lenny agreed to come over. "Things were kind of awkward, but he enjoyed seeing his little girl grown up and looking so pretty. That was my turning point," recounts Phyllis. "After Darlene left for the prom, we sat for hours and just talked."

Shortly thereafter, Darlene was in a very bad car accident. Lenny, remarried by then, came immediately to support his first family. "I believe that he realizes how precious life is. The bond Darlene has with him now is incredible."

These days, Phyllis regularly invites Lenny and his new wife to family functions; the three sometimes go out to dinner. "I know, I know—it's strange," says Phyllis, chuckling, "but it works." Apparently, Lenny's new wife grasps an important axiom about ex-spouses: it's not continued contact that threatens a new marriage; it's continued conflict, because the exes are still enmeshed —through their anger.

"All the children respect Lenny," says Phyllis. "They've seen how we both have grown." When Lenny moved to Florida a few years ago, he tried to entice Phyllis to move there too. But she thought life there would be "too boring." Recently, however, Lenny made her the proverbial offer she couldn't refuse. "He bought me a condominium! I lost my job because of the economy, and I figured, 'Why not move to Florida?' I'm taking a course to get my broker's license, so maybe I'll go into real estate. I'm only here two months, but I like it."

Being too friendly with an ex can have a down side, as Phyllis points out. "We speak on the phone all the time. Sometimes, he'll call me up, screaming about something, and I'll have to remind him that we're not married anymore!"

Moving On

Does the friendship ever tug at Phyllis's heartstrings? "Sure, there are times I say to myself that I should never have gotten the divorce—that I should have just let him get his flings out of his system. At other times, I say I couldn't have lived through it —and I certainly wouldn't have grown if I had. He was my first love, and I guess I'll always love him in a way, but we're two different people now."

Everything Old Is New Again

Many women might find Phyllis May's attitude and her relationship with her ex-husband incredible, and many second wives might bristle at the thought of their closeness. However, from her point of view—and the study confirms it—letting go of the rage and resentment and making peace with a tumultuous, hurtful past is vital to the healing process. "When there's anger and hurt, it turns into a fiasco—and the only ones who make out really well are the attorneys," contends Phyllis. "You can only hang on to your anger for so long. You've got to let it go and get on with your life."

Phyllis has seen women divorced ten years or more, who are still in a fury. "If you don't let go of the anger, how are you going to be productive in your own life?" She answers her own question: "You can't be, because your thoughts are always on him—on that constant anger. Meanwhile, your husband has turned his life around, and you're still out there feeling hurt!"

Whether you can or cannot develop a friendship with an ex-husband is not the point. Some women do—with varying degrees of civility—but others are unable to maintain any kind of post-divorce relationship with their exes. However, all women are capable of at least reviewing the memories of their marriage from a new vantage point. A woman who makes peace with the past in this way, not only makes her own life better, she enriches her children's lives and helps maintain all family ties as well.

Which women are most likely to achieve this kind of emotional truce with the past? Once again, the findings reflect the developmental profile. *A woman can redefine relationships from the past only when she has a separate identity and a clear picture of who she is.* Among the participants of the "Divorce Over 40" study, this principle was evident in three important domains:

211

Relationships with children: Even Judith Wallerstein, whose longitudinal analysis of divorce and its aftermath was published in *Second Chances: Men, Women, and Children a Decade After Divorce,* admits, "the single most important protective factor in a child's psychological development and well-being over the years is the mother's mental health and the quality of her parenting." Our research confirms that opinion. The findings also demonstrate that when a woman discovers what *she* needs out of life, she becomes a more responsible adult who can help her children through the trying aftermath of divorce. Her strong sense of identity also strengthens the mother-child bond, and she gets better at being what her children need most: a conscientious parent.

Relationships with ex-spouses: Many women were able to at least reach an amiable postdivorce détente with their exes; some couldn't. If a woman is able to stop blaming her ex-husband and to "forgive" her marriage, she can honestly assess her own part in the breakup and move through the rediscovery process. She is also less likely to engage with her estranged spouse in a deadly tug-of-war over the children.

Relationships with parents, other family members, and the "ex-family": Just as family pressure often influences a woman's decision to marry, parental perceptions may also have a tremendous impact on her divorce. Even though some parents—especially mothers —initially criticized their daughter's divorce, most women in the study were able to field family criticism and to stand up for themselves. Some women even maintain a connection to their "ex-family," who are, after all, still related to their children.

Unquestionably, *all* relationships improve when a woman grows and changes. She is able to integrate what happened in the past and has a sense that she can survive in the future. The study also establishes that a woman who forges a separate identity is able to make sound choices. Rather than compromise her own needs— as she is likely to have done in the past, both in her family of origin and in her marriage—she finally gets what she needs and wants from family relationships.

Children as Mirrors of a Marriage

Children often illuminate marital problems. Marilyn Haupt-man, a native of Germany, married an American when she was eighteen. Over the next twenty years, Marilyn's husband shamed her unceasingly. He was overbearing and repressive, alternating fits of rage with bouts of morbid depression.

Marilyn thought it was her "job" to put up with her husband's wrath. Still quite young in developmental terms, she was unable to identify the problem or command the respect due her. For years she did little more than plead, "Please don't yell, Oscar, please don't yell."

With each of their three children, the wedge between Marilyn and Oscar grew wider. When she was thirty-two, Marilyn's five-year-old son, her youngest, inadvertently opened her eyes. "It was when I first started to see that things were wrong with our marriage. I remember one day, I was standing in the hallway and Gregory was coming toward me, talking to me—yelling—just like his father, and I didn't like that!"

It was evident in many of the interviews that a child's problem—tantrums, withdrawal, difficulty in school, involvement in drugs and alcohol, sexual promiscuity—was often a red flag in these marriages. Teenagers, in particular, can be the conduit through which marital tensions are expressed, although it some-times takes a while before mothers view their children's behavior as symptoms of serious problems in the marriage.

"My oldest child was beginning to have problems in school—cutting classes, getting into fistfights," says Patsy Marconi, recalling the last few years of her marriage. A therapist, whom the school recommended for Patsy and her son, quickly identified the problem. He explained to her that when a marriage falters, it is common for a parent to "triangulate" a child—usually the oldest—overburdening him or her with responsibility and form-ing an alliance against the other parent. "He felt that my son and I were tied emotionally."

At that juncture, Patsy couldn't muster the courage to leave her ill-tempered and volatile husband. Her self-esteem was shat-tered, her identity weak. She unintentionally continued to lean on her son, because she wasn't ready to stand on her own. Then, a few years later, she saw a sudden transformation in their second child, a daughter who had always been "perfect."

"Angie's personality changed dramatically. She went from being a bubbly child to becoming sullen and aggressive," observes Patsy. "I had thought that as long as there was no screaming, no violence, it wasn't hurting them. But when Angie, who was fifteen at the time, started getting out of hand, I finally admitted to myself that our way of life was affecting the children."

Over the years, Patsy, a Slow Motion, had begun to work on herself. She did not yet know exactly what she wanted out of life, but she knew enough about herself by then to know what she *didn't* want. So, when her husband wouldn't move out, she did.

"My children tell me that I am much better without their father than I ever was with him," she notes five years after her divorce. Clearly, Patsy, now forty-seven, *is* better. But it's not simply a case of good riddance to a bad husband. In Patsy's case, her husband happened to be a bad guy—cruel, insensitive, at times obscene. However, in the vast majority of the marriages we observed, fault is hardly the issue; development is. Because of societal conditioning, men *and* women are deprived of vital, yet different, pieces of the developmental pie. Neither gender has been given a complete package that would equip them to be *both* independent (traditionally male) *and* loving (traditionally female). Sadly, most of these partners were conditioned to be one or the other.

The Challenge of Children in Mid-Life Divorce

In order to survive after divorce, a woman must acquire the skills and qualities denied her in the confines of her marital roles. However, she also faces certain challenges that are indigenous to mid-life, one being that her children are typically in early adolescence or college age.

Nearly half of the women in the study had one or more children leaving home at the time of the divorce. Fifteen percent of the women in the study had teenagers: wisecracking, fast-talking kids that even happily married parents find taxing. These older children tend to see more, understand more, and complain more aggressively than their younger counterparts. To further complicate matters, they are often struggling to accomplish a comparable developmental task: to separate and differentiate themselves from their parents. Lo and behold—their mothers are going through the same thing!

Unlike women in shorter-term marriages, mid-life and older women also have long histories with many memories to sort through. It's harder to redefine *family* after so many years. "It's very hard breaking up the home, selling things off. The house was built for four of us, not one," writes a survey respondent. "We're not just dealing with the empty nest; we're dealing with a *broken* nest," adds Gwenn Banning, forty-nine, whose two sons are in their early twenties.

Finally, unlike younger women who are relatively youthful when they divorce, one out of five women is caring for an ailing parent or mourning the death of a parent at the same time she loses her husband. She is doubly distressed. She must help her children—and herself—cope with the death of their grandparent (her parent) *and* the death of the marriage.

Maternal Guilt

While sixty-five percent of the mid-life women in the study believe divorce benefits their children, seven out of ten are also concerned about how divorce affects their children. This is not surprising; some might wonder why all women aren't worried. The truth is, in many divorces children are—inadvertently or purposely—put into positions of choosing sides. This tug-of-war is apparent in a number of scenarios, but no matter which one was played out, it's the *mothers* who usually felt guilty.

When the father leaves: Maggie Prince was relieved when her husband left, but, like many women, she was worried about how she would fare as a single parent and how the children, aged four and five, would take the news. She felt so guilty, in fact, that she tried to "protect" her children by not telling them! "Dean and I were separated for six months before the kids knew. I made him come over every night after work and play with them until they went to bed, which was at seven-thirty, so it wasn't that hard. When I finally told them, they both cried. For a long time they kept asking me questions like 'Why doesn't Daddy live here anymore?' "

Over the following years, notes Maggie, "The hardest part was coping with them blaming me for this terrible situation and helping them understand why their father and I had to divorce. I was very careful not to put their father down by expressing any of my bad feelings about him to them," says Maggie. When Maggie and the kids had to move, it made matters more difficult. "It was a terrible adjustment, because I constantly had to find new baby-sitters, which was upsetting to them and me."

(It's worth mentioning that although having such young children at the time of separation was rare among the women in the study, this may be a trend in the future. Many women now delay motherhood well into their thirties or forties. If they get divorced, they will have children younger than those of the women in the "Divorce Over 40" study.)

When the mother leaves: Even when it is her choice, guilt is especially lethal when a woman surrenders custody of the children to her ex-husband. She worries that her children will never understand and will blame her for the breakup of the marriage. Not only has she "broken" her family, she has abandoned it.

Debby Black's two daughters, fourteen and fifteen when she left, were "devastated." She tried to explain that she wanted them to stay with their father because she didn't want to disrupt their lives, their proximity to school. "I had talked to them about it, but he was screaming at the same time," recalls Debby. "So they were hearing me say, 'I need some space for me,' and 'Don't worry—I'll be close by,' while he was yelling, 'She's leaving us! She's leaving!' They got angrier and angrier. How dare I break up their happy family!"

Debby literally paid for her guilt, a situation we saw replicated for other interviewees who left their children. They walk out of the marriage with little more than the clothes on their backs. Debby even paid for a housekeeper "So that my kids would not have to clean house."

When children have divided loyalties: Marilyn Hauptman moved out of her husband's bedroom, into the basement, and finally left the house when her daughters were seventeen and fifteen, and her son eleven. "I knew he would fight me for custody, and I thought that would have done more damage to the kids." She never asked her children to choose. "I think it is a cruel thing for parents to say, 'Who do you want to live with?' "

Vera Castro's children's loyalties split along gender lines, and they let her know in no uncertain terms what they thought of her decision to divorce their father. "My sons had a rough time, saying that I had abandoned the family, that I wasn't Mom anymore. One son commented that he didn't know what was going to happen at Christmas and Easter. It just wasn't fair that he had all these houses to go to." Quite the opposite, her daughters were supportive and "handled it well."

When the couple lives in a small community: "The hardest part of the first year was the lack of support from married friends and the feeling that the gossip would never die down," admits Paula Oslow, who had lived in the same community for seventeen of the twenty-one years she was married. As their house-of-cards marriage was collapsing her husband accused her of having an affair. "It was ridiculous, but the guy went berserk, and said that he wanted to let all our friends know about it." Ultimately, he made life so unbearable that Paula finally sat her seventeen-year-old son down and told him, "It's really me who needs to leave." Her older child, a daughter, was away at college.

Paula had always been involved in the community—on the school board, supporting the school teams, Girls Scouts, teaching Sunday school—and she tried to remain active after she left her husband, too. "But then my son called me and said he didn't want me to come to the basketball games anymore. Weeks later, I finally talked to one of the coaches to find out what was going on. Apparently, his teammates were saying that I was not married anymore, and I was hanging out with the coaches," says Paula, recalling the hurt. "I knew that at some point he would come to understand me—which he has—but it was very traumatic. All I could think about was that my son was rejecting me."

A Developmental Prescription for Change

In each of the above cases, the factor that eased the loneliness and maternal guilt and changed the children's attitudes toward their mother was her personal growth. "The hardest part was for me to stop trying to get my son on my side," admits Paula Oslow, who realized that when she walked out on her marriage, she was sorely lacking in survival skills. She immediately had to take steps to make herself financially solvent and socially independent. "When I finally started concentrating on getting my own life together and resigned myself to the situation, a new relationship developed. My son and I are close now."

The conclusion is inescapable: *when a woman becomes autonomous, her relationships with her children change.* A woman who is sure of her identity doesn't have to prove anything. She doesn't tug at children to choose sides, lean on them, or inappropriately share with them her fears and insecurities—pitfalls for many newly divorced women. In short, she doesn't need to use her children, because she can stand up on her own. And no matter how rebellious, manipulative, guilt-provoking, or angry her child becomes after divorce, her strong sense of identity inoculates her against taking her children's feelings personally.

Many women in the study witnessed a transformation over time; as they changed, relationships with their children changed. In Irene Presto's case, her relationship with her son was the barometer. "He had a hard time. He was very, very angry for years afterward. He would always throw up to me that I had said to the kids, 'Everything was going to be okay,' and it wasn't! Things got worse financially," recalls Irene, whose son and daughter were sixteen and fourteen respectively when she first separated.

Things got worse before they got better. Irene lived alone with her children; her ex saw them on weekends. "I was angry that Ted had freedom, and I didn't. Perhaps I wasn't there for my kids at first. It was a very hard time, and a very lonely time."

The conflict between mother and son escalated. "I didn't think I was going to survive him," admits Irene, who now knows that her real battle was not with her son—it was with her dependency. Looking back, she knows it was the feelings of abandonment and the suddenly-single life-style that troubled her. Seething at her husband and feeling quite desperate, every time her son balked, or asked her for something that she couldn't or wouldn't give him—be it permission to hang out at the mall or a new pair of high-tech basketball sneakers that she couldn't afford—his adolescent temper flared up. *And so did hers!* "I'd scream at him, 'You're just like your father!' "

The situation changed when Irene got her priorities straight. She eventually realized that Ted's ominous prophecy might be true—that she wouldn't find another man to support her. Rewinder that she was, Irene was forced to finally face her dependency. By allowing herself to experience the full range of her feelings, talking with other divorced women, and working on becoming financially self-sufficient, Irene began to rebuild her self-confidence and her relationship with her children.

"I made us have a family life. I went out of my way to do things with other divorced families, so my kids would know that they were not that different," she remarks. "Even with the loneliness and being alone and dealing with all that I had to do, I began to see how much I had grown. I was able to take care of myself."

Coincidentally, Irene could then hear her children without feeling guilty. She could let them know that the divorce was neither all Dad's fault nor all hers. She could step out of the defensive, self-centered posture that so many newly divorced women assume. And she was able to see that while her son might resemble her ex-husband in looks, the boy was a different person.

"My son and I learned how to communicate. I remember one day, in the heat of anger, I blurted out, 'You're just like your father.' He shot back with, 'But you *hate* my father!' Even though it wasn't the first time that happened, it was the first time I *heard* him." Irene could finally see her son as a separate person, because she was finally beginning to see herself as a separate person.

Early in the divorce process, women in the study often report, they are self-conscious about parenting alone. They try to compensate for their children's loss. They twist themselves inside and out, becoming overly solicitous or trying to provide "balance" to make up for an errant or missing father. Eventually, however, most realize that they don't have to be special to protect their children or to be good role models. They just have to be comfortable with who they are.

Two years into her divorce, the Mother's Day entry in her diary illustrates Lorraine Feldman's awakening. Understanding her own limitations, she lets go of her guilt. She can only be who she is; and that, in fact, is all her children need.

Mother's Day—5/10/81. It was a nice day.
I am a mother.
I was, I am, and I will be a special Mom.

I'm not super. I do not intend to be.
I care deeply for my children.
I am honest with them, and I love them deeply.

In contrast, if a woman doesn't feel up to the task of taking care of herself, if, deep inside, *she* feels like a homeless child, it's hardly reasonable to expect her to feel confident about her ability to be a single parent. "Not having the support of a husband seems to weaken my role as mother when there is no one there to back me up and support me in interactions with the children," fears Christine Moss after less than a year of solo parenting. "With all this stuff being dumped on me, I often feel that I'm losing control of the kids."

When fifteen-year-old Jerry doesn't get in until four in the morning, Christine says he becomes defensive when she tries to reprimand him. "Jerry feels that he can do whatever he wants. If I tell his father, he'll say that he'll talk to the boy, but I still have the burden of disciplining the boy on a daily basis."

The survey shows that personal independence enables a woman to become a responsible parent who can set limits for her children. The farther Christine gets from the divorce experience, probably the more she will begin to trust her own judgment and the less she will rely on her ex-husband. For most women it takes at least a year for this shift to begin to occur and three to five years for a profound transformation.

Support: A Two-Way Street

Despite a mother's growth, some adolescents and young adults remain ambivalent about accepting their mother in new roles. "I have changed," announces a survey respondent in her mid-fifties. "Some of those changes have been difficult for my children to accept. Their mother, who used to fix big Sunday dinners in polyester slacks and was always available to baby-sit, now spends weekends at the lake with a man. I try to protect their image of the Virgin Mary, but they also have to give me some slack!"

Regardless of how old they are, children's expectations of what a mother should be frequently don't fit with the new picture— Mom dating, engaging in new activities, acting different from her usual milk-and-cookies self. That is not to say that children don't have wavering feelings about their fathers too. But father ambivalence is different, because in most families it's still Mom who wipes kids' noses and lays out their school clothes the night before.

Because children are indoctrinated by the culture too, such expectations may be there even when Mom doesn't fit the traditional mold, as was often the case with our Rewinders. "I didn't bake them cookies. I gave them ten bucks to go buy them," says Debby Black of her daughters. Now thirty and thirty-one, "the girls" are still smarting, as Debby discovered when she decided to go to Europe a few years ago.

"I had saved enough money to afford not to work for a while. I had no idea how long I was going to be away, so I said to the girls, 'I could be gone for one month, two months, three months—I don't know.' I stayed six. The kids were devastated and, I think, shocked by my behavior."

Debby acknowledges, "I think they're somewhat proud about what I've accomplished, and they let me know by saying, 'Most people give their children a ticket to visit their parents in Florida, but when we have children, we'll have to buy them a Eurail pass to find their grandmother!' They say it with a sense of pride, but I think to some degree they're also giving me a little dig."

Debby's daughters are in the minority. Based on the findings, most children are, in fact, more encouraging of than ambivalent about their "new" mother, especially when they see Mom thriving and being independent. They're grateful that they don't have to worry about their mother or take care of her. In most cases, the support washes both ways: the mothers bolster their kids' growth, and, in turn, their children reinforce their mothers' development.

Moreover, children are motivated by their mother's making a conscious attempt to prevent the divorce from splintering the family; their cooperation and backing help solidify the sense of family unity. "One's family need not be destroyed. My four children are closer now than they ever were," writes a survey respondent. "We are a very close family—just without a father. If you have the courage and fortitude, you can make your family a strong one. There are many days of loneliness, but keep in mind that your children love you."

On the questionnaire, when asked who championed them during the crisis, six out of ten women five years past the divorce answer, "my children." In interviews, too, we heard this theme expressed. Maggie Prince asserts, "My greatest source of support and comfort in my life are my children." Paula Oslow's married daughter, then twenty-two, became her "immediate support," often accompanying her mother on trips and attending events that Paula "always wanted to but couldn't because my husband would never go." And Marilyn Hauptman's college-age daughter brought her mother to a fraternity party over parents' weekend. "I told her it was the biggest compliment she could have given me!"

"Thank God for my children!" exclaims a grateful Lorraine Feldman in her diary when she recounts their support on the night her husband announced over a Sunday night take-out dinner, "Guys, I have something heavy to tell you. I have a dream for the future, and my dream doesn't include your mother."

The room was completely silent, recalls Lorraine, chronicling the heartbreaking moment. Her three children were then in their late teens and early twenties.

> It was heavy, but I knew the kids had known. It was a final step into reality. They, too, had their "clicks," storing a little of this and that into the recesses of their minds. And they were glad it was out in the open. Now their inner doubt and inner pains were in the open, and they now longer had to carry their secrets.

At the end of the several-page entry about each of her children's individual reactions to her ex-husband's announcement, Lorraine sums up her feelings: "My children are more mature than I suspected. They will be my future strength and comfort."

Women Without Children

Since one out of ten women in the study didn't have children —by choice or because they were unable to—we would be remiss if we didn't address mid-life women who are divorced and childless. Do they have fewer avenues of support after divorce? Not according to the survey. Not surprisingly, women without children generally have had more time and energy to develop careers or to invest in interests and activities outside marriage than women with kids.

Gisella Morgan, who had no children, was easily able to segue into single life. Gisella "always worked" during her marriage. By the time she got divorced, she had changed careers several times. Being without a husband naturally had a great impact on her life, but Gisella, a Player, was also prepared. "Of course, I lost the status at first—I was no longer the doctor's wife. But I always had my own life too."

Often, women like Gisella create alternate forms of "family," especially if they don't have large families of origin. (Her family is still in her native Germany.) Sometimes a favorite niece or nephew or a best friend's child may become a kind of surrogate child for a childless woman, which can develop into a very gratifying and supportive relationship. After all, the woman gains an intimate and tender relationship with a child, without the problems of day-to-day parenting!

"The Father of My Children"

The greatest gift a divorced woman can give her children is to call a truce and stop the war. "We worked very hard to remain friends," writes a respondent who calls her friendship with her ex-husband "unusual." On one hand, her perception is correct: friendship may be impossible after a divorce. On the other hand, the gap between acrimony and friendship spans a continuum. We see increasing evidence that many women are aware of the importance of being at least civil to an ex-spouse, motivated by the proverbial bottom line, as this woman expresses it: "It is much better for the kids. I still care for him and want the best for him, but I don't love him and can't live with him."

Part of the forgiveness process is recognizing the implication of such a long shared history. Even after divorce, the couple continues to be parents of their children and always will be. "I taught my children to love their father no matter what difficulties he and I had in our marriage. We have already attended our son's wedding together, and we managed to be nice to each other in public," remarks Joann Cress.

Based on our findings, a cease-fire happens only when a woman can come to grips with her part in the dissolution of the marriage. Evelyn Dorrin recaps what many women who reach the point of forgiving the marriage ultimately feel: "I wonder sometimes if the person I have become could have somehow existed while I was in that marriage—and, if so, would I have been divorced today? I can't really envision being married to the guy again, nor can I even imagine how life might be with him. But there was and is so much history. He was not really a bastard. And he is the father of my two terrific children. I never thought he'd leave me, and I lived my life with him fully when we were together."

Ask any marriage counselor: both partners' behavior plays an important role in ending the marriage. Even a woman who is left is not a "victim." And when she begins to understand this basic axiom and concentrates on herself instead of her ex-spouse, her perception of him changes. She is able to let go of the anger.

Among women divorced at least a year or more, we observed an unmistakable pattern: women in the process of rediscovery allow feelings of increased self-esteem to fill the holes and the hurt. In effect, they switch their focus. The ex-spouse simply becomes "the father of the children." How he acts—or doesn't act—loses its former power to determine her behavior. Instead, these women look at what they can do in their own lives.

Ten years after the fact, Fran Sargent is completely at peace with her past. "When I first got divorced, I used to worry about what would happen at holidays or family events," she confesses. But Fran has since coproduced a number of milestone events for their children with her ex-husband: birthday parties, high school and college graduations. "I certainly don't worry anymore about who's going to walk down the aisle at the children's weddings. We'll always be their parents, no matter what."

When Resolution Is Not Possible: Severing the Bonds

Regrettably, the tug-of-war sometimes continues, and feelings of rancor persist. Sometimes, a woman simply can't bear the pain of repeated contact with her ex. One survey respondent, for example, describes an on-again, off-again separation that finally ends when she files for divorce. "In five months, he came again and told me that he was wrong, and that I should postpone the divorce. I decided I wouldn't stop the proceedings but agreed to be his friend. It didn't work," she reports. "It was too painful, to have him come in and out of my life. I don't wish to see or talk to him."

Disagreements with an ex-husband can also be fueled by a woman's perception that her children are not being treated well or adequately supported by their fathers. Or, a woman purposely keeps away from her ex, fearing that contact with an abusive spouse will continue to poison the family.

Patsy Marconi is happily removed from her coarse and insulting ex-husband, but the separation may have come too late to salvage her children's low self-esteem. "This is very scary. They say children who come from abusive homes end up doing the same thing or seeking out similar kinds of relationships. But I never thought a daughter of mine would do that—especially after all she saw!" Patsy says that eighteen-year-old Angie "hooked up with this guy who is just like her father—he's controlling, he undermines her, he's abusive! She doesn't see it, but Angie is doing exactly what I did."

An armistice with an ex, or at least a redefinition of the relationship, also may not possible because of the man's reaction. "I have seen Mike on several occasions, both of which were terrible," reports Debby Black. "Whenever I meet him, he cordially shakes my hand—say, at a funeral or a college graduation. One time, I took my daughter to the emergency room, and he met us there. But he doesn't communicate. He won't talk to me."

In much the same way, Lorraine Feldman's ex-husband has steadfastly refused to mend the fences between them. Her last attempt took place at their son's graduation—eight years after the divorce. By then, Marvin's girlfriend had become his wife, and Lorraine had come a long way. She had begun to earn a comfortable living selling real estate; she had many friends and a full, active social life. The man she was dating at the time accompanied her to the graduation. Lorraine, who no longer saw herself as a victim, was ready to put the animosity behind her.

"After the ceremony, I walked up behind Marvin and put my hand on his shoulder and said, 'Congratulations, Marv. I guess we must have done *something* right!' He just kept walking!" remembers a still-astonished Lorraine. "He muttered something, like 'Congratulations,' but he just kept walking, that bastard!"

Lorraine has since stopped trying to figure out Marvin. "For eight years, I talked to a wall. Then I realized, it's over. I will never get through to this man. I'll never know the answer. I'm one of those people who likes to put things to bed, but I guess

I'll never understand his anger. Maybe he's furious because I didn't curl up and die when he left me!"

This is a vital point: a women can continue to grow despite vestiges of anger and resentment toward her ex, as long as it doesn't poison, embitter, or paralyze her. Nowadays, Lorraine puts all her energies into herself. She can withstand Marvin's rejection and get on with her life in spite of it.

It's a Family Affair

It's not just the specter of the ex-spouse's judgment that haunts a newly single divorced woman—it's often the whole family. Not surprisingly, nearly a third of women express concern about family criticism. Divorce reverberates up and down the generations, especially for mid-life women whose children are often old enough to have children of their own. Hence, a woman's parents may worry about the effects of the trauma on their grandchildren, as well as its impact on their divorced daughter.

Some mothers and fathers are supportive; they feel that their daughter is bettering her life by getting divorced. "My parents thought my first husband was a nice guy, but they didn't think he was loving and tender nor that he would want a family," recalls Bonnie Lenza, who disregarded the hints her parents dropped when she was first engaged. As it turned out, they were right. Though her father had died by the time Bonnie got divorced, her mother was right there. "My Mom was very glad, and she offered to help me in any way. My whole family was supportive."

Debby Black's mother applauded her determination. "You are the person I used to know," she told Debby after her divorce. And when she later learned that her divorced daughter had decided to "wing it" through Europe for a few months, she told Debby, "This is who you were when I was raising you!"

Melanie Spade, whose parents helped out with money, acknowledges, "I had my mother and father behind me. They didn't have a lot, but they would never have let me sink!" Florence Hacker is also depending on her parents to finance the initial period of her divorce. They are helping her keep up the mortgage payments so she won't lose her house; and they loaned her money for the lawyer's fee, as did Fran Sargent's father. "The lawyer wanted a five thousand dollar retainer. I didn't have that kind of money," admits Fran.

Many women *expect* support from their fathers; they are less optimistic about getting their mothers' blessings. While it's dangerous to generalize, parents' ability to provide support is frequently affected by their gender perspective. Perhaps because fathers do not identify with "women's roles," they may be more unconditionally accepting of their daughter's life-style changes than mothers who expect daughters to follow in their footsteps. Also, as men grow older and their interest in work and career diminishes, they seem to have an increased capacity to nurture family relations.

Caroline Breed, who calls her father "my safety net," says that in the later years of his life, her father inspired and cheered her on, in ways that he didn't when she was younger. "He had a very fifties mentality when I was growing up: the man goes out to make the money, and the woman takes care of the emotional needs. At the same time, he had no sons, so he had no one to project his male dreams onto." After her divorce, says Caroline, her dad helped her out financially too.

"I could write a book about my father!" Anne Garner exclaims about her dad—a lawyer who worked his way through college, a great writer, a commanding presence in her life who was always supportive of her, even when she got divorced. Conversely, her mother was devastated. Somehow, Anne's mother feared that she must not have done her job correctly to have a daughter who defected from the marital fold. Angry and disappointed, Anne's mother didn't try to hide her feelings. "Even to this day, my mother says, 'You could have stayed.' "

Witness how the "little girl" in Anne remembers her father in this excerpt from "Reflections in Mahogany," a poem she wrote to commemorate him.

Oh, Papa, it's finally happened
You slipped away quietly in death
As you quietly lived life.
A steady, somber, shy man.
Captive amid the garrulous magpies of the world.

I am now a fatherless child.
The "Read me a story, Daddy," long gone.

227

OUR TURN

"Can I borrow the car, Pop?" just an echo.
"Straight A's, Dad," just a memory.

It's not that I will never see you again
Or that I consign you to the quiet earth
Or that your leaving leaves a void in me
Never felt before.

It's just that with you gone,
I will never again be

                                    your little girl.

Compared to how she felt about her dad, that same "little girl" in Anne's poem entitled "Mama" is angry about the tradition of self-sacrifice that so many mothers conferred on their daughter.

> Quick kiss on a parchment cheek
> A hug that lasts too long
> Making me squirm to escape.
>
> I've never really known you, Mama,
> The real you, all this time.
> You've always been there,
> Yet, like strangers, we say
> What's new? How are the kids?
> Thanks for the rice pudding.
> Give my love to Dad.
>
> I know you'd forgive me if you knew.
> You've forgiven me all else,
> And I thank you for that.
> I only wish I could forgive you,
> Mama, for being you,
> Because it has been so hard for me
> To be your little girl.

Many other women in the study found their mothers to be harshly critical. Jody Burke remembers, "My mother had the classic words. She told me, 'You must have done something terribly wrong.'" Other mothers implied, "You made your bed; now lie in it . . . I did." Conversely, Paula Oslow's mother found fault with her daughter for just the opposite reason: "I did not get any emotional support from my mother, who had been

228

divorced for years. She thought that I should have stayed married, because she didn't!"

In the face of such parental censure, a woman needs a strong sense of identity to fend off family negativity and judgment. However, she also needs to at least *hear* the criticism, because her ideas about marriage and gender roles have been "cooked" in the family crucible over the years. They led her to the alter; and they influence her feelings about divorce.

Bear in mind, too, that so many of these women went from parents to husband. Living an independent life-style was never part of their worldview. Compounding the problem, many of them were unable to formulate separate identities in the context of their marriages. Hence, in a developmental sense, they were still looking for Mom and Dad's approval when they got divorced.

A woman who is still yearning for her parents' recognition, will naturally experience their criticism as a harsh, rejecting slap in the face. However, by no longer conceiving of her identity as that of a child but as that of an adult, a divorced woman can shift the balance.

Rediscovery is a gradual and strenuous process. A woman doesn't wake up one morning with a new, improved identity, able to slay all the dragons of her past in one fell swoop! Typically, it takes at least two years after divorce for her to build up an arsenal of inner resources. She is then fortified with her own insights and her own aspirations—her true self. She is independent. And, in not so many words, she can finally say to a faultfinding parent, "I hear your concerns, and I thank you for caring about me. I know that you *believe* that you know what's best—but only I know what's right for *me.*"

The Ex-Family

Sadly, members of the ex-spouse's family often divorce themselves not only from their ex-daughter-in-law but also from the children. This puts further strain on a divorcing mother, who must reformulate her "new" family without the support of an extended family on both sides:

"My ex-husband's family—his parents, his sisters and their spouses—totally abandoned my children as soon as we separated," notes one survey respondent. "This was especially devastating as

I am an only child, so there are no aunts and uncles on my side. I believe this put additional pressure on my parents and me."

Lorraine Feldman didn't worry about her children losing the grandparents, because her ex-husband's large extended family stayed in touch with them after divorce; she bemoaned her own loss. In her diary, Lorraine fondly recalls how Marvin's family welcomed her.

> When we met so many years ago, I was introduced to your side of the family. I loved your family. Your aunts and uncles, cousins and friends, made me feel at home with them, as my family and friends welcomed you. Your family is now my family.

As the divorce drags on, Lorraine can't fathom her husband's coldness. "He doesn't give a damn about my family, but I am very wrapped up in his," she writes when she finds out that Marvin's father is ill and her ex-husband hadn't bothered to inform her. And when Marvin's father dies a year later, she writes, "I will miss him dearly. I have lost a friend and confidant."

She is not alone. Remember that many of these women's marriages span twenty or thirty years. Understandably, ties to their ex-families are important. Moreover, when they were courting, many women were initially as drawn to their young suitors' parents and family as they were to their husbands-to-be!

The Legacy of the Past: What They Tell Their Children

Women who reclaim their own lives have no regrets; they can look back without anger, forgiving their ex-husbands, their families—and themselves. This is even true in cases where there are lingering hostilities on the part of the ex-spouse or when children still haven't fully accepted the reality of their mother's life today.

"There are times that I'm lonely, times that I have the feeling that I'd like the whole family around," admits Debby Black. "But I take care of myself when it comes to Passover or Christmas or Thanksgiving, and I take care of myself because I know how to do it now. I didn't always know how. I love the old memories, I cherish them. I've probably blocked out most of the bad times."

The study indicates that when a woman forges a strong sense

of her own identity, the benefits are apparent in many aspects of her life. Five years after divorce, eighty-four percent feel positive about themselves. Of women who perceive divorce as a "better situation" for their children, seventy-seven percent also have improved relationships with their children; the majority foster better relationships with their ex-spouses, their own parents, and their siblings as well.

Statistics notwithstanding, most revealing of their personal growth are the kinds of messages these women, who have blossomed into self-assured Players, impart to their children. Most often, they bequeath a legacy of empowerment.

"The reason she is a lawyer and not moving to the country with a white picket fence is me," boasts Melanie Spade, referring to her stepdaughter. Melanie, forty-six and childless at the time of her second marriage, to a widower, became an instant mother to his five children. "The youngest was twelve, and she lived with us. She needed a mother desperately. She was wonderful. She needed me as much as I needed her."

Caroline Breed recognizes that knowing what she wanted for her children motivated her to strive for independence. Filling in the gaps in her own growth has helped her see that her daughters and sons will need different strengths to survive adulthood, different pieces of the developmental pie. "I always hoped that my son would become self-sufficient—to be able to do laundry, cook for himself—because I wanted him to choose a wife, not because he needed someone to take care of him, but because he wanted someone to *be* with."

As for her daughters, Caroline wants them to learn how to support themselves. "I don't want them in dependent relationships, where they'd have to stay with some man because they can't take care of themselves," insists the woman who, at first, was so lacking in survival skills she couldn't even fill out the renewal form for her driver's license!

When all is said and done, these Players relegate the past to its proper perspective. Evelyn Dorrin concedes, "I have no regrets. Nothing lasts forever—that's what I discovered from this divorce. I am very pleased and proud of both my children. The fact that I'm divorced but I still communicate with my ex-husband makes me feel good too. Divorce is a big trauma for the children; regardless of their age, it's very difficult."

Evelyn, whose sons are now thirty and thirty-four, speaks for many women when she says, "I like to think of myself as a good role model for my children. I do feel that I am the most important person—certainly not perfect, but if I have to do something, I do it. I may get frightened, but I do it. I am making up for all those years . . ."

When Evelyn thinks back to her girlhood, she knows she was, like most of her peers, "programmed" to get married and have kids. But she never wanted a marriage like her parents'. "My father made it very clear that he was the king. The more I observed, the more I said to myself, 'Hey! No way!' "

The young Evelyn Dorrin believed marriage should be a partnership, but hers never quite fit the bill. After her divorce, nearly thirty years later, she is finally becoming the person she was meant to be. "This idea of getting through my divorce was traumatic, but it also made a whole lot of growth occur. I guess I was a late developer—the potential was always there. And I just had to bring it out."

She is also struck by an irony: "I used to think of my mother as a very selfish woman—she always came first. At a young age, I interpreted her attitude differently, but now, being in my fifties and having children of my own, I have news for you: I know *I* come first!"

9

Do as We Say, Not as We Did:
Lessons from Players'
Pocketbooks

I was angry with myself for not gaining job skills, for believing a husband
when he said he would always be there to take care of me, and for being
so ill-informed about financial matters. I've added up the investments of
my life: one husband—now gone; four kids—now grown; and a $300,000
house—too expensive to keep. The legal system assumed that after thirty
years, with no marketable skills and a dusty degree from a junior college,
I could run out and be gainfully employed. I didn't even have a credit
card in my own name. I abdicated my life to another person, and now I
feel like I have to start over. Don't make the same mistakes I did!

—Survey respondent, answering: "What would be the most important
advice you would give a woman going through a divorce and building
a new life?"

$$\Diamond$$

From Awesome to Awful . . . and Back

Caroline Breed is not fabulously wealthy these days. Like most
women in the study who live at less than half of their former
standard of living, her postdivorce life-style doesn't come close
to the opulence she enjoyed as a married woman. But Caroline
became a Player. Instead of despairing at her situation, she
tapped her inner resources and learned to stand on her own.

Five years after her divorce, Caroline is working as a counselor
for the Displaced Homemakers Network, a national organization
that provides vocational counseling and job-placement services
for divorced women and widows. "I think probably ninety-five
percent of the women who come here are one paycheck away
from the street—and, until recently, that included *me*," maintains
Caroline. "We've all gone through life changes that lead to
tremendous growth, but money is a problem. It's hard to catch
up with twenty years of not building a career."

Caroline Breed's rocky road to financial security makes her a

233

wonderful role model for other divorced women who must rediscover themselves and learn how to manage their finances. "These women have a great deal of anxiety about what's in front of them."

With good reason. The "Divorce Over 40" study confirms that economic recovery after divorce is an uphill battle. Individual success stories notwithstanding, the overall statistics for most women are quite grim: almost two thirds are forced out of the family home; ninety-three percent receive no money for job training; three-quarters get no compensation for their years as homemakers; and eighty-five percent are deprived of their husbands' health and pension plans. Not surprisingly, eighty-nine percent admit to not having any long-term financial goals. They probably feel that they have nothing to invest in their futures!

"My life-style went from awesome to awful! It was a mess!" admits Caroline. Gone was the six-figure income she enjoyed as Mrs. Thomas Breed and, with it, the $350,000 home, the swimming pool, the chic parties, the private planes. A jet-setter with clipped wings, Caroline was devastated at first. "I couldn't imagine how I was going to manage on one thousand dollars a month in alimony and three hundred dollars a month in child support," she admits.

"I remember one day in my car, waiting for a red light to change, I started worrying, 'I've got to pay the college bills, one of the kids needs glasses, and I need a new crown on my tooth.' I just panicked for a few minutes. But then I said to myself, 'Stop it! Everything is okay today. You've got a good meal on the table, a nice home to live in, a job—you have everything you need today. Just take care of today.' "

Caroline now admonishes other women to have a similar perspective. "You have to stop negative self-talk. Say positive things to yourself, out loud if necessary, until you get into the mental habit. Otherwise, it will drag you down. Write notes to yourself if you have to and put them on the refrigerator. The point is, you've got to hold a vision out in front of you. When you start seeing yourself wherever you want to be, it will happen."

A Slow Motion in her marriage, Caroline bolstered her confidence with a gradually rising sense of independence that began when she went back to college. "About halfway through, I realized that getting a degree was not just for fun, as I had originally thought—it was going to be *essential.*" As it turned out, Caroline's last exam fell on the day her husband left.

Around that same time, Caroline's mother died, so she decided to relocate to Florida, where her dad was living. "My father was very supportive. And I had other family there." Obviously, the backing of her family helped Caroline and so did the fact that Tom sent her alimony and child-support payments "like clockwork." Most important, Caroline had already learned an important lesson: she could not, and would not, depend on Daddy or her ex for the rest of her life.

"I guess I had foresight too: I sat down with a pen and a paper and said, 'In order to overcome the twelve-thousand-dollar-a-year decrease when my alimony discontinues in 1995, here is what I need to be making—in three years, four years, five years, and so on.'" Caroline's first job was an entry-level position at a social service agency. She was making $12,000 a year. "I was devastated at the pay."

Over the next four years, Caroline was promoted twice. "I knew basically that I had to double my income in eight years, and I have already done that. I'll make another jump in the next year to thirty-two thousand dollars and plan to be completely self-supporting," she reports four years after her divorce.

"Quite frankly, I've been smart enough to change jobs enough times and work real hard to get where I'm going—that's half planning and half luck! You have to be really ready to take advantage of every opportunity and recognize them when they come—if they come, that's the luck part. They came for me, but you can be sure, I was looking for them!"

The Case of the Disappearing Nest Eggs

Not all women have Caroline Breed's luck or her ability to conceive a financial game plan immediately after their divorce. The majority take longer to move past the fear; and a few never do. However, a woman is not truly autonomous if she still depends on others to pay her way. For most women in the study, however, the personal-responsibility slice of developmental pie, of which financial independence is an important part, is the toughest to swallow and digest.

In the long run, an inability to become financially self-sufficient also compromises whatever growth a woman has attained in other sections of the pie. For example, thirty-eight percent of women say that a lack of money prohibits them from making friends after divorce, which certainly cuts into their social life; seventy-eight percent cited a lack of money as the hardest part of being single. Those worries undoubtedly drag women down emotionally, as well.

A lump-sum divorce settlement can certainly help a woman readjust to her new life more quickly—but that's not always the case. If a woman doesn't see herself as capable and independent, and is therefore not developmentally ready to manage her own finances, the money tends to slip through her fingers. In short, it's not her bank balance that determines her survival; it's her attitude toward it.

"I wish I had socked away even a quarter of my settlement," laments Rewinder Fran Sargent, who was awarded over $300,000 in a lump sum. Though Fran's divorce settlement was far and above in the top range among women in the study, no amount of money would have been enough to make her feel secure. "I kept saying to everyone around me, 'I really need to talk to a financial adviser.' I knew that you don't just leave that kind of money lying around in a bank."

Despite her resolve, Fran, a free-lance graphic designer always more in touch with the arts than with business, was no different from the vast majority of women in the study. Nearly two-thirds worked outside the home, averaging between six and ten years on the job at the time of the divorce proceedings, so one could not classify the majority as homemakers. From the interviews it is clear, nevertheless, that many worked not to support themselves, but to ease their boredom or to escape the strains of the marriage. Like Fran, who made only a fraction of her husband's income, they considered their earnings "pin money" and used it "for the extras." In fact, although twenty-eight percent were professionals and twelve percent worked at the managerial level, it was husbands who had the *careers;* wives merely held *jobs.*

"I paid the household bills and wrote all the checks, but I never really knew what we were worth. I never asked! I signed the joint tax returns, but I didn't read them." Fran's husband, an investment banker, regularly lost large sums of money. "But he always seemed to be able to make it back, so *I* never worried. I'd have to say it was very much like living with my father: the money was just always there."

Fran never considered herself as "sheltered" as other women she knew, who virtually ignored family finances and handed over paychecks to their husbands. In many respects, however, she was no different from the six out of ten survey respondents who never made major financial decisions prior to divorce, the eight out of ten who had no investment knowledge, or the sixty-five percent who didn't understand or know how to do their taxes.

After her divorce, just *thinking* about managing her money made Fran feel "like a kid." She felt embarrassed and ashamed, afraid to ask anyone for help. Because she had always relegated money management to the men in her life, she doubted her ability to even *choose* a competent financial adviser. How would she assess the advice? "I didn't trust anyone. You hear stories about women turning over their money to so-called advisers who either steal it or invest it unwisely. Then poof—it's gone!"

Fran was making about $30,000—hardly enough to support the $200,000 Tudor home she bought in Evanston, Illinois. Instead of getting advice about what she could afford on her suddenly-single income, Fran assumed that she could "coast" on the nearly $100,000 she had left over from her settlement. It was quite a sizable nest egg.

Over the next several years, Fran discovered how wrong she was. "It sounds like a lot, but you can't believe how fast you can spend that amount of money—a little here, a little there—especially if your income just covers the mortgage!" Fran continued to live and spend money the way she did during marriage, paying for her new home, taking her children on expensive vacations. "I had to constantly subsidize myself by dipping into my savings." A financial Armageddon was inevitable.

Fran, like most women, was never an adult when it came to money. After her divorce, rather than face the fact that she was no longer Daddy's little girl—or her husband's—she admits, "I was paralyzed. And for a long time I deluded myself into believing that I wasn't in trouble. Things *looked* good in my life—I had a great house, money in the bank, a social life, and the divorce was something I wanted—so I was fine emotionally . . . until reality hit, that is!"

Amy Brown's nest egg, which was considerably smaller than

Fran's, all but disappeared too, but for another reason common to the women in the study: she felt she owed something to her children. "I got a lump sum from my husband—fifteen thousand dollars, which was a lot of money for us. He did right by me—but that's probably because he felt guilty about having a girl-friend," maintains Amy.

A year or so after her divorce, Amy's oldest daughter got engaged. "What with my ex-husband running around like a playboy, he just wasn't very interested in being a father. I felt badly for all of the children, so I tried to make up for what he was doing."

Amy spent seven thousand dollars on her daughter's wedding. "It made her so happy. I thought it was the least I could do." Then her nineteen-year-old son wanted a car. "How could I not help him out too—especially after I had spent so much on the wedding?"

Disregarding her own needs entirely and never once question-ing what she might require in the future, Amy, a Pauser during her marriage, was just beginning to fill in the social and emotional gaps. She didn't even consider her financial identity. In the end, she dissipated the bulk of her settlement by "paying back" her children for the trauma of a divorce that she never wanted in the first place! At least, Amy managed to find work as a recep-tionist at a lumber company. She now makes $27,000 a year. But it's unlikely that she'll ever replenish her nest egg.

The shock of reality hits hard. "If I had some of that money now, I would use it to invest in myself—go back to school, or at least take some courses," Amy laments. It's no mere coincidence that, for the first time since her divorce, Amy, who is now forty-five, is finally beginning to think about what *she* wants out of life. "That money could have been my way out, but I was so focused on my children, I couldn't think of other options."

No doubt, a woman who receives an ample divorce settlement is certainly better off initially than a woman who doesn't, since she has a substantial foundation on which to build an economic base. However, women like Fran and Amy share the same cultural mindset as their less fortunate counterparts: they were brought up to think of themselves as commodities, not breadwinners. "Some man will take care of you if you please him and bear his children" was the message of the day.

Furthermore, when it comes to learning new financial skills after divorce, the majority of women usually fly by the seat of their pants: sixty-nine percent admit that they use the trial-and-error method to make money decisions—an immature and irresponsible strategy at best. Error is more common than success.

Kate McKinley, one of our interviewees, is now a financial consultant who makes $60 an hour telling other people—women *and* men—how to spend money. Typically, she advises clients to put money into different types of investments, with varying degrees of risk—some quite conservative, others riskier but with potential for growth. "It's never good to have all your money in one place."

Some clients don't heed Kate's warnings—like one divorced woman who ended up with a $100,000 settlement. The woman never returned for a second appointment; Kate wasn't surprised, especially when she heard from a mutual acquaintance that the woman had squandered her money. Kate has seen the same pattern before in other newly divorced women—and in men who are not accustomed to handling money. "She never had any money of her own. Before that, she lived like most people—from paycheck to paycheck. Because she didn't have any experience, she did what, according to the experts, most people do with lump sums of money: they spend it all in two years!"

Lack of experience is only one facet of the problem. Another mechanism is at work in many cases: procrastination and denial. In varying degrees, depending on how much of the developmental pie they've focused on, divorced women deal with money the way they handled problems in marriage—by sweeping them under the rug. No wonder ninety-five percent of our survey respondents advise other women to do as they say, not as they did. "Get job training so that you'll have an income," "Save for the future," or simply "Learn about money," are the most commonly offered pieces of advice from survey respondents—warnings to all women that marriage does not guarantee a happily-ever-after financial future.

Fear of Trying: More Cautionary Tales

Some women, particularly Rewinders, have more trouble than others dealing with the third piece of the pie. "I hadn't ever taken responsibility for myself. Even my immigrant refugee parents never forced me to take a *job!*" confesses Helga Gross. For a long time after her divorce, Helga saw no reason to look at her options in the work world. She was awarded the $150,000 beach house, and when she sold it, she invested part of the proceeds in the stock market. The balance, which the buyer paid out over the next ten years, netted Helga a monthly income of $800.

"I didn't worry about what I was going to *do*," admits Helga, who was then forty-eight. Eight hundred dollars a month was far less than she spent living in suburban Philadelphia, among her well-heeled cronies. But as a born-again hippie in New Mexico, that money went a long way. Besides, she was watching her money double in the stock market.

When the market crashed in 1989, so did Helga. "It made me realize that I was still looking for someone—or something—to take care of me. This time it was the stock market, and that failed me too!"

Helga admits, "I was like a teenager who didn't want to go out to look for a summer job. I just wanted to sit in my room and smoke pot and listen to rock and roll!" Because she was still collecting money from the sale of the summer house, Helga delayed the inevitable until a therapist made her grow up.

"I had about twenty-five thousand dollars in the bank, and I was telling my group how frightened I was about money. The therapist looked at me and said, 'You probably have more money than anyone in this room. The way I see it, you have a choice: you can be the kid who runs through every nickel before you face your situation—or, you can deal with it now. It's not money you're worried about; it's the idea of taking care of yourself that makes you panicky.' I knew he was right, and that really scared me."

A few weeks later, Helga was driving downtown. "For some reason—I can't explain it—I found myself parked in front of a paralegal school in Albuquerque. I went in to ask for information, and I left promising to send a check!"

"I fought it every step of the way. I'd say to myself, 'What am I doing here? All these people are assholes!' But I knew I would come out with something that I could *do*."

Looking back, Helga admits, "All of my money decisions have been emotional. Enrolling in paralegal school was not a rational decision, either. It was a lot of money to do the training—five or six thousand dollars. But because of how tight I am about spending money, as often as I wanted to quit, I couldn't give myself a good enough reason to throw that money away!"

Helga still doesn't love being a paralegal, but today her freelance business pays the bills. "What I do for a living isn't as important as my getting over the hump of facing that nobody else was going to take care of me. Some days it is still hard for me to force myself to make phone calls!" she admits. "But now I feel really good about getting my business to work and knowing that people depend on me," she acknowledges. "I guess it boils down to the fact that I'm finally taking care of my own ass!"

Unlike Helga, Rewinder Lisa Frazier had no cushion after her divorce. Her husband paid only $60 a week in child support and $20 in alimony; even in 1981 that didn't begin to cover her expenses: her rent alone was $1,000 a month. As a result, Lisa quickly dissipated the $18,000 settlement she received, her share of the profit on the house.

Still, Lisa was just as recalcitrant as Helga Gross when it came to supporting herself. Somehow, she *expected* that her financial needs would just be "taken care of." She *expected* that Jeff, her married air traffic controller, would leave his wife. Lisa *expected* to live like a princess.

As a result, she acted impetuously and never planned for contingencies—in much the same way as adolescents tend to attack problems. "I *trusted* Jeff. I moved out and got an apartment. I was supposed to move in with him and that never happened. That's how I came to be single."

In retrospect, Lisa knows, "Selling my house was the worst thing I ever did. I have not had a home of my own since then, and I probably never will. My son is furious about that. Now he wants to go live with his father! That is absolute heartbreak to deal with."

As we explained in Chapter Eight, problems with children can persist when a woman doesn't define her own identity. When she was first interviewed, Lisa, separated for seven years but not yet divorced, was worried about her fourteen-year-old son. She didn't realize that she was having trouble parenting her son because she was hardly acting like an adult herself! Eternally impractical and unwilling to settle for "just a job," she dabbled in one money-making scheme after another, never earning enough to support them.

Clinging to the image of herself as a "princess," Lisa delayed her own growing-up process and squelched her self-respect. Instead, she unwittingly projected what she needed onto her son. "I've been encouraging him to be more independent, like getting a job at Burger King and working nine to five. It would be great for his self-esteem." How ironic! What about *her* self-esteem?

At that time, Lisa recognized, "Money is the issue right now. It can get me a better car, can get my kid a tutor." Still, she had no respect for process. Like the headstrong Rewinder she was, Lisa Frazier wanted what she wanted *now*. Instead, she needed to get out there and do something with her life and to grow up!

Happily, at a follow-up interview, almost two years later, we noticed a critical difference. Realizing that a steady paycheck afforded her more stability than her pie-in-the sky notions of independence, at forty-two, Lisa finally got a job. "I'm using my skills and getting paid, which thrills me to no end. My income went up, and it changed my life entirely. It improved my self-esteem."

Lisa came to see that money represents power and respect in the real world. "I have a paycheck coming in—what a relief! I'm not so anxious, and I have much more patience with my son. I can be a better mother, because I have more to give from inside myself. I'm not threatened that I'm going to be homeless. I've had eight years of anxiety about that. I found out that I can survive anything. I am much more courageous than I ever thought."

Work: The Best Medicine

While many mid-life divorced women are twice disadvantaged, having to cope with the emotional trauma *and* seek work for the first time, the study highlights that they also gain an unexpected benefit: *the intrinsic value of working can heal even the deepest wounds.*

"I was a displaced homemaker at age fifty-three," offers Doreen McBride. "How I loathe that description. It conveys the image of a barbed-wire enclosure around a herd of displaced women!" Doreen, who put her architect husband thorough school and watched his career skyrocket over the years, was understandably bitter at first. "Twenty-five years of marriage vanished like smoke, because he found a young girlfriend." That was five years ago. Today, Doreen realizes how much good has come to her since.

"After brushing up on my typing at a nearby high school, I found a job at a local radio station as a typist. With encouragement and hard work, I'm now a production assistant—at my age! I feel reborn, although the rebirth was not without pain and depression and lots of mistakes. I'm older, but I'm also better and happier than I have ever been—for I've learned to stand alone."

Work enables a mid-life woman to see that she can rise to new challenges. She meets new people. She is exposed to new ideas. Most important, she can paint a new self-portrait.

"I feel so free after years of role-playing and being stage-managed by everyone but me," shares a forty-four-year-old survey respondent, who went back to school after twenty-three years to train as a computer programmer. She is proud of the fact that after school she researched a number of companies, asked intelligent questions, and, in the end, landed a great job.

"Gaining confidence from a job I love and making new friends has made me feel like my life is continuing to unfold and surprise me at every turn! I finally feel that I'm operating on my own steam. My life is under my control, and it is just starting."

Many of the women in the study were finally able to do what they never did as adolescents: figure out what they wanted to be when they grew up. Whereas young boys are urged to examine their strengths and weaknesses, consider their likes and dislikes, think about their career interests, and survey their options, our women were not similarly encouraged when they were younger.

To an adolescent, earning a paycheck means growing up. It marks the first real separation from one's parents. Gainful employment also engenders feelings of mastery and builds self-esteem. But mid-life women who grew up in the forties and fifties were denied this reward. Instead, they were told to go out and "make some man a good wife."

Consequently, many mid-life divorced women don't have a clue about what they want to do or be. They only know what they once were, mothers and wives, and their only "investment" was their families. Their fears are universal:

"Who would want me?"

"I haven't typed in twenty-five years; how will I master a computer?"
"Will I catch on as fast as younger employees?"
"What if I make mistakes?"

As in other areas of postdivorce adjustment, how gracefully a woman shifts gears, from marriage and home to being in the workplace, is related to where she is developmentally. In her capacity as a counselor for the Displaced Homemakers Network, Caroline Breed recognizes that she has to "start further back" with certain women, women we call Pausers.

"They were raised, as so many of us were, to believe that compared to their duties as wives and mothers, everything else is secondary." When these women are questioned about what they'd like to do or be, their answers are predictable: "nurse's aid" or "child-care worker" or "housekeeper." Caroline explains, "That's all they think they can do. Most can do *more*. A good counselor tries to help them identify what that 'more' is.

"Those women don't have a clear idea of who they are," Caroline points out, "but everybody has dreams." She first asks a client to pretend that she doesn't have any problems. She can do anything she wants to do. Nothing is holding her back. "It's basically a way for me to start some dreaming on their part. I tell them we'll deal with reality later!"

That is not to say that a woman shouldn't use the skills she has already honed as a wife and mother. She can barter her services—for example, ask an accountant to do her taxes in exchange for child care. One woman in the study managed to keep up her mortgage payments by renting out rooms vacated by her grown children. Another, a client of Kate McKinley's, who was "an incredible cook, cleaner, and organizer," hired herself out as a *wife!* "Do you know how many working women would be willing to pay for a trustworthy woman to come in when the kids get home from school, cook, and stay for a few hours until they get home?" says Kate. "I would love to have someone who has dinner ready when I walk in the door!"

For divorced women who have been involved in activities outside the cocoon as well as caring for their families—Slow Motions or Rewinders—the transition may not be as difficult. Caroline Breed comments, "Some may not realize how many transferable skills they have. But they don't need as much—just a little push."

Caroline, once a Slow Motion herself, says, "The plus side—and I've seen it in myself—is that these women get to a point where they realize that they *do* have skills and experience, that they actually *do* have a great deal in the areas of management, organization, and planning."

Indeed, when women in the study began to redefine their identities, many were able to apply their skills to paying jobs or to turn talents into businesses of their own. A woman, who loved to shop and had an eye for fashion, became a personal shopper. A gourmet cook became a caterer. Another, whose meticulously organized closets were legendary among her friends, launched a service called Clean Sweep. She helped her upper-income clients empty and reorganize their closets and then sold their no-longer-worn items to thrift shops, splitting the proceeds with her customers and also getting a fee for her time.

As one survey respondent explains, "When I was married I spent a lot of time refinishing the furniture—stripping, staining, and varnishing chairs, cabinets, tables. When I divorced, that was the only skill I had." She started with friends and neighbors at first. "Eventually, my business grew out of my garage and expanded to a building downtown. I have hired three more people to work for me, because business is so great!"

These women are both optimistic and realistic. They realize that a temporary or entry-level job can be an important initial step. "My first job was a temporary position with a florist, answering the phone and taking orders," reports a survey respondent who watched and listened carefully to everything happening around her. One busy day, when the florist asked her to fill in for a sick assistant, she recalls, "I found out I was good at making arrangements and liked doing it. Three years later, someone else answers the phone, and I am now considering opening my own florist shop. As a matter of fact, several customers who really love my work have even offered to back me!"

Whether it's a first-time-ever job, the launching of a serendipitous enterprise, or commitment to a career once thought of as secondary, work trumpets a long overdue separation from both parents and husbands. A woman's newfound income, like an adolescent's first paycheck, is tangible evidence that she is, finally and truly, on her own.

Because divorced women in mid-life are so often late bloomers who haven't had a chance to build up pensions or set aside funds for the future, six out of ten say that they will continue to work after age sixty-five because of financial need. However, the other reasons these women cite for working long past retirement indicate that the majority perceive the intrinsic as well as the practical value of work: fifty-six percent "want to use their talents and skills," sixty-one percent "want to stay busy," sixty-five percent believe their "self-image as a productive person is important," and eighty-three percent "feel work gives a sense of purpose to life."

Investing in the Future

As a financial consultant, Kate McKinley frequently advises women to "invest in the future and invest in themselves." That doesn't mean buying a fur coat or a fancy car—a possible trap for some divorced women who felt deprived of material things in marriage. In contrast, when her marriage ended, Kate's first "investment" was further training, which secured her future.

Kate had been an art history major in college and a teacher when she was first married. For some women, reviving a teaching career might have been the obvious and most accessible choice. "I knew I could have gotten a job, making somewhere between twenty and thirty thousand dollars a year—and that's fine for some women. But I wanted to earn more, so I made a decision not to go back to work right away. I gave myself the time to get an education."

Kate, who had done most of the family money management while she was married—budgeting, paying bills, preparing the family tax returns, making some investments—opted for a settlement that would allow her to get a degree in financial management. "I didn't want to be tied to him, so instead of taking spousal support, I took a lump sum of thirty-six thousand dollars, a payment that amounted to three years' worth of alimony. Eventually, I knew I'd make more money that way."

Even for a Player like Kate, the first several years were a struggle, but it was more than bearable for one key reason: she had a *plan*, with concrete goals and landmarks that allowed her to gauge her progress along the way. No matter how much she had to watch her pennies and worry about grocery bills, Kate could see an end to her troubles. Equally important, she was building her self-esteem.

Kate doesn't regret her decision to take a lesser amount of alimony in a lump sum, instead of getting ongoing spousal support. "Maybe my life would have been easier if I had collected money from him over a longer period of time. On the other hand, I didn't have him picking at me, asking about my income. No matter how hard the struggle or how desperate I felt at times, at least I was on my own."

Making savvy investment decisions has given Kate increasing faith in herself and in her judgment. "I actually ended up better off than my ex-husband. The property I own has since skyrocketed in value. I knew it would go up."

A wonderful role model, Kate McKinley now helps other people conceive retirement plans. "I show them inflationary figures. I ask them what they're living on per month today, and then I tell them this is what you're going to need in twenty years when you retire, in order to be living the way you're living now. That usually scares them!" Kate points out. And learning that they'll be lucky if their social security check buys groceries certainly doesn't brighten the picture.

"I've had women who come and say to me, 'I haven't come 'til now, because I didn't want to know.' But at least I can give them a figure. It's a nice road map." Kate explains that with many retirement plans she simply "runs the numbers backward." For example, if a woman wants to maintain a particular life-style, she may have to save $400 a month, but if she can only put in a hundred a month, she knows she's either going to have to make it up down the road or live in a very awful position in retirement.

Whenever it's at all feasible, Kate also advises her clients to pay off their mortgages, "so that they have a rent-free retirement. Often, the ideal retirement plan is impossible, so we then talk about different options. Maybe she can only semiretire. We just start searching for other possibilities."

Granted, it's harder for a woman to look toward the future when she is concerned about supporting herself or worrying about whether a husband will continue paying child support, which, statistics indicate, half of their husbands won't. If a woman has barely enough money to live on, rarely is she inclined to seek professional investment help, let alone consider an IRA retirement account or an investment.

In fact, eighty-nine percent of the women in the study admit that they have no financial game plan for the future. Nearly half say they lack the necessary information, forty percent are too scared to consider the future, and a minority are still holding out for Prince Charming—or King Midas! Making matters worse, seventy-eight percent of these women have not looked into new job possibilities, and eighty-nine percent have not done anything to prepare for a new career.

It's not just their financial picture that's bleak. Of divorced women who are stuck in the present and haven't made provisions for the long run, the vast majority have also failed to consider what they will do with their time and energy when they retire. They have not become involved in either volunteer work or other activities and interests that might fulfill them. They have no intention of traveling, nor do they have plans to spend more time with friends and relatives. Almost of third of these women think of the future as being too far away to start planning for it!

"They're wrong," insists Grace Dunkirk. Divorced at age forty-five after twenty-five years of marriage, Grace now runs financial workshops for the National Center for Women and Retirement Research. "The future is around the corner and everyone has to make provision for it. We're all up to our noses in expenses! No matter what part of the economic ladder a woman is on, she should put away *something*, even if it's just five dollars a week. In the seminars we tell women, 'Pay yourself first.' It's a struggle, but you have to do it."

Grace, a former teacher, understands how many divorced women feel. "I was typical," she admits. Her husband suddenly up and left one day, abandoning her and their four children, who were nine, eleven, fifteen, and seventeen, at the time. The owner of his own business, prior to divorce he made $150,000 a year ("not counting the extras"). Knowing he was leaving, her husband sold the business and went to work for the new owner —at $20,000 a year.

"That was a pretty big shock. I was only teaching part time, making sixteen thousand dollars. Luckily, I found a job at the center, just as I was going through the divorce process. They were writing the financial handbook* around that time, so I got a lot of good information, and I put it to use. Now I have a very secure financial future."

Of course, each divorce and set of financial circumstances is vastly different, acknowledges Grace, so a woman should ferret out specific information about her own situation. However, she adds, a woman who seeks help has already made a positive first step. Just by reading a book, attending a financial seminar, or seeking the help of a professional counselor for the first time, she is acknowledging, "I'm on my own now—I have to learn how to do this." All women have to be made aware, stresses Grace. "They have to start planning *NOW!*"

The Players' Club: What They Do Right

Women who become Players after divorce get their lives back on track because they figure out how to support themselves financially. They realize that being socially adept and emotionally stable aren't quite enough. To be totally independent, they also have to fill in that last piece of the developmental pie.

Though their circumstances are vastly different, and they traveled the road to rediscovery via different paths, several key themes are evident in their stories. Keep in mind that becoming a Player is a matter of developmental growth. A woman can become a Player regardless of her ex-husband's income, her own earning capacity, or how great or small her divorce settlement.

They know where they stand. When they get divorced, women on the road to rediscovery don't put on blinders when it comes to money. "It frightened me to sit down that first time," admits Joann Cress, "but I needed to know where I was—and where I was going!" They look for documents, and they organize, file, and label all records, including family birth certificates, loan papers, bank statements. They list assets, pore over bank books, draw up budgets. And they know exactly what they spend and what they owe—no matter how frightening it is.

Helga Gross recalls, "I didn't want to balance my checkbook, because I didn't want to find out how much money I had. And

---

* See page 264 for a list of the handbooks produced by the National Center for Women and Retirement Research.

I didn't want to look at my bills, because I didn't want to know how much money I owed!" Today Helga knows what she has and what she spends.

They make plans. They are realistic about their living expenses and about how much they must earn in order to survive; sixty-three percent try to keep debt down. They also know they must have savings, so they consider the long-term picture, factoring in the effects of inflation, money for emergencies, and what they will need to retire. More than half buy IRA's; a third make investments; fifty-five percent contact the Social Security Administration to find out how much their retirement benefits will be. If a Player can't manage health insurance, disability, and retirement plans on her own, she tries to find employment that offers them. As Grace Dunkirk puts it, "If one entry-level job pays four hundred dollars a week and the other three hundred and fifty dollars a week but includes good benefits, take the latter."

In every respect, Players make a concerted effort to meet their needs. "I had a goal," says Ellen Garland, who was working part-time at odd jobs before her divorce, "to finish school and get a job that I liked. I kept putting a lot of money away. I found my present job by looking in the paper. I got my degree in the meantime. It's perfect, and I've been able to build it to what it is today."

They invest in themselves. They take time, and they take action. They figure out what they want to do, what they have to offer, and, if necessary, they fill in the gaps. In short, they "do their homework," whether it's figuring out what kind of training is needed, investigating schools, finding out about scholarships and loan programs, researching companies.

A Player is also alert to using government financial aid—outright grants for tuition or low-rate loans—for both their children's and their own education. "It takes a lot of time and effort to fill those forms out, but it's well worth it," notes Grace Dunkirk.

The payoff is immeasurable, as this respondent reports: "I won two full scholarships to study for my doctorate twenty-four years ago. My first semester, I fell in love, quit school, and married. Over the years, I became a gourmet cook, great party giver, and could move our family at the drop of a hat. Now I'm learning to start over," she notes. "I received financial aid and am finally finishing my doctorate. I feel like I had been sleepwalking for over twenty years!"

They are willing to sacrifice. Especially true of women who had high-income life-styles before divorce, many have to cut back and reassess their priorities. A woman may be forced to do work she doesn't relish, but she is nevertheless able to distinguish between her needs and her desire for a "dream job."

"Whenever business is slow and I have to market myself to new clients, I immediately get to the point of saying, 'Fuck it! I hate what I'm doing anyway,'" confesses Helga Gross. She explains that the stubborn teenager is still inside her; but Helga no longer allows Rewinder tendancies to control her actions. "I've finally learned to listen to a new voice inside of me that says, 'You're running away from responsibility again. You need to earn a living, and this is a good and not very difficult way to do it.' So, I start making the phone calls."

Sometimes the twinges are painful, as Caroline Breed points out: "Everyone I socialize with is at a point in their lives where they're very comfortable; they can afford to travel and shop." But when a woman views the sacrifices she has to make as part of a long-range plan that will ultimately get her out from under, the concessions are infinitely more palatable.

"When I was married, I never bought clothes that someone else had worn," remarks Caroline, who had to invest in a work wardrobe but lacked the funds to do it. "But a lot of women I worked with were in the same position, so we scrambled around together, going to thrift shops. We found ways to build our wardrobe—and we had fun!"

They have a positive attitude. They don't hold on to resentments. Rather, they express their emotions and talk about their disappointments. They don't poison themselves with might-have-been's and what-if's. "Sure, I've had to downplay some of my expectations," owns Caroline Breed, "but that's life. My financial situation could have changed whether I got divorced or not."

Belief in oneself and faith in process are also paramount. "I feel that I'm in exactly the right place, and it's the right time in my life. Everything is coming together!" Ellen Garland declares emphatically—an attitude typical of a Player.

They ask for help. Many of these women have had no prior financial experience, or very little, but they read books and take seminars that will help them. They are not afraid to ask someone to show them how to balance a checkbook, to consult a career counselor about how to figure out what job skills are transferable, or to go to a financial consultant to explain whatever they need to know—from their insurance needs to investment instruments to retirement plans. "Women have to really keep abreast of things, because laws change and economics change," notes Grace Dunkirk.

They are great role models for future generations. This is a sometimes overlooked return that some of our women have already begun to experience: Fran Sargent's daughter, Nicole, who graduated from college last year, decided to take a year off after graduation before deciding whether to go on to graduate school—a road taken by many of our respondents' children. She's essentially on her own for the first time, making between $200 and $300 a week, waitressing and baby-sitting.

Fran reports, "All year, I've been telling her to not to do what I've done, to learn from my mistakes. Try to sock away a little here and there—*pleeeease!* Yesterday, she informed me, 'You'd be very proud of me, Mom. I've saved around one thousand dollars. Actually, I have about sixteen hundred dollars in the bank, but rent is due!' "

"I thought I'd faint!" Fran exclaims. "Maybe there is hope for the next generation of women after all!"

Epilogue

Where Are They Now?
Parting Words from Women
on the Road to Rediscovery

Final Conversations

Joann Cress's license plate says it all. On the first line, it says,
"I spell relief . . ." and written below are the letters:

D–I–V–O–R–C–E

"I guess that sums it up," says Joann, laughing. "You should
see the response I get from people on the road. Women wave to
me; even men sometimes!"

Six years have passed. Joann, forty-eight, is happily involved
in her relationship with Ken; and she has a tight bond with both
sons, now in their twenties. "Divorce is tough, but I think if you
believe in yourself, your life will come together. What I took on
was major, but the divorce was one of the best things I've ever
done. It has turned out all right. And I see how far I've come."

As the writing of this book neared completion, Joann was one
of several women—Pausers, Slow Motions, Rewinders, and
Players—whom we called for a final check-in. Now that divorce
is no longer the focal point of their lives, we asked, what have
they learned that they would like to pass on to other women? We
also wondered where their lives had taken them.

Keeping a Positive Outlook

"The whole thing is, a woman has to believe in herself," says
Debby Black, summing up a pervasive message. "Know that if
she puts her mind to it, she can do it." Debby lives by her own
example. Two summers ago, after several financially flush years

that afforded her, among other things, a new house, Debby's thriving interior design business was dragged down by the recession. So was she.

"I said to myself, you can be depressed and worried sitting in your office shuffling papers and waiting for the phone to ring or you can be depressed and worried on the beach. I chose the beach." Over the next few months, Debby, then fifty-three, got a great tan, read books on Tibet, learned about the culture, and decided to contact the Peace Corps. "I figured I'd rent my house, go away, and donate my time until things got better!

"My friends said, 'You're incredible!' " Discouraged by the two-year enrollment requirement, Debby never joined the Peace Corps. Besides, the phone started ringing again, and business—though not as great as it was in the eighties—picked up again. "I have always had the strength inside me to say this is who I am and this is what I want to do. And since my divorce, I don't give a damn what anyone else thinks!"

At sixty-eight, Elizabeth Harkness is active in her community, she is the president of a national professional organization, *and* she is enrolled in college. Of the divorced women she sees, Elizabeth comments, "Some take longer than others to get over the situation, but I think most eventually do. A woman can't just sit there and wallow in self-pity."

Elizabeth proves her own philosophy. "It's never too late to keep trying for something bigger and better. Here I am, sixty-eight, and finding it delightful to go back to school. If I do nothing more than get my degree, that's an accomplishment—and that's fine." Elizabeth will be seventy when she graduates.

Stand by Yourself

An extraordinary metamorphosis enabled most women in the study to change their lives—and to rewrite the stand-by-your-man credo that sustained them in marriage. Ten years past her divorce, and now earning a good living as a real estate broker, Lorraine is proud of her self-sufficiency. It's the "little things," she says, that so often emerge as milestones of growth and change. Like the fact that when her new mailbox arrived a few months ago, she never asked the man in her life to install it. Instead, she went to the hardware store, found out what she needed—and did it herself.

Because so many of these women finally learned to stand on their own after years of depending on husbands and putting their own needs aside, Lorraine and other women's messages center on finally taking control of one's own life. "A woman shouldn't relinquish to any man what she is capable of doing on her own. She should be open to adventure," Lorraine urges, "and do what *she* wants, *not* what the outside world says she should!"

Evelyn Dorrin, fifty-six, who works as the office manager of a computer company, cautions, "Sure, it's hard work for a woman not to dwell on the man who left her or whom she left. It's like a child growing up in a new environment. But divorced women have to look at themselves, see how far they have come, and realize that they can do it on their own."

Evelyn encourages other women to "work on themselves during marriage too, so they see what they can do and see that they're worthwhile." She also adds, "If they are mothers, they should try to teach their children that lesson too!"

In her work at a divorce information center, Karen Marshall meets women at different stages of turmoil—on the way to a divorce, single for the first time in decades, or long past the crisis and still struggling. She stresses that leaving one's husband is *not* the issue. "A woman has to build a life for herself. I tell each one I meet to make friends with other women, learn about herself, be proud, and recognize her own inner strengths and her abilities. We have so much inside us that we can use!"

Anne Garner, who is now sixty-two, runs self-awareness groups for divorced women and men, as well as holding down a full-time job as the manager of a million-dollar company. Anne observes that divorced women are often surprised at what they can accomplish, albeit gradually. "It's like lifting a calf each day. When it becomes a two-thousand-pound cow, you can still lift it, because you've been doing it each day!" Anne continues to take courses; she writes short stories and plays and hasn't given up on the idea of getting her work published. "I'm always finding out new things about myself. I'm enjoying life."

Feeling the Strain

Divorce also "takes a toll," as Joann Cress puts it. For all their growth and joy, some women also evidenced stress and ambivalence during these final conversations. In the past four years, for example, Gwenn Banning, a Pauser who once asked her ex-husband to balance her checkbook, has worked diligently on every piece of the developmental pie. She has many good friends ("it's the most important thing"), earned advanced degrees, got awards and honors. She also hired an accountant. "I decided I was never going to be emotionally or financially dependent on *anyone.*"

At the same time, Gwenn is eternally exhausted and still angry. "I'm scarred now, but it's not the raw carnage that was there before," she reflects. "I've proven to myself that I can do it. You have to. After divorce, it's time to grow up—quick!"

Gwenn admits with more than a hint of sadness in her voice, "Some days I'd still like to hide, and at times I'd still like to be taken care of." For all her ambivalence, however, Gwenn has come to terms with her dependency. "I regret seeing my marriage deteriorate and not doing something about it. I knew a good five years before he left. Maybe my marriage would have been healthier if I had been less emotionally dependent on him. I see more women being Players today, and I think their marriages are all the better for it."

Not surprisingly, a lack of money is the most common source of debilitation. Even a woman who has taken responsibility for her own welfare may have trouble finding work in an ageist, sexist workplace—not to mention, a depressed economy. Education, the ability to network, and uncommon courage in the face of terrifying odds seem to be the most effective ammunition, but it's often an exhausting, uphill battle.

"I don't feel young. I feel old and tired," says Lisa Frazier, now forty-four. "My mind wants to do so many things. I love life so much. I get frustrated." Lisa still views selling her house as the biggest mistake she has ever made. "My advice to young women is to get a good education so you can call your own shots. I dropped out, because I couldn't go to school and clean a house and take care of a kid. But if I had been educated at twenty-three, I'd be an MSW [social worker] today. As it is, I'm trying to start now."

Money problems aside, some women have also been buffeted by unexpected adversities. "To be honest I have mixed emotions about how I am," confesses Irene Presto. It's not hard to understand why. Irene is one of several women in the study who were hit hard not only by dire financial circumstances, but also by illness and other misfortunes beyond their control. Irene was bilked out of her life savings by an embezzler who promised to make her money grow; shortly thereafter, she was diagnosed with breast cancer. "Cancer made the divorce look like light work!" contends Irene. "I was off the wall nuts. But eventually, I came around. I decided I was going to beat it. So I got information, and I fought hard." Irene is currently in remission.

Other women report similarly serious problems, but each has found a way to deal with her pain and unearth important lessons from the depths of despair.

• Elizabeth Harkness's four daughters turned against her when her ex-husband died two years ago, because he had excluded them from his will. "They thought I went off and left a poor old sick man to die." Three of her daughters no longer blame Elizabeth, but the oldest recently instituted a lawsuit. "My daughter never dealt with her father's alcoholic past." While Elizabeth is saddened, she refuses to let her oldest daughter's actions stop her. "I like me and I like my life. It may never be the same between my oldest daughter and me, but you have to go on. You can't sit there and let your sorrows fester."

• Marilyn Hauptman was shaken when the man she had been dating, a Vietnam veteran, was hospitalized for manic depression. "I hated him for being sick, but it made me realize that I never wanted to be a caretaker again." Dealing with her problems has also taught Marilyn to allow a trusted inner voice to determine her decisions about future relationships. "When you really let go, and you see yourself, you realize *you* are the message. When you must change something in your life, nothing else will matter if it's right. *You will know.*"

• Betty Duprey's twenty-two-year-old daughter committed suicide while Betty was in the thick of the divorce. "The deepest pain was my daughter. The divorce was a process; and I really wanted out. The women's movement gave me the strength to get through it; so did other women." Today Betty also finds solace in her new life. "My philosophy is to let go of things you can't control. I read a lot, and I've been in therapy.

"Of course, there's still emotional pain, and I'm still struggling with money. But I keep my dignity. I have a glamorous appearance: my hair is cut or permed at a good beauty parlor, and I wear good clothes. I just can't go to fine restaurants or take my kids away on vacations anymore. So, my friends and I use discount tickets to go to Broadway shows, and I haven't given up on restaurants altogether! I've really gotten *myself* back."

Fran Sargent, forty-eight, reminds us that even divorced women who don't face such terrible calamities nevertheless have much in common with survivors of other types of trauma. "I'm amazed when I talk to friends who have had cancer or other women in Alcoholics Anonymous. We all went through tremendous growth as a result of our pain; we all had to learn to live a new way. I used to feel sorry for myself—that I had to deal with my alcoholism *and* learn to live on my own. But in retrospect, I also know I'm a stronger person for it."

Final Observations

Surprising though it may be, neither divorce nor tragedy can obliterate most women's dreams. When her son graduates from high school, Lisa Frazier would love to get a job as a "pink jeep guide" and live in a mountain cabin in Arizona. She can imagine herself "in the denim skirt, the boots, the Indian feathers," conducting Indian rituals and chauffeuring visitors to see the spiritual sights of Sedona. "That's the real me. I want to live with nature."

Without realizing that she is using our analogy, Lisa then summarizes the essence of every divorced woman's journey: "All the parts that make up the real me are like pieces of a pie. I'm just trying to get them together."

The women in the "Divorce Over 40" study are still working on the developmental pie; growth, change, and the search for one's identity are lifelong endeavors. While the study in no way advocates divorce, for most of these women, the process inspires an astounding transformation. In every arena, they see indications of their progress. They have begun to date again, and to reawaken their sexual selves. They have learned the value of friendships with other women. They have become better mothers; most have redefined other family relationships as well. They take themselves—and their health—seriously. They recognize the value of working, of saving money, of taking responsibility for their own lives. Some have come so far that they shine a beacon of hope for other divorced women.

They may have made mistakes along the way; they may find themselves in circumstances beyond their control. The bottom line is that, even when they have to roll with some devastating punches, mid-life and older divorced women continue to meet life on life's terms. Despite the scars, the enduring anger, the pangs of loss, and the concerns about money, the vast majority continue to flourish after divorce. Like the phoenix who rises from the ashes to recreate itself, out of divorce, each woman soars with newfound strength and happiness. She begins life again, with renewed confidence in herself and in her ability to effect change.

"Our Turn!" exclaims Marilyn Hauptman when she hears the title of this book. "That's perfect—it's just how I feel. It *is* our turn, but it's also okay to include your past in that too. Because of what we've learned and what we've been through, we are who we are today, and I'm grateful for that!"

◇

Appendix

About the Center:
The National Center for Women and Retirement Research

Background

The National Center for Women and Retirement Research, based at Long Island University, Southampton, New York, is the first academic entity in the country to focus on the preretirement planning needs of mid-life women. Established in 1988, by Dr. Christopher L. Hayes, the center addresses three broad mandates.

• *Research* To undertake applied studies that uncover and articulate the economic, psychological, and social needs of mid-life women prior to retirement.

• *Education* To foster an increased awareness of the need for women to plan for retirement during the middle adult years in order to avoid impoverishment later in life.

• *Training* To sensitize community, public, and corporate leaders regarding the needs of mid-life women.

The PREP Program

A major activity of the center, the Pre-Retirement Education Planning for Women (PREP) Program, was launched in 1986 with a $300,000 grant from the Administration on Aging, Department of Health and Human Services. PREP was established to provide women with the information and skills needed to create a secure and independent future. The overall goal of PREP is to ensure that we don't produce another generation of destitute older women in our country.

By attending PREP seminars and using specially designed handbooks, women are provided the tools to gain financial knowledge and confidence in building their own financial re-

Appendix

sources. Along with addressing the financial needs of women, PREP focuses on other life-planning skills about which women need to be aware, such as health and fitness, knowledge about employment, and the emotional issues associated with the aging process.

Since 1986, more than 100,000 women have contacted PREP and participated in life-planning seminars nationwide. Professional facilitators help women build a strong foundation in understanding how to navigate through the variety of transitions that mark the middle years of life. Special attention has been given to organizing seminars within business, union, university, and community settings.

The PREP program has been featured on such programs as *Good Morning America*, the *Today* show, *Sonya Live*, and in numerous women's magazines. Women can contact PREP for seminar, research, and publication information by calling, toll-free: (800) 426–7386. The following handbooks and audiovisual materials are produced by the center:

Looking Ahead to Your Financial Future

Social and Emotional Issues for Mid-Life Women

Employment and Retirement Issues for Women

Taking Control of Your Health and Fitness

Long-Term Care Issues for Women

Mid-Life Women and Divorce

Women and Money: Things Your Mother Never Told You About Finances (videotape)

Preparing for Your Financial Future (audiotape)

Future Research

The "Divorce Over 40" study represents the center's first major study. Recognizing that self-esteem is at the heart of a person's identity, the center plans to break new ground in the area of self-esteem research. The proposed "Gender Rhythms and Self-Esteem" study will attempt to identify similarities and differences in self-esteem between men and women over the life span. The study will also explore how various events, people, and social factors influence how men and women feel about themselves.

The "Gender Rhythms and Self-Esteem" study will be noteworthy from the perspective that no national comparative studies have been done on the self-esteem patterns of men *and* women. Also, no research has attempted to view the changing nature of self-esteem throughout the course of life. Men and women, representing different ages and different socioeconmic and cultural backgrounds will be part of this national study.

The "Divorce Over 40" Study:
Method and Sample

◇

Overview

In 1989, the National Center for Women and Retirement Research undertook one of the most ambitious efforts to date to explore the impact of divorce on women forty years of age or older. The purpose of this research study was to examine how mid-life women adjusted psychologically, socially, and economically after the dissolution of a long-term marriage. The specific areas of inquiry revolved around four broad concerns: psychological adjustment, adaptation by utilization of social support networks, present and future economic needs, retirement and overall well-being.

The intitial underpinning and design of the study was guided by a group of scholars who met for a four-month period to design the research instrument and discuss strategies for obtaining the sample. During this period, an exhaustive literature search was conducted to ascertain popular and academic literature that addressed the needs of divorced mid-life women. This literature search provided an understanding of previous work in the following areas: (1) existing research on the similarities and differences between the divorce transition for younger versus older women; (2) self-help materials that identify the critical tasks that women must address in the divorce transition; and (3) existing gaps in knowledge concerning the psychosocial and financial needs of divorced mid-life women.

267

Appendix

Research Sample

The sample of 352 females consisted of recently divorced women, forty to seventy-five years of age (eighty-five percent were between forty and sixty), who had been in long-term marriages ranging in length from twenty to forty-eight years (eighty-five percent were married thirty years or less). A major criterion for the sample was that the women must have been divorced over the age of forty and had to have been married a minimum of ten years.

The national sample was obtained by utilizing the center's mailing list, through public-relations activities, and with the assistance of a variety of women's networks and organizations, such as the Displaced Homemakers Network.

Demographics

The racial and ethnic background of the sample was predominantly white (ninety-five percent). Religious affiliation was mostly Protestant (fifty-five percent), Catholic (twenty-five percent), and Jewish (six percent). The majority of the sample had some college education, with twenty percent holding either a Master's degree, Ph.D., M.D., or J.D.

The average length of years post divorce was four. The average number of years married was twenty-three. The average age at the time of the divorce was forty-five. The number of children from the (first) marriage ranged from none to twelve, with the average being two. The mean age of children at the time of the divorce was twenty years.

A total of sixty-five percent of the women were employed at the start of the divorce proceedings. The median number of years working predivorce was six to ten years. A quarter of the sample was employed in clerical positions predivorce; and over thirty-four percent were in administrative, managerial, or professional occupations. The majority of the sample worked full-time prior to the divorce transition.

Research Instruments

The primary research instrument was the 77-item questionnaire, which has been reprinted on pages 273–93. Prior to dissemination, the questionnaire was pilot-tested, utilizing forty-two subjects who matched the established criteria. In addition to the questionnaire, an interview schedule was designed and administered to eighty-six subjects.

The questionnaire contained nine sections, covering the following areas: background information (current age, religious affiliations, and highest educational level obtained), marital background, employment status (pre- and postdivorce), financial status (pre- and postdivorce), legal matters, emotional health, utilization of support networks, perspectives on retirement, and open-ended questions that asked the respondent to offer personal insights regarding the divorce transition.

The 96-item interview schedule provided women with an opportunity (within a two-hour time frame) to discuss their prior marriage and their divorce transition. Included were such topics as: early childhood influences, how the couple met, perspectives on marriage, marital roadblocks, areas of personal growth during and after the dissolution of the marriage, impact of the women's movement, knowledge of finances during and after the dissolution of the marriage, present-day concerns.

Methodology

Initial Contact   A total of 352 subjects completed the questionnaire. Respondents were asked at the conclusion of the questionnaire whether they were willing to be interviewed by a member of the research team. A striking sixty-seven percent of the sample from around the country indicated a desire to be interviewed. In-depth interviews were ultimately conducted with seventy women.

The initial interviews were typically two hours in length. Some women were interviewed in person; others were interviewed over the telephone. Initially, the interview schedule was followed very rigorously to ensure that each interview was uniform. After several interviews were conducted, the research team opted for a more flexible, open-ended format, which allowed women to share the richness of their experiences and, at the same time, cover the topics within the interview schedule.

Each interview was recorded, transcribed verbatim, and then developed into a case study, which included the overall impressions of the interviewer. Overall themes were coded and quantified for statistical analysis.

Follow-up Interviews Over the next three years, a total of seventy women were reinterviewed, with over a third being contacted three or four times, including a final follow-up intereview shortly before the writing of this book was completed. The purpose of these follow-up interviews was to assess how these women were continuing to adjust after the dissolution of their marriages. Often, these contacts provided women with the opportunity to share with the team new insights they had developed, as well as on-going concerns about their life-style, social situation, psychological issues, and economic needs. Insights from these interviews provided the team with a "snapshot" of the significant exigencies and triumphs that divorced mid-life and older women experienced over time.

Data Analysis

The responses to the questionnaire were loaded into a computer using the Statistical Program for Social Sciences (SPSS) Program. The first stage in our data analysis involved developing simple frequencies for each of the questions, in order to arrive at specific percentages. Each of the open-ended questions underwent content analysis, wherein common themes were identified and tallied.

To further the team's understanding of the data, responses to the questionnaire were analyzed in four distinct ways. Each "cut" provided a different "landscape" of the data.

- *Cut #1* Age at the time of the divorce: 40–44, 45–49, and 50–59.

- *Cut #2* Age at the time of the divorce: 40–49 and 50–59.

- *Cut #3* Age at the time of the divorce was at least 40 years (or older) and age at the time of filling out the questionnaire was 40–44, 45–49, 50–59, and 60+.

- *Cut #4*   Number of years since the divorce: up to one year; two to four years; five years or more.

The three different ways of looking at the age variables gave the team an opportunity to view women's lives from alternative perspectives. For example, a woman's age at the time of her divorce is critical for understanding her social or financial well-being in 1989, so cuts #1 and #2 were the most appropriate ways to analyze the data. However, if the team wanted to look at women who were at least forty years of age or older at the time of the divorce, but who were between the ages of forty and sixty when they responded to the questionnaire to understand women's social or financial well-being, then Cut #3 was more appropriate.

Cut #3 also gave the team an opportunity to look at women's lives retrospectively. For example, women who were between forty and forty-four years of age in 1989 were between twenty and twenty-four years of age in 1970, the beginning of the women's movement. Thus, the team was able to regard women in the context of their historical experiences.

Cut #4 provided the team with an understanding of the effect of time as a variable that affects a woman's adjustment during specific periods of the divorce process.

The data were further analyzed by developing correlations among certain social and emotional variables and financial variables within the questionnaire—for example, how "concern with making decisions alone" was related to "worry about growing older," or "perceived more control" was related to "feeling positive." Statistical significance was set at .10 or less. This meant that at least ten percent of the time, the relationship between the two variables was meaningful and could not be attributed to chance alone.

The Questionnaire

DIVORCE AFTER 40:
A NATIONAL SURVEY

To understand how divorce affects women age 40 and over, the National Center for Women and Retirement Research at Long Island University has developed the following survey. Information from this survey will be used to develop materials and programs to help women facing mid-life divorce.

We invite you to join with other women throughout the country and share your divorce experiences with us. **If you were divorced after age 40**, please fill out the following survey. **All responses will be completely confidential.**

The survey includes sections on *Employment, Finances, Legal Matters, Emotional Concerns, Building a New Life,* and *Retirement* (a special concern of the National Center). On the last page, there is space for you to write in personal comments if you wish.

If you have any questions about the survey, please call the National Center at 1-800-426-7386. Thank you for your cooperation and your willingness to share your experience so that other women can benefit.

Note:
If you have been divorced more than once, limit your answers to the first divorce which occurred after age 40.

Appendix
BACKGROUND INFORMATION

1. **What is your age?** _____

2. **What is your racial/ethnic background?** (Circle the appropriate letter.)
   a. White
   b. Black
   c. Asian
   d. Hispanic
   e. American Indian
   f. Interracial
   g. Other: _____

3. **What is your religious affiliation?**
   a. Protestant
   b. Catholic
   c. Jewish
   d. Other: _____

4. **What level of education have you completed?** (Please circle all that apply.)
   a. Less than eighth grade
   b. Eighth grade
   c. Some high school
   d. Completed high school or GED
   e. Vocational/technical school
   f. Secretarial school
   g. Nursing school
   h. One to two years of college
   i. Associate degree
   j. Three to four years of college
   k. College graduate
   l. Some graduate school
   m. Master's degree
   n. Ph.D., M.D., or J.D.
   o. Other: _____

MARITAL INFORMATION

5. **How many years has it been since you divorced?** _____

6. **How many years were you married?** _____

7. **How old were you at the time of your divorce?** _____

8. **How many children did you have from the marriage?** ____

9. **How old were your children at the time of the divorce?** ___

EMPLOYMENT

10. **Were you employed outside the home at the time the divorce proceedings began?**
    a. Yes   b. No

11. **If yes, approximately how long were you working before your divorce?**
    a. Less than 1 year   d. 4 to less than 6 years
    b. 1 to less than 2 years   e. 6 to less than 10 years
    c. 2 to less than 4 years   f. Over 10 years

12. **What type of work were you doing before the divorce?** ___

13. **How many hours did you usually work per week?** _____

14. **What type of work are you doing now?** (i.e., clerical, teaching, administrative, etc.) _____

15. **How many hours do you usually work per week?** _____

16. **How much do you usually earn per week before deductions?**
    _____

17. **What benefits are you receiving in your current job?** (Circle all that apply.)
    a. Health insurance   c. Disability coverage
    b. Pension coverage

18. **If you have chosen not to work, why?**
    a. Enrolled in school or in job training program
    b. Job hunting
    c. Could not find appropriate job
    d. Experienced age discrimination in job hiring
    e. Caring for children still at home
    f. Caring for parents or other relatives
    g. In ill health
    h. Retired
    i. Other: _____

19. **What job-related changes happened after the divorce?** (Circle all that apply.)
    a. None
    b. Began to look for work
    c. Increased work hours
    d. Decreased work hours
    e. Began new career or job
    f. Upgraded job held before divorce (won promotion, expanded job description, etc.)
    g. Changed employers but for same type of work
    h. Sought employment counseling
    i. Attended employment workshops
    j. Took part in vocational/technical training
    k. Attended college or graduate school
    l. Started own business
    m. Other: _____

20. **What job-related goals do you have for the future?** (Circle all that apply.)
    a. None
    b. Return to work
    c. Upgrade present job
    d. Begin new career
    e. Stay in same line of work but find new employer
    f. Seek employment counseling
    g. Attend employment workshops
    h. Take part in vocational/technical training
    i. Attend college
    j. Attend graduate school
    k. Retire
    l. Start own business
    m. Other: _____

FINANCES

21. What category best represents your income?

Household Income Level During Marriage	Household Income First Year After Divorce	Household Income Now
a. $ 0–9,999	a. $ 0–9,999	a. $ 0–9,999
b. $10,000–14,999	b. $10,000–14,999	b. $10,000–14,999
c. $15,000–19,999	c. $15,000–19,999	c. $15,000–19,999
d. $20,000–24,999	d. $20,000–24,999	d. $20,000–24,999
e. $25,000–34,999	e. $25,000–34,999	e. $25,000–34,999
f. $35,000–39,999	f. $35,000–39,999	f. $35,000–39,999
g. $40,000–44,999	g. $40,000–44,999	g. $40,000–44,999
h. $45,000–49,999	h. $45,000–49,999	h. $45,000–49,999
i. $50,000–59,999	i. $50,000–59,999	i. $50,000–59,999
j. $60,000–79,999	j. $60,000–79,999	j. $60,000–79,999
k. $above $80,000	k. $above $80,000	k. $above $80,000

22. Before starting divorce proceedings, did you understand the financial details of: (Circle all that apply.)

a. Joint ownership of your marital property?
b. Ownership of property in your name?
c. Ownership of property in spouse's name?
d. Joint bank accounts?
e. All your credit accounts?
f. Investments (stocks, bonds, real estate) made during the marriage?
g. Insurance policies?
h. Spouse's health coverage and your related benefits?
i. Spouse's pension and your related benefits?
j. Other: _____

23. **Before divorce proceedings, did you:** (Circle all that apply.)
    a. Look over tax returns, checkbooks, financial records?
    b. Work up a budget to determine financial needs after divorce?
    c. Seek financial advice from a professional?
    d. Seek financial advice from a friend, family member, or coworker?
    e. Clear or reduce debts?
    f. Discuss finances with spouse?
    g. Find out eligibility for spouse's health, pension and Social Security benefits?

24. **What were your most pressing financial needs immediately after the divorce?** (Circle all that apply.)
    a. Finding a part-time job
    b. Finding a full-time job
    c. Upgrading present job
    d. Getting financial advice
    e. Finding a less expensive home
    f. Keeping up payments on home, including repairs, utilities, and rent or mortgage payments
    g. Paying for children's needs
    h. Paying for health insurance
    i. Other: _____

25. **What financial skills did you have when you divorced?** (Circle all that apply.)
    a. Budgeting
    b. Keeping track of bills and paying them on time
    c. Doing taxes
    d. Making major financial decisions, such as buying and selling homes, cars, etc.
    e. Balancing a checkbook
    f. Shopping for low credit interest rates
    g. Applying for credit
    h. Using credit wisely
    i. Investing in stocks, bonds, real estate, etc.
    j. Setting long-term financial goals

26. **In learning any of these skills, did you use any of the following resources?**
    a. Female friends
    b. Male friends
    c. Family members
    d. Professionals (accountants, counselors, etc.)
    e. Workshops
    f. Hints in books or magazines
    g. Bank personnel
    h. Personal trial-and-error method
    i. Other: _____

27. **What financial skills would you like to develop?**
    a. Budgeting
    b. Keeping track of bills and paying them on time
    c. Doing taxes
    d. Making financial decisions, such as buying and selling homes, cars, etc.
    e. Balancing a checkbook
    f. Understanding credit (interest rates, annual fees, etc.)
    g. Using credit wisely
    h. Applying for credit
    i. Investing
    j. Setting long-term financial goals
    k. Other: _____

28. **Where did you/do you live?**

During Marriage	*After Divorce*	*Now*
a. Home owned jointly with husband	a. Home owned jointly with husband	a. Home owned jointly with husband
b. Home owned by self	b. Home owned by self	b. Home owned by self
c. Home owned by husband	c. Home owned by husband	c. Home owned by husband
d. Rented home/ apartment	d. Rented home/ apartment	d. Rented home/ apartment
e. With relatives	e. With relatives	e. With relatives
f. Other: _____	f. Other: _____	f. Other: _____

LEGAL MATTERS

29. **Did you use a lawyer?**
    a. Yes   b. No

30. **If yes, how did you select the lawyer?**
    a. Recommendations from a friend or coworker
    b. Recommendations from family member
    c. Recommendations from women's counseling service
    d. Recommendations from family lawyer
    e. Through union
    f. Through advertisement or yellow pages
    g. By convenient location
    h. Other: _____

31. **Did your lawyer specialize in divorce?**
    a. Yes   b. No

32. **How satisfied were you with your lawyer?**
    a. Very satisfied   c. Somewhat dissatisfied
    b. Moderately satisfied   d. Very dissatisfied

33. **Did your lawyer:** (Circle all that apply.)
    a. Help you understand immediate financial needs?
    b. Help you understand long-term financial needs, including retirement?
    c. Help you understand what you were entitled to?
    d. Work out a good settlement?
    e. Work out the best settlement possible?
    f. Seem sensitive to your situation?
    g. Treat you as a responsible adult?

34. **If you were not satisfied with your lawyer, circle all that indicate why.**
    a. Failed to give you a clear picture of immediate financial needs
    b. Failed to give you a clear picture of long-term financial needs, including retirement
    c. Did not help you determine actual entitlements
    d. Failed to work out a good settlement
    e. Failed to be sensitive to your situation
    f. Failed to treat you as an adult
    g. Other: _____

35. **Did anyone else help you with financial information during the divorce process?**
    a. Yes   b. No

36. **If yes, circle all that apply.**
    a. Relatives   e. Financial advisers
    b. Female friends   f. Counselor/therapist
    c. Male friends   g. Other: _____
    d. Accountants

37. **If you had underage children, what type of custody was granted?**
    a. Custody of mother   c. Joint custody
    b. Custody of father   d. Other: _____

38. **Did you have to negotiate child support payments?**
    a. Yes   b. No

39. **What were your requirements for a good settlement?** (Circle all that apply.)
    a. Security for children
    b. Secure living arrangements
    c. Money for job training or starting a business
    d. Compensation for years spent as homemaker or for role in family business
    e. Continued health insurance coverage through ex-spouse's policy
    f. Future security through access to ex-spouse's pension benefits
    g. Other: _____

40. **What were you awarded in your settlement?** (Circle all that apply.)
    a. Child support
    b. Additional financial benefits for children (trust fund, etc.)
    c. The family home
    d. Money for job training or starting a business
    e. Compensation for years spent as homemaker or for role in family business
    f. Continued health insurance coverage through ex-spouse's policy
    g. Future security through access to ex-spouse's pension benefits
    h. Other: _____

41. **Do you think this settlement was fair?**
    a. Yes   b. No

42. **If you now feel you settled too quickly, what influenced you?**
    a. Desire to end emotionally painful experience
    b. Lack of information on own financial needs
    c. Lack of information on husband's finances
    d. General lack of information
    e. Divorce process made difficult by spouse
    f. Desire to spare children stress and tension
    g. Desire to be fair outweighed self-interest

EMOTIONAL HEALTH

43. Did you seek joint counseling before the marriage ended?
a. Yes   b. No

44. If yes, was it helpful in some way?
a. Very helpful   c. Not helpful
b. Moderately helpful

45. If you did not consider joint counseling, why?
a. Did not believe it would   d. Subject never discussed
    help   e. Other: _____
b. Spouse refused to partici-
    pate
c. Financial cost

46. Did you seek counseling for yourself?
a. Yes   b. No

47. If so, was it helpful?
a. Very helpful   c. Not helpful
b. Moderately helpful

48. What were your major concerns about going through with a divorce? (Circle all that apply.)
a. Family criticism
b. Lack of support from friends
c. Effect on children
d. Custody fight over children
e. Loss of financial security
f. Loss of home
g. Taking care of household responsibilities alone
h. Managing finances alone
i. Making decisions alone
j. Living alone
k. Lack of male companionship
l. Loss of sexual relationship
m. Growing old alone
n. None of above
o. Other: _____

49. **When the divorce proceedings began, what did you consider to be the major benefits of the divorce?** (Circle all that apply.)
    a. Being in control of own life
    b. Relief from the stresses of the marriage
    c. Peace and quiet
    d. Better situation for children
    e. More time to take care of self
    f. More time for family
    g. More time for friends
    h. Chance for a new life
    i. Renewed self-confidence
    j. None of above
    k. Other: _____

50. **What activities and/or persons helped you through the various stages of divorce?**

Before Decision to Initiate Legal Proceedings	*During Divorce Proceedings*	*First Year After Divorce*

People

a. Children	a. Children	a. Children
b. Other family members	b. Other family members	b. Other family members
c. Female friends	c. Female friends	c. Female friends
d. Male friends	d. Male friends	d. Male friends
e. Counselor/ Therapist	e. Counselor/ Therapist	e. Counselor/ Therapist
f. Clergy, Priest/ Rabbi, etc.	f. Clergy, Priest/ Rabbi, etc.	f. Clergy, Priest/ Rabbi, etc.
g. Support group	g. Support group	g. Support group
h. Financial adviser	h. Financial adviser	h. Financial adviser
i. Lawyer	i. Lawyer	i. Lawyer
j. Intimate partner	j. Intimate partner	j. Intimate partner
k. Other: _____	k. Other: _____	k. Other: _____

Before Decision to Initiate Legal Proceedings	During Divorce Proceedings	First Year After Divorce

Activities

a. Prayer	a. Prayer	a. Prayer
b. Church services	b. Church services	b. Church services
c. Work or job	c. Work or job	c. Work or job
d. Exercise	d. Exercise	d. Exercise
e. Hobbies	e. Hobbies	e. Hobbies
f. Volunteer work	f. Volunteer work	f. Volunteer work
g. Educational opportunities, classes, etc.	g. Educational opportunities, classes, etc.	g. Educational opportunities, classes, etc.
h. Other: _____	h. Other: _____	h. Other: _____

51. **At the time of your divorce, what other changes were taking place?**
    a. Menopause
    b. Moving from residence
    c. One or more children left home
    d. Child(ren) returned home
    e. Developed health problems
    f. Caring for ailing parent or relative
    g. Death of parent
    h. Death of relative or close friend
    i. Change in employment
    j. Developing new intimate relationship
    k. Other: _____

BUILDING A NEW LIFE

52. **What positive things have been happening since your divorce?** (Circle all that apply.)
   a. Developing and enjoying new skills, interests and/or hobbies
   b. Feeling positive about self
   c. Having privacy and independence
   d. Starting counseling or therapy
   e. Experiencing more sexual enjoyment
   f. Maintaining a closer relationship with parents
   g. Maintaining a closer relationship with siblings
   h. Maintaining a better relationship with children
   i. Developing new friendships
   j. Developing better relationships with female friends
   k. Finding more freedom and time for work or employment
   l. Feeling relieved not to be torn between needs of spouse and children
   m. Feeling free to be own self and meet own needs
   n. Feeling less turmoil and more peace of mind
   o. Feeling of strength because of ability to survive difficult times
   p. Feeling of achievement through own resources

3. **What special concerns do you now have as a divorced woman in mid-life?** (Circle all that apply.)
   a. Worry about money
   b. Have less time for self
   c. Have problems with ex-spouse
   d. Have problems raising children as a single parent
   e. Reactions to divorce on part of children
   f. Miss having an ongoing intimate relationship
   g. Miss having a regular companion for social events
   h. Miss having a peer to share daily responsibilities with
   i. Have difficulty meeting men and dating
   j. Worry about growing older

54. **As a result of the divorce, with whom do you now live?**
    a. Self only
    b. With female roommate
    c. With male roommate
    d. With husband
    e. With children
    f. With other relatives
    g. With intimate partner
    h. Other: _____

55. **Since your divorce, how have your friendships changed?**
    (Circle all that apply.)
    a. Not at all
    b. Have given up previous friendships through own choice
    c. Have lost previous friendships by their choice
    d. Women friends during marriage are still friends
    e. Friendships with other women are now closer
    f. Made new friends, both single and married individuals
    g. Still trying to find new friends who understand and support my new life
    h. As a private person, I am satisfied with only one or two close friends
    i. Have a new intimate partner, and we have made new friends together

56. **Where do you meet potential friends?**
    a. Work
    b. Church or synagogue
    c. Support group
    d. Women's organizations
    e. Social events
    f. Through new intimate partner
    g. Through children
    h. Through siblings, parents, relatives
    i. Through other friends
    j. Volunteer work
    k. Clubs and activities
    l. Other: _____

57. **Have any of the following kept you from making new friends?** (Circle all that apply.)
   a. Being too tired after work
   b. Being too busy with work
   c. Being too busy with school
   d. Too busy with children
   e. Lack of money for activities with friends
   f. Lack of money for activities where I would meet friends
   g. Limited opportunities to socialize
   h. Spending time caring for parents
   i. Lack of invitations as a single woman
   j. Not meeting people who share interests and viewpoints
   k. Meeting people who are too busy to respond to my requests to socialize
   l. I am putting my time and energy into opportunities to find another male partner

8. **How do you feel about remarriage?** (Circle all that apply.)
   a. Opposed
   b. Somewhat interested
   c. Undecided
   d. Very eager

59. **If you want to remarry, why?** (Circle all that apply.)
   a. Financial security
   b. For my children's sake
   c. Companionship
   d. Sexual intimacy
   e. Social and traveling companion
   f. Someone who can care for me when I'm ill
   g. Someone to love and care for
   h. Someone to grow old with
   i. Other: _____

60. **If you don't want to remarry, why?** (Circle all that apply.)
    a. Prefer freedom
    b. Find it difficult to find appropriate partner
    c. Afraid of making a mistake
    d. Did not enjoy married life
    e. Like being financially independent
    f. Children are opposed
    g. Disillusioned about marriage
    h. Do not need marriage for an intimate relationship
    i. Other: _____

RETIREMENT

61. **Do you plan to retire from full-time work?**
    a. Yes   b. No

62. **If you plan to retire, at what age?**
    a. Before age 65   d. After age 70
    b. At age 65   e. Haven't decided yet
    c. Between the ages of 65 and
       70

63. **Are you planning to work at new career after retirement?**
    a. Yes, part-time   c. No
    b. Yes, full-time

64. **If you plan to work after age 65, why?** (Circle all that apply.)
    a. Financial need
    b. Want to use talents and skills
    c. Feel it gives a sense of purpose to life
    d. Like the companionship the workplace offers
    e. Self-image as a productive person is important
    f. Like the routine and structure it provides
    g. Want to stay busy
    h. Other: _____

65. **What financial preparations have you made for retirement?**
(Circle all that apply.)

    a. Found out about Social Security benefits and how to collect on own or ex-spouse's work record

    b. Am vested in a pension plan

    c. Started buying IRAs or similar plans

    d. Considered places for relocation and evaluated cost of living in those areas

    e. Have made investments (real estate, stocks, etc.)

    f. Keep personal debt down

    g. Make purchases only after considering long-range benefits

    h. None as yet

    i. Other: _____

66. **What other preparations have you made for retirement?** (Circle all that apply.)

    a. Looked into new job possibilities

    b. Enrolled in an educational or training program to prepare for a new career after retirement

    c. Planned activities and interests to pursue in retirement

    d. Enrolled in educational or training program to prepare for new activities and interests

    e. Planned volunteer activities

    f. Set travel goals

    g. Made plans with friends and relatives to spend more time together

    h. None as yet

    i. Other: _____

67. **Where do you want to live after retirement?**

    a. In same home as now

    b. With children in their home

    c. In a different home

    d. In a rented house or apartment

    e. In a retirement complex or community

    f. Other: _____

    g. Have not made a decision

68. **If you have not yet started planning for retirement, why?**
    a. Too far away
    b. Don't have time
    c. Don't have necessary information to plan
    d. Scared to consider prospects for the future
    e. Still feel healthy
    f. Still hope to find a new long-term partner and make joint plans
    g. Never make long-range financial plans

69. **When you look ahead to your retirement years, what do you see?**
    a. Financial security
    b. Financial stress
    c. Health and productivity
    d. Sickness and dependency
    e. Time with family
    f. Time with friends
    g. Loneliness
    h. Involvement in interests and activities
    i. Boredom
    j. Other: _____

FINAL COMMENTS

(If you do not have enough room to write your answers on these pages, please put them on an additional page and include in the return envelope.)

70. **What were your strongest feelings at the time of the decision to divorce, during the divorce proceedings, and during the first months after the divorce was finalized?**

71. **What was the hardest part of the first year(s) after the divorce, and how did you cope with it?**

72. **Was your health affected in any way during the divorce? If so, explain briefly what happened and how you dealt with it.**

73. **What information should women know if they are facing divorce after age 40?**

74. **What would be the most important advice you would give a woman going through a divorce and building a new life?**

75. **Please describe any additional experiences you want to share or comments you want to make.**

76. **Would you be willing to discuss some of your experiences further with an interviewer from the National Center for Women and Retirement Research?**
   a. Yes   b. No

77. **If so,**
   a. In person (give phone number with area code): _____
   b. By telephone (give phone number with area code): _____

Acknowledgments

We are truly indebted to the many people who relegated their self-interests to second place so that this study and book might become a reality. The foundation of the study was guided by an advisory group that included Dr. Jane Deren, Dr. Jane Porcino, Dr. Sara Rix, and Dr. Doris Francis. Dr. Lois Tepper, of Long Island University, and Dr. Deborah Pearlman of the Brookdale Center on Aging provided extensive assistance during the data entry and analysis stage of the research. We are particularly grateful to Maurice L. Hayes, M.D. for spearheading the transcriptions of each of the interviews and developing interview summaries.

The dissemination of the survey could not have been accomplished without the assistance of the Displaced Homemakers Network in Washington, D.C., and Jill Miller, Executive Director, who provided on-going support in working with local chapters to ensure that the survey would reach a wide audience.

The support of Ms. Dottie Clarke, Ms. Jean Plitt, and Joette Stef at the National Center for Women and Retirement Research cannot be overstated. We also want to acknowledge the help of our two University interns, Wendy Barrington-Bennett and Nancy Leistman.

The study could not have been completed without the blessing of the administration and faculty at Long Island University, particularly Provost Tim Bishop, Dean Alvin Siegel, Dr. John Strong, Dr. Walter Jones, and Ms. Mary Lai. The enthusiasm and backing of Dr. Donald Baker was particularly helpful throughout the study.

We are indebted to Sherry Henry, who helped to set in motion our goal of writing this book. Throughout the next two years,

295

we were grateful for the enthusiasm we received from our agent, Loretta Barrett, and our editor, Julie Rubenstein.

Our Turn is a story about growth and change. Unlike the women who embarked alone on a voyage of discovery after divorce, the coauthors of this book set out on a joint expedition. During the last two years of this project, we were fortunate in working with a writer and collaborator, Melinda Blau, who not only helped shape and articulate the material but also possessed a rare gift—that of nurturing and strengthening our individual talents. The success of the study and the resulting book is a testament to her writing abilities and who she is as a person. Melinda fostered our growth and change throughout the process and, for this, we will always be indebted.

Finally, we are truly grateful to our respective family members who prodded us on, giving us emotional succor during the times when we questioned whether the end would ever come.

> —Christopher L. Hayes, Ph.D., and Deborah Anderson
> National Center for Women and Retirement Research
> Southampton, New York

The writing of this book represents a true meeting of the minds. It is rare that a journalist is given the opportunity to work with researchers who are so willing to collaborate. Chris Hayes and Deborah Anderson provided me with a wealth of background material, which enriched the study's findings and gave the interview transcripts an historical context. However, I am even more grateful for their unceasing cooperation, their openness to new concepts, and their willingness to constantly adapt, reformulate, and review ideas conceived during the writing process. Each brought to this project a different strength and a different vision; both inspired me to cultivate my intuition.

Certain women who participated in the study granted me additional interview time after their initial and follow-up sessions with Chris and Deborah. To my delight, the interviews were more like conversations between friends: besides confiding about their

Acknowledgments

own lives, these women also compared notes with me—a fellow divorced woman in mid-life. Most important, they validated our insights. Without them, the final pieces of the puzzle might never have fallen into place. To preserve their anonymity, I thank them by listing the "stage names" used in the book: Gwenn Banning, Debby Black, Caroline Breed, Joann Cress, Janet Cummings, Evelyn Dorrin, Grace Dunkirk, Betty Duprey, Lena Entemann, Lorraine Feldman (and her diary), Lisa Frazier, Ellen Garland, Anne Garner (and her poetry), Helga Gross, Florence Hacker, Alice Hampton, Elizabeth Harkness, Marilyn Hauptman, Anita Parsons, Bonnie Lenza, Gail Leperk, Patsy Marconi, Karen Marshall, Phyllis May, Kate McKinley, Gisella Morgan, Irene Presto, Nancy Rolfing, Fran Sargent, Melanie Spade, Jane Wharton, and Annette Winwood.

I also am grateful to Loretta Barrett whose foresight about this project brought my coauthors and me together and who has always been an ardent supporter of my career; and to Julie Rubenstein, who brought editorial skill and sensitivity to our book and, on many occasions, brightened my day.

Finally, no writer can exist without family and friends who love and support her. I am fortunate to have an abundance of both. Special thanks go to Ellen Lefcourt, who diligently and (to my constant amazement) enthusiastically read every page of this manuscript, and to Carol Clarke, who is always in my corner. Although my children's reassurance was delivered via long distance phone calls, I also thank Jeremy, who said, "Hang in there, Mom," when I was ready to give up, and Jennifer, who reminded me that finishing this book would "build your character." It did.

—Melinda Blau
Northampton, Massachusetts

Bibliography

Adams, B. N. 1986. *The family: A sociological interpretation*. New York: Harcourt Brace Jovanovich.

Arafat, I., and B. Yorburg. 1976. *The new woman: Attitudes, behavior, and self-image*. Columbus, OH: Charles E. Merrill Publishers.

Atchley, R. 1985. *Social forces and aging*. 4th ed. Belmont, CA: Wadsworth.

Baruch, G., R. Barnett, and C. Revers. 1983. *Love prints: New patterns of love and work for today's women*. New York: New American Library.

Beauvoir, de, S. 1952. *The second sex*. New York: Alfred Knopf.

Belenky, M. F., B. M. Clinchy, N. R. Goldberger, and J. M. Tarule. 1986. *Women's ways of knowing: The development of self, voice, and mind*. New York: Basic Books.

Bernard, J. 1989. The good provider role. *Marriage & family in a changing society*. Ed. J. M. Henslin. New York: Free Press.

Blair, M. 1970. Divorcées adjustment and attitudinal changes about life. *Dissertation Abstracts* 30, 5541–5542. (University Microfilms No. 7–11, 099.)

Blau, Z. S. 1985. *Current perspectives on aging and the life cycle*. Greenwich, CT: Jai Press.

Bloom, S. L. 1992. The national dilemma: Can we heal ourselves? *Journal of Psychohistory* 19 (3): 281–306.

Bohannon, P. 1970. The six stations of divorce. *Divorce and after*. Ed. P. Bohannon. Garden City, NY: Doubleday.

Brody, J. 1992. Maintaining friendships for the sake of your health. *The New York Times*. February 5: C12.

Cain, B. S. 1982. Plight of the gray divorcée. *The New York Times Magazine*. December 19: 89–95.

Cherlin, A. J. 1981. *Marriage, divorce, and remarriage*. Cambridge, MA: Harvard University Press.

Bibliography

Dickson, P. 1990. *Timelines*. Reading, MA: Addison-Wesley Publishing Co.

Dyer, E. D. 1983. *Courtship, marriage, and family: American style*. Homewood, IL: Dorsey.

Estes, C., L. Gerald, and E. Clarke. 1984. Women and the economics of aging. *International Journal of Health Services* 14 (1): 55–68.

Faludi, S. 1991. *Backlash: The undeclared war against american women*. New York: Crown Publishing Group.

Fischer, C. S., and S. Oliker. 1980. *Friendship, gender, and the life-cycle*. Working paper No. 318. Institute of Urban and Regional Development, University of California, Berkeley.

Garnets, L., and D. Kimmel. 1991. Lesbian and gay male dimensions in the psychological study of human diversity. *Psychological perspective on human diversity in America*. Ed. J. D. Goodchilds. Washington, DC: American Psychological Association.

Gettleman, S., and J. Markowitz. 1974. *The courage to divorce*. New York: Simon and Schuster.

Gibbons, A. 1992. Chimps: More diverse than a barrel of monkeys. *Science* 255 (January 17) 287–288.

Gilford, R. 1986. Marriages in later life. *Generations* 10 (4): 16–20.

Gilligan, C. 1982. *In a different voice*. Cambridge, MA: Harvard University Press.

Goode, W. 1956. *After divorce*. Glencoe, IL: Free Press.

Gove, W., M. Hughes, and C. Style. 1983. Does marriage have positive effects on the psychological well-being of the individual? *Journal of Health and Social Behavior* 24 (June): 122–31.

Hagestad, G. 1987. Divorce. *Encyclopedia of Aging*. Ed., G. L. Maddox, R. C. Atchley, L. W. Poon, G. S. Roth, I. C. Siegler, and R. M. Sternberg. New York: Springer Publishing Co.

Hancock, E. 1989. *The girl within: Recapture the childhood self, the key to female identity*. New York: E. P. Dutton and Co.

Henslin, J. M., ed. 1989. *Marriage and family in a changing society*. New York: Free Press.

Hess, B., and E. Markson. 1985. *Growing old in America: New perspectives on old age*. New Brunswick, NJ: Transaction Books.

Hetherington, E., M. Cox, and R. Cox. 1977. The aftermath of divorce. *Mother-child, father-child relations*. Ed. J. H. Stevens and M. Mathews. Washington, DC: National Association for the Education of Young Children.

Hill, R. 1949. *Families under stress*. New York: Harper and Row.

Bibliography

Hutter, M. 1991. *The family experience.* New York: Macmillan Co.

Kahn, R., and T. Antonucci. 1980. Convoys over the lifecourse: Attachment roles and social supports. *Life-span development and behavior.* Ed. P. Baltes and P. C. O'Brien. New York: Academic Press.

Kaslow, F. W., and L. L. Schwartz. 1987. *The dynamics of divorce: A life-cycle perspective.* New York: Brunner/Mazel.

Katchadourian, H. 1987. *Fifty: Midlife in perspective.* New York: W. H. Freeman and Co.

Kegan, R. 1982. *The evolving self: Problem and process in human development.* Cambridge, MA: Harvard University Press.

Keith, P. M. 1985. Work, retirement, and well-being among unmarried men and women. *The Gerontologist* 25 (4).

Leslie, G. 1982. *The family in social context.* New York: Oxford University Press.

Lowenthal. M. T., and D. Chiriboga. 1975. *Four stages of life.* San Francisco, CA: Jossey-Bass.

McGrath, E., G. Keita, B. Strickland, and N. Russo. 1990. *Women and depression: Risk factors and treatment issues.* Washington, DC: American Psychological Association.

McGoldrick, M., and E. Carter. 1980. Forming a remarried family. *The family life cycle: Framework for family therapy.* Ed. E. Carter and M. McGoldrick. New York: Gardner Press.

Mercer, R. T., E. G. Nichols, and G. C. Doyle. 1989. *Transitions in a woman's life: Major life events in developmental context.* New York: Springer Publishing Co.

Milardo, R. 1987. Changes in the social networks of women and men following divorce. *Journal of Family Issues* 8 (1): 78–96.

Miller, J. B. 1976. *Toward a new psychology of women.* Boston: Beacon Press.

Nemiroff, R. A., and C. A. Colarusso. 1990. *New dimensions in adult development.* New York: Basic Books.

Scanzoni, J. 1979. A historical perspective on husband-wife bargaining power and marital dissolution. *Divorce and separation: Context, causes, and consequences.* Ed. G. D. Levinger and O. C. Moles. New York: Basic Books.

Scarf, M. 1981. *Unfinished business.* New York: Ballantine Books.

Settlage, C. F. 1990. Childhood to adulthood: Structural change in development toward independence and autonomy. *New dimensions in adult life.* Ed. R. A. Nemiroff and C. A. Colarusso. New York: Basic Books.

Bibliography

Shaw, L. B. 1983. *Unplanned careers: The working lives of middle-aged women.* Lexington, MA: Lexington Books.

Sheehy, G. 1976. *Passages: Predictable crises of adult life.* New York: E. P. Dutton and Co.

———. 1991. The silent passage: Menopause. *Vanity Fair.* (October): 222–263.

Silverstein, O. 1988. Single women: Later years. *The invisible web: Gender patterns in family relationships.* Ed. M. Walters, B. Carter, P. Papp and O. Silverstein. New York: The Guilford Press.

Steinem, G. 1983. Words and change. *Outrageous acts and everyday rebellions.* New York: Plume Books.

Stone, R., 1985. *The relationship between retirement and change in functional health among unmarried women.* Paper presented to the Annual Meeting of the American Public Health Association, November, pp. 17–20.

Tavris, C. 1992. *The mismeasure of woman: Why women are not the better sex, the inferior sex, or the opposite sex.* New York: Simon and Schuster.

Turner, N. W. 1980. Divorce in mid-life: Clinical implications and applications. *Mid-life: Developmental and clinical issues.* Ed. W. H. Norman and T. J. Scaramella. New York: Brunner/Mazel.

Uhlenberg, P., T. Cooney and R. Boyd. 1990. Divorce for women after midlife. *Journal of Gerontology: Social Sciences* 45 (1): 3–11.

Vanderbilt, H. 1992. Incest: A chilling report. *Lear's* 4 (12): 49–77.

Wallerstein, J. S., and S. Blakeslee. 1989. *Second chances: Men, women, and children a decade after divorce.* New York: Ticknor and Fields.

Walters, M., B. Carter, P. Papp and O. Silverstein. 1988. *The invisible web: Gender patterns in family relationships.* New York: The Guilford Press.

Weitzman, L. 1985. *The divorce revolution.* New York: Free Press.

———. 1991. Divorce and the illusion of equality. *The family experience.* Ed. M. Hutter. New York: Macmillan Co.

Wiseman, R. S. 1975. Crisis theory and the process of divorce. *Social Casework* 56: 205–12.

Women's Studies Program and Policy Center at George Washington University, *The economics of aging.* 1980.

◇

Index

Printed in the United States
1073100002B/94-129